100 GREATEST TRIPS

**TRAVEL+
LEISURE**

In front of Harlem's Il Caffe Latte,
in New York City.

TRAVEL+
LEISURE

100 GREATEST TRIPS

SIXTH EDITION

FROM THE EDITORS OF
THE WORLD'S LEADING TRAVEL MAGAZINE

TRAVEL+
LEISURE
BOOKS

AMERICAN EXPRESS PUBLISHING CORPORATION
NEW YORK

TRAVEL+LEISURE
100 GREATEST TRIPS
SIXTH EDITION

Editor Jennifer Miranda
Consulting Editors Laura Begley Bloom, Irene Edwards
Art Director Wendy Scofield
Photo Editor Beth Garrabrant
Production Associate David Richey
Editorial Assistant Dorkys Ramos
Reporters Rebecca Dalzell, Jane Margolies, Madhu Puri
Copy Editors David Gunderson, Mike Iveson, Ed Karam, Sarah Khan, Libby Sentz
Researchers Kristina Ensminger, Gabriella Fuller, Joseph Harper, Pearly Huang, Tomás Martín, Charles Moore, Paola Singer, Marguerite A. Suozzi, Rory Tolan

TRAVEL + LEISURE
Editor-in-Chief Nancy Novogrod
Creative Director Bernard Scharf
Executive Editor Jennifer Barr
Managing Editor Laura Teusink
Associate Managing Editor Patrick Sheehan
Arts/Research Editor Mario R. Mercado
Copy Chief Kathy Roberson
Photo Editor Whitney Lawson
Production Director Rosalie Abatemarco-Samat
Production Manager Ayad Sinawi

AMERICAN EXPRESS PUBLISHING CORPORATION
President and Chief Executive Officer Ed Kelly
Chief Marketing Officer and President, Digital Media Mark V. Stanich
CFO, SVP, Corporate Development & Operations Paul B. Francis
VP, General Managers Frank Bland, Keith Strohmeier
VP, Books & Products Marshall Corey
Director, Book Programs Bruce Spanier
Senior Marketing Manager, Branded Books Eric Lucie
Assistant Marketing Manager Stacy Mallis
Director of Fulfillment & Premium Value Philip Black
Manager of Customer Experience & Product Development Charles Graver
Director of Finance Thomas Noonan
Associate Business Manager Uma Mahabir
Operations Director Anthony White

Cover: The skyline in Shanghai's Pudong district. Photographed by Morgan & Owens

Copyright © 2011 American Express Publishing Corporation

All rights reserved. No part of this book may be reproduced or transmitted in any form or by any means, electronic or mechanical, including photocopying, recording, or by any information storage or retrieval system, without permission in writing from the publisher.

ISBN 978-1-932624-38-0

Published by American Express Publishing Corporation
1120 Avenue of the Americas
New York, New York 10036

Distributed by Charlesbridge Publishing
85 Main Street, Watertown, Massachusetts 02472

Printed in Canada

The spa at the Royal Mansour
Marrakech, in Morocco.

An Elvis impersonator
on Hollywood Boulevard,
in Los Angeles.

contents

12
UNITED STATES & CANADA
WEST CHELSEA, NEW YORK CITY **14**
HARLEM, NEW YORK CITY **18**
HUDSON, NEW YORK **20**
MONMOUTH COUNTY, NEW JERSEY **24**
CHARLESTON, SOUTH CAROLINA **28**
ATLANTA **30**
THE EVERGLADES, FLORIDA **32**
MIAMI **34**
CHICAGO **38**
COLUMBUS, INDIANA **39**
NEW ORLEANS **40**
SAN ANTONIO, TEXAS **44**
CONTINENTAL DIVIDE **46**
LAS VEGAS **48**
PARK CITY, UTAH **50**
PORTLAND, OREGON **52**
SAN FRANCISCO **54**
HOLLYWOOD, CALIFORNIA **56**
KAUAI, HAWAII **58**
HONOLULU **60**
FOGO ISLAND, NEWFOUNDLAND **62**
MONTREAL **64**
COWICHAN VALLEY, BRITISH COLUMBIA **66**

68
CARIBBEAN
PUERTO RICO **70**
OCHO RIOS, JAMAICA **72**
SAMANÁ PENINSULA, DOMINICAN REPUBLIC **73**
BARBADOS **74**
NEVIS **78**
ST. MARTIN **82**
ANGUILLA **84**
MARTINIQUE **86**

90
MEXICO & CENTRAL & SOUTH AMERICA
92 MEXICO CITY
96 ACAPULCO, MEXICO
100 SAN MIGUEL DE ALLENDE, MEXICO
102 VERACRUZ, MEXICO
104 JICARO ISLAND, NICARAGUA
106 CAYE CAULKER, BELIZE
107 LIMA, PERU
108 SACRED VALLEY, PERU
110 PATAGONIAN LAKES REGION, CHILE
112 EASTER ISLAND
114 BUENOS AIRES
116 IGUAZÚ FALLS, ARGENTINA
118 COLONIA, URUGUAY
120 SÃO PAULO, BRAZIL

122
EUROPE
124 ICELAND
128 DUBLIN
130 COLONSAY, SCOTLAND
132 LONDON
134 EAST SUSSEX, ENGLAND
135 SINTRA, PORTUGAL
136 ASTURIAS, SPAIN
138 PARIS
140 BEAUNE, FRANCE
142 CAP FERRET, FRANCE
146 THE ALPS
147 GHENT, BELGIUM
148 ITALIAN LAKES
150 SALENTO, ITALY
154 FLORENCE
155 COPENHAGEN
156 VIENNA
158 SKOPELOS, GREECE
159 GOZO, MALTA
160 ISTANBUL
162 ST. PETERSBURG, RUSSIA

Riding a bike
in Hanoi, Vietnam.

166
AFRICA & THE MIDDLE EAST
MARRAKESH, MOROCCO **168**
LAMU, KENYA **172**
NAIROBI, KENYA **176**
ZAMBIA **178**
JOHANNESBURG, SOUTH AFRICA **180**
CAPE WINELANDS, SOUTH AFRICA **184**
TEL AVIV **186**
RODRIGUES, MAURITIUS **188**

190
ASIA
TOKYO **192**
HONG KONG **196**
SHANGHAI **198**
HANGZHOU, CHINA **202**
BEIJING **204**
SINGAPORE **205**
BANGKOK **206**
KOH KONG, CAMBODIA **207**
HYDERABAD, INDIA **208**
MUMBAI **212**
PUDUCHERRY, INDIA **213**
GOBI DESERT, MONGOLIA **214**
LHASA, TIBET **215**
PENANG, MALAYSIA **216**
CON DAO, VIETNAM **220**
VIETNAM **222**
BALI, INDONESIA **226**
ROTE, INDONESIA **228**
KOH SAMUI, THAILAND **230**

232
AUSTRALIA & NEW ZEALAND
234 SYDNEY
238 SURRY HILLS, AUSTRALIA
240 MORNINGTON PENINSULA, AUSTRALIA
244 MELBOURNE
246 TASMANIA, AUSTRALIA
248 SOUTH ISLAND, NEW ZEALAND
250 GREAT BARRIER ISLAND, NEW ZEALAND

252 THE GUIDE
280 TRIPS DIRECTORY
282 INDEX
284 CONTRIBUTORS
286 PHOTOGRAPHERS

The entrance hall at the
Awaiting Table Cookery School,
in Lecce, Italy.

introduction

IT IS A HAPPY REALITY OF MY PROFESSIONAL LIFE that many of the things I love to do—traveling to far-flung destinations, trying new restaurants, visiting museums and galleries, and even shopping—are relevant to my editorial responsibilities at *Travel + Leisure*. In fact, the same can be said for most of my colleagues on the editorial side of this magazine. One of the greatest pleasures is passing on tips about the places we love to our readers to help them plan journeys of their own.

With this in mind we present the sixth book in *Travel + Leisure*'s annual series *100 Greatest Trips*, a compendium of ideas and itineraries for travelers culled from the thousands of inspiring destinations we've featured in the magazine over the past year, as well as from our five international editions. Organized by continent, country, and region, this volume has something for every kind of traveler: polished aesthetes; thrill-seeking explorers; committed gastronauts; eco-adventurers. Regardless of which category you fall into, like me, you are probably seeking authentic experiences of place. That's just what you'll find in each of the locations detailed in *100 Greatest Trips*.

Ecotourism and adventure travel continue to grow by leaps and bounds—a trend reflected in our coverage. Our collection of epic excursions ranges from road trips (a drive through the changing landscapes of America's Continental Divide) and desert expeditions (a quest for dinosaur fossils in Mongolia's rugged South Gobi province) to jungle treks (a hike to Argentina's Iguazú Falls) and safaris (Zambia, Africa's next great escape). The interactions with the natural world that these trips provide are likely to result in the memories of a lifetime.

For those seeking an urban escape, there's a story about one New York City neighborhood's transformation from gritty wasteland into cultural spawning ground; an intimate look at the hidden quartiers of Paris that most tourists never see; and a sojourn in Shanghai that goes from street-level hawker stalls to vertiginous skyscraper hotels.

And, of course, food is always a draw—whether it's a dizzying romp through the tempura joints and *kushiage* restaurants of Tokyo; a look at the locavore-friendly food trucks of Portland, Oregon; or a stroll through the lively lunch counters on Marrakesh, Morocco's Jamaâ El Fna square.

At the back of the book, we've provided a resource section to help you search for hotels, restaurants, and activities by location, as well as a comprehensive trips directory that sorts the contents by category (adventure, arts and culture, shopping, and more). Whether you're headed to new places or revisiting the ones you think you know, we're entirely delighted to guide you to the very best experiences these destinations offer.

NANCY NOVOGROD EDITOR-IN-CHIEF

The Egyptian Theater,
in Park City, Utah.

UNITED STATES & CANADA

W YORK CITY HARLEM HUDSON NEW JERSEY CHARLESTON ATLANTA T
ERGLADES MIAMI CHICAGO INDIANA NEW ORLEANS SAN ANTONIO CON
VIDE LAS VEGAS UTAH PORTLAND SAN FRANCISCO HOLLYWOOD HONO
WFOUNDLAND MONTREAL VANCOUVER NEW YORK CITY HARLEM HUD
RSEY CHARLESTON ATLANTA THE EVERGLADES MIAMI CHICAGO INDIAN
LEANS SAN ANTONIO CONTINENTAL DIVIDE LAS VEGAS UTAH PORTLAN
ANCISCO HOLLYWOOD HONOLULU KAUAI NEWFOUNDLAND MONTREA
NCOUVER NEW YORK CITY HARLEM HUDSON NEW JERSEY CHARLESTO
E EVERGLADES MIAMI CHICAGO INDIANA NEW ORLEANS SAN ANTONIO

NEW YORK CITY

WEST CHELSEA'S ART AND ARCHITECTURE MOMENT

New York City's
West 22nd Street.
Opposite: At work
in West Chelsea.

Wines stacked above the bar at Ovest Pizzoteca. Clockwise from right: West Chelsea locals; a shop that sells art publications on 10th Avenue; Carlos Couturier in the Hôtel Americano's lobby.

A sleepy stretch of the High Line. Below: The "diavolo" pizza, made with mozzarella and spicy salami, at Ovest Pizzoteca.

FIRST CAME THE HIGH LINE—A BOLDLY LANDSCAPED STRIP OF public space atop an abandoned elevated freight railway—which opened to endless acclaim in 2009. Now the park, which draws 2 million visitors a year, has opened a second section that stretches from 20th Street to 30th Street. All you have to do is look at the buildings that have sprung up alongside it to realize that the gritty neighborhood of West Chelsea is in the throes of a design revolution.

The slick Hôtel Americano, the first U.S. outpost of the splashy Mexican chain Grupo Habita, materialized, surprisingly, in the middle of a block best known for its warehouse-scale nightclubs. ("It feels like the Meatpacking District ten years ago," says hotel owner Carlos Couturier.) A wall of a stainless-steel apartment building wraps around the gas station at 245 10th Avenue; the minimalist HL23, an angular 14-story condo tower, muscles its way into the airspace; and a new Renzo Piano–designed branch of the Whitney Museum is under construction (it will open in 2015).

Hundreds of galleries populate the nearby Chelsea art district; stroll through the showrooms at Bryce Wolkowitz, Paul Kasmin, and Gagosian, then follow local gallerinas to Bottino, the art world's semi-official cafeteria, for expertly crafted sandwiches and salads. Trestle on Tenth specializes in Swiss-inspired cuisine such as duck with huckleberries, while Ovest Pizzoteca turns out perfectly charred pies from its wood-burning oven. Of all the tapas bars that have sprung up, each as skinny and crowded as a subway car, the most accommodating is Txikito, where you can actually sit while sipping your *zurracapote*, a Basque variation on sangria.

Meanwhile, the neighborhood's reinvention continues apace. The as-yet-unrestored third section of the High Line might one day run right through Hudson Yards, a 13 million-square-foot development slated to begin construction in 2012 or 2013. In 20 years, West Chelsea may well be an extension of midtown. The grit, for better or worse, will be history.

Dining at Red Rooster. Right: A tree-lined path in Central Park's Conservatory Garden.

HARLEM

INFUSED WITH NEW ENERGY

THERE'S BEEN A LOT OF TALK ABOUT HARLEM'S RENAISSANCE over the past decade. Rents rose and big-box stores moved in—along with the tech-savvy Aloft Harlem, the first major hotel built here in over a century—yet in the midst of it all, something peculiar happened in this upper Manhattan neighborhood: the community's unique character endured.

Among the landmarks that have stood since Harlem's Jazz Age heyday, celebrating the stories of a bygone era, is the legendary Apollo Theater, on 125th Street. Harlem's biggest attraction, the Apollo still stages modern musical productions, concerts, and its infamous weekly

One of Harlem's scenic corners. Left: Grabbing a bite at Il Caffe Latte.

amateur night. From there it's a short stroll to the Studio Museum in Harlem, where chief curator Thelma Golden showcases rising talent in a building whose cool interior balances the street's frenetic spirit. Not far is the edgy Maysles Cinema, which screens compelling films such as those in the Harlem Homegrown series.

At housewares boutique Swing, the contemporary designs could easily hold their own in Stockholm. But nowhere is the area's diversity better demonstrated than in its dining scene. Ethiopia-born, Sweden-raised chef Marcus Samuelsson's Red Rooster dishes up comfort food that honors Harlem's Southern culinary traditions (blackened catfish with fried pickles and black-eyed peas; collard greens; fried "yard bird"). Low-key Il Caffe Latte makes bracing espressos and flaky French croissants. And the authentic Amor Cubano serves an excellent roast-pork sandwich with fried plantains that's a hit with the local Spanish-speaking population.

Even in a neighborhood as vibrant as this, there's a dedicated oasis of calm nearby: Central Park's Conservatory Garden, six acres of hedges, lawns, and fountains located just off Fifth Avenue at East 105th Street. The leafy expanse is unfamiliar to many a die-hard Manhattanite—and proves the city hasn't lost its capacity to surprise.

PLEASE
DO NOT PASS
THIS LINE
UNTIL TRAIN
HAS COME TO
A STOP

HUDSON
A SOPHISTICATED SMALL-TOWN RETREAT

Apple, the pet potbellied pig at Kaaterskill Inn, just outside the village of Catskill. Opposite: The Hudson train station.

The Carrie Haddad Gallery.
Left: Strolling through Poet's
Walk, a park in nearby Red Hook.
Right: Dill-baked Arctic char
"Södermalm" at DA|BA.

A view of the Hudson River. From far left: Antiques shop Neven & Neven Moderne; endless volumes at Hillsdale's Rodgers Book Barn.

CITY SLICKERS WILL DO A DOUBLE TAKE WHEN THE TRAIN pulls into the historic town of Hudson after only a two-hour ride upriver from Manhattan. All sorts of fashionable industries, from whaling to shipbuilding, once seduced this colorful riverside getaway; its recent transformation comes courtesy of antiques dealers and gallery owners, who were followed by a wave of restaurants to impress even the most jaded New Yorker.

On Warren Street, Hudson's main drag, Nantucket-style houses give way to elaborate Victorian and Italianate structures, a veritable dictionary of American architecture. You could spend an entire afternoon browsing through the merchandise at Neven & Neven Moderne, from a gleaming Bruskbo rosewood bench to a 1940's chrome Vornado fan. Across the street at Historical Materialism, an Edwardian-period sofa shares the space with prewar German silver candleholders and an Arts and Crafts hanging Lantern. The intimate, sometimes mildly disturbing works at Carrie Haddad Gallery—Hudson's first gallery—never fail to amuse. And in nearby Hillsdale, bookworms would do well to stop by Rodgers Book Barn, where more than 50,000 tomes and mint-condition records make it *the* place to spend a rainy country afternoon.

The shops may have turned Hudson into a destination, but a surprising array of restaurants have brought the city some serious buzz. At DA|BA, chef-owner Daniel Nilsson's Swedish DNA is evident in his weekly specials, like the toast Skagen, with its judicious use of dill, cold shrimp, and whitefish roe. Everyone goes to Swoon for the crisp shoestring fries—just don't ask for ketchup (the owners don't believe in it). The menu offers new dishes daily: linguine topped with duck prosciutto and escargots; grilled octopus with ramps and sugar snap peas; curried mussels with sweet potatoes and chorizo. And in the back of Hudson Supermarket, a 7,000-square-foot antiques and vintage-accessories emporium, interior designer Chris Hebert has opened Café @ Hudson Supermarket, a Mexican counter serving complex creations such as roasted-poblano pork soup and shrimp marinated in chipotles, garlic, beer, and lime.

There are many historically accurate and meticulously restored B&B's, but for a genuinely rural experience, bed down for the night at the Kaaterskill, an inn just outside the village of Catskill, across the river from Hudson. Rooms face out to the distant peaks and a path winds past a brook and a herd of happy-looking goats—the subject of some pleasant rubbernecking.

MONMOUTH COUNTY

THE OTHER FACE OF THE JERSEY SHORE

A staff member at Le Club's rooftop pool, in Long Branch. Opposite: A Pipeline suite at Long Branch's Bungalow hotel.

Outdoor dining overlooking the Atlantic at Avenue, in Long Branch. Clockwise from right: Bungalow's front desk; tchotchkes in the hotel's lobby; Le Club's rooftop pool.

LONG BEFORE SNOOKI AND THE SITUATION GAINED notoriety for their signature orange sheen, the world's elite summered along the Jersey Shore. That legacy endures today in the sunbaked seaside enclaves of Monmouth County, an hour from New York City. With good food and shopping, not to mention 27 miles of blue-tinged coast, this is a destination that deserves a second look.

You can have oysters and rosé by the beach near Bungalow, a chic property in Long Branch's Pier Village shopping and dining complex that has access to a St.-Tropez–style oceanfront club. The public spaces are decorated with eclectic pieces: a pearl-button portrait of Queen Elizabeth by British artist Ann Carrington; old-school surfing photos; vintage furniture found at flea markets in Paris, London, and Brazil. You'll also find stores like Nirvana, which sells Hudson jeans and Splendid tees, and Avenue, a restaurant and open-air nightclub that serves lobster *pot-au-feu* and impressive towers of *fruits de mer*. Everything is within walking distance, including the train from New York City.

Neighboring towns have their own appeal. Once-derelict Asbury Park—where Bruce Springsteen occasionally plays at the Stone Pony—is undergoing a discreet revival, thanks to its early-20th-century architecture and rows of antiques shops. Horse-racing fans head to Monmouth Park Racetrack, in nearby Oceanport; summer's biggest competition is the Haskell, where past Kentucky Derby and Belmont Stakes winners are invited to take the field. For live music, there's the 1926 Count Basie Theater, in the jazz great's hometown of Red Bank, a picturesque landing on the Navesink River. Best of all: not a single MTV reality star in sight.

Le Club's cocktail waitresses in uniform. Above: The beach at Pier Village, in Long Branch.

Shrimp and grits with crisp Benton's bacon at Husk restaurant. Above: Bowen Island restaurant's famous oysters.

CHARLESTON

A DOWN-HOME FOOD QUEST

PIG-LOVING CHEFS, RAMBLING ROADHOUSES, AND GENTEEL charms make Charleston the pride of the Lowcountry. The city's evocative Southern heritage tends to work its spell on even the most forward-thinking newcomers, but there's a youthful energy coursing through the historic food scene.

At the restaurant Husk, in a 19th-century house on stately Queen Street, chef Sean Brock sources Ossabaw pigs from a farm north of Charleston for his fried pork skins, pleasantly gamy pork rillettes, and silky pork butter (yes—pork butter). A city institution since 1946, the seafood dive Bowens Island, perched on a muddy bank of the Folly Creek about 25 minutes from City Hall, has been reincarnated as a pavilion on stilts that preserves the unhinged rusticity of the original: graffiti walls; mismatched furniture; shell-collecting buckets. The atmosphere can seem spartan, but the beers are cold, and the house-harvested oysters—which you shuck yourself before delivering them to the pit master in the open-air roasting room—are sublime.

Back downtown, the nightlife is diversifying beyond its college-centric sensibilities. On Percy Street, a jewel box of a bar called Enoteca serves an array of Italian beers with enough esoteric depth to humble even Mario Batali. At Belmont, a decidedly grown-up single-barrel-bourbon-focused establishment, the doorman enforces a civilized 46-person maximum. The Charleston Pour House incorporates a Cuban restaurant and two stages for live music under one roof; order a pint of HopArt IPA from North Charleston's Coast Brewing Company, made with organic grains in bio-diesel-fired kettles. Lofty though they may seem, these additions are physically and intellectually connected to this place, reaching back to the past to find a new way forward. As it turns out, in this bastion of Southern hospitality, so many of the buzzwords of post-recession America—sustainability, community, artisanal—have been evergreen for centuries.

Walking along Charleston's
historic Queen Street.

Ann Mashburn boutique.
Left: The "all share"
course of cod, pork, and
tripe stew at Abattoir.

ATLANTA

A NEIGHBORHOOD'S NEW LEASE ON LIFE

AT THE TURN OF THE 20TH CENTURY, ATLANTA'S MEATPACKING District was the last place you'd call a cultural hotbed. Fast-forward about a hundred years and it's the most fashionable address in town. Rechristened the Westside, the once-industrial area is now the site of vigorous creative discourse—and the sybaritic pleasures that tend to follow it.

Dip into the energy every third Saturday, when galleries in the Westside Arts District host lectures, talks, and guided tours of the various showrooms that have taken root. Not to miss: Saltworks, with cutting-edge video and sculptural installations by emerging

The dining room at JCT. Kitchen & Bar. Left: Miller Union's executive chef Steven Satterfield.

talents from Atlanta and beyond, and Jennifer Schwartz Gallery, which showcases fine-art photography.

If it's more-commercial art you're after (namely, fashion) you'll be better off spending the day in the Westside Provisions District, a former meatpacking plant. The bespoke suits and gentlemanly accoutrements—silk-tartan ties; Forge de Laguiole pocket knives; Caran d'Ache pens—at Sid Mashburn's namesake haberdashery fill the bill. Across the way at Ann Mashburn, run by Sid's wife, poplin shirtdresses from her own label and ballerina flats are stylishly preppy staples.

Good food is also in abundance. In a space originally occupied by stockyards, chef Steven Satterfield's Miller Union embraces New Southern cuisine, with dishes such as farm eggs baked in celery purée and house-made ice cream sandwiches. The fried chicken regularly sells out at JCT. Kitchen & Bar, named for the railroad junction that once transported livestock to the area. At Yeah Burger, chef Shaun Doty's mix-and-match menu focuses on organic ingredients, from a grass-fed bison patty to its gluten-free bun. Nose-to-tail cooking is the specialty at Abattoir, French for "slaughterhouse"—an apt reminder of just how far the neighborhood has come.

A still-clean Swamp Buggy Queen.

Kayaking around the
Ten Thousand Islands.
Left: Firefighters in
Everglades City.

THE EVERGLADES

AMERICA'S LAST FRONTIER

COMPARED WITH THE NATION'S OVERLY MANICURED suburbs, the Everglades are a jolt of fear and freedom—a vast expanse of subtropical wetlands that shelter dilapidated crab shacks and 12-foot alligators alike. In fact, the UNESCO World Heritage site is as variegated and weird as America itself—full of eccentric characters and big enough for all manner of dreams.

The Tamiami Trail, a 270-mile road that goes through Miami, Naples, and Tampa, offers easy access to this wonderland. Driving west near Ochopee, you'll find the Fakahatchee Strand Preserve State Park, where biologist Mike Owen conducts guided swamp walks through a 20-mile-long slough filled with tropical ferns, otters, egrets and roseate spoonbills, Everglades mink, eastern diamondback rattlesnakes, the occasional bald eagle, and delicate ghost orchids.

From there it's a 10-minute drive to Everglades City, the unofficial capital. The town is the perfect jumping-off point for

exploring the Ten Thousand Islands, a mangrove-filled archipelago along the coast, by airboat. The working dock of City Seafood Café & Market is still authentic and funky, with patrons chucking the shells of just-eaten stone crabs into the water. At the Camellia Street Grill, the day's catch (often grouper) is prepared with homegrown herbs. Down the road, the eco-friendly Ivey House hotel offers guided kayaking tours morning, noon, and night.

On or off the Tamiami Trail, the Everglades have remained wild at heart. Swamp buggies are cheap, jury-rigged affairs of old truck parts and giant tractor tires. During the Swamp Buggy Races—a ceremonial ritual of mud and supercharged engines held in Naples every January, March, and October—they morph into bellowing dinosaurs charging down the straightaway. At the end of the day, the anointed Swamp Buggy Queen, dressed in a gown and tiara, jumps into the cold, muddy water. It's a splendidly absurd finale to the epic adventure that is the Glades.

MIAMI

A STYLE CAPITAL'S LATEST TRANSFORMATION

Brickell Key, as seen from the
JW Marriott Marquis Miami.
Opposite: Works by Ugo
Rondinone and Rachel Harrison
at the de la Cruz Collection of
Contemporary Art.

The beach at Soho Beach House Miami. Clockwise from above: The hotel's pool; Wynwood Kitchen & Bar, in the Design District; co-owner Arel Ramos at his shop, Stripe Vintage Modern.

FORTY YEARS AGO, THE FIGHT TO PRESERVE SOUTH BEACH'S Art Deco district jump-started the first resurrection of Miami. Today, it is Frank Gehry's New World Center that is helping put the city on the global cultural map.

Though Gehry's performing arts venue looms large as you approach the entrance to Lincoln Road, it's meant to serve as an everyday social arena. Visitors to the adjacent park can watch the New World Symphony rehearse through a six-story glass curtain wall, or take in concert broadcasts and video-art murals on a 7,000-square-foot screen. Just north of the structure, the Collins Park arts district features a lawn studded with sculptural installations that stretch from the Bass Museum of Art to the beach. It's a 10-minute bike ride along the boardwalk to South Pointe Park, a 17½-acre former wasteland transformed into a maze of serpentine trails, winding through dune grasses to a waterfront promenade lined with 18 light-emitting pylons.

See them all before retreating to mid-Miami Beach's Soho Beach House, the newest outpost of the London-based boutique hotel and social club. Public spaces include heavy ye-olde-English-club leather chairs and a 150-plus-piece contemporary art collection curated by Francesca Gavin. Downtown's most recent addition is the JW Marriott Marquis Miami, inside a 41-story tower that also houses the boutique Hotel Beaux Arts Miami, the debut of Marriott's new luxury brand.

Smaller Miami communities are also being reenergized. Bal Harbour, primarily known for its luxury shopping, now hosts free movie screenings by the water and concerts. Off the beach, in the Design District, high-end boutiques and showrooms join the 30,000-square-foot de la Cruz Collection of Contemporary Art, the latest in a series of museums opened by eminent Miami collectors. On the other end of the style spectrum, there's Wynwood Walls, a graffiti garden with a restaurant and bar created by Tony Goldman, an early South Beach pioneer who jumped from Art Deco to street art.

In a city known for reinventions, the classics are just as alluring. Head north on Biscayne Boulevard, and you'll discover row upon row of Miami Modern motels that unfurl like a ribbon of joy—all statues of cavorting sea nymphs and trapezoid forms resembling 1955 Cadillac fins. Little Haiti lies a few blocks west, its atmospheric landscape filled with artists' studios and fantastic murals by Serge Toussaint. Farther south, in the heart of Little Havana, music and art take center stage: on the last Friday of every month, the Viernes Culturales street festival includes late-night gallery openings and sophisticated Afro-Cuban *timba* music. It's a party no visitor should miss.

A biker in South Pointe Park. Below: The Shops at Bal Harbour.

Chef Cary Taylor's take on
poutine, at the Southern.
Right: The El in Bucktown,
near the restaurant.

CHICAGO

SAMPLING THE MIDWEST'S EXOTIC FLAVORS

ALTHOUGH IT'S HOME TO PLENTY OF NITROGEN-CANISTER-wielding megachefs, Chicago also lays claim to one of the country's greatest back-to-basics food communities. From Bucktown to the Ukrainian Village, a tour of the city's neighborhood restaurants proves that the heartland's palate is more adventurous than ever.

Stop by Bucktown on a Monday night and the Bristol is likely to be sprinkled with off-duty chefs, all wondering what they'll find on Chris Pandel's wildly unpredictable daily menu. One thing's for sure: Pandel doesn't play coy with flavors. When you see the brined, braised, and fried pig ear with Vietnamese noodles, coriander, and Illinois soybeans, floating in a meaty *pho*-style broth tinged with palm sugar, grab it. Pandel may never offer it again.

At the Southern, also in Bucktown, chef Cary Taylor is a Georgia homeboy who makes good on his promise of "the dirtiest fried chicken north of the Mason-Dixon." Turning out bar-centric food in a sleek version of a lake house, Taylor straddles Southern and Midwestern cooking with hybrids such as his Cajun send-up of Canada's beloved *poutine*: layers of freshly cut potato drenched in house-made tasso gravy, then topped by Wisconsin cheese curds and served with a side of Taylor's amiable Southern-fried storytellin'.

Come Sunday, when you're desperate to avoid typically treacly brunch food, get in line at Jam, in the Ukrainian Village. Chef Jeffrey Mauro blankets braised lamb neck and Asian pears with nutty buckwheat crêpes. His French toast (custard-soaked brioche) is vacuum sealed and cooked *sous vide* before it even hits the griddle. Even the eggs Benedict land someplace unexpected: neat stacks of crisped, cured pork belly and English muffins are the foundation for silky poached eggs and a sweep of butternut-squash hollandaise with pumpkin seeds. Mauro rarely looks up from the busy open kitchen. Once your food arrives, neither will you.

The Miller House & Garden, designed by Eero Saarinen.

COLUMBUS

REDISCOVERING A MODERNIST RETREAT

DESIGN-SAVVY TRAVELERS HAVE A NEW DESTINATION FOR architectural thrills. In the somnolent town of Columbus, Indiana, 50 miles south of Indianapolis, the J. Irwin & Xenia Miller house is a high-concept marvel that has been called the most significant Modernist residence in America. A block-long wall of neatly clipped evergreens is the only clue to its presence on a placid suburban street, but once inside, you'll wonder how anyone could miss it.

In 1957, Eero Saarinen designed the residence, which Miller heirs recently bequeathed to the Indianapolis Museum of Art, to look like nothing else in the vicinity. The result is a minimalist box supported by white steel columns and wrapped in black Virginia slate, joined by floor-to-ceiling glass. Terrazzo-paved terraces surround the four sides of the house, with open-air living and dining areas reachable through sliding glass doors. In contrast with the subdued façade, the interiors are a carnival of opulent colors and graphic patterns—blue glass mosaic walls; folk art from Mexico; mirrored pillows from India—the work of *Mad Men*–era architect and textile designer Alexander Girard.

The residence ranks alongside such classic landmarks of modern design as Frank Lloyd Wright's Fallingwater, Ludwig Mies van der Rohe's Farnsworth House, and Philip Johnson's Glass House. But unlike those structures, Miller House has some of the most beautiful gardens in the United States. Walk through the highly ordered grounds, and you'll begin to understand why landscape architect Dan Kiley favored spare plantings and clean geometry. Beds of ivy and arborvitae, allées of honey locusts, and sculpted hedges make the abode a haven that is all but invisible to its neighbors. But now that the site is finally open to the public, it won't be a secret for long.

Musicians Ben Jaffe (left) and Charlie Gabriel of the Preservation Hall Jazz Band, outside the French Quarter club. Opposite: The corner of Royal and Orleans at twilight.

NEW ORLEANS

INDIVIDUALITY IN THE SPOTLIGHT

Dressed up for Mardi Gras. Clockwise from above: Locals gathered on the French Quarter's Toulouse Street; New Orleans-born singer and songwriter Paul Sanchez; the Dungeon Room at Antoine's restaurant.

A CRAWFISH IS A STRANGE-LOOKING CREATURE, AND learning how to eat the thing is one of the subtle markers on the path to understanding, or at least enjoying, New Orleans. This kind of eccentricity is in NOLA's marrow. For all its problems, the city once ravaged by Katrina and plagued by the Gulf oil spill is blessed with an innate sense of style that wafts up and down Oak Street: from the Oak Street Café—with its picture windows, green-and-white-checked tablecloths, and a piano in the corner that give it the feeling of time pooling—to Z'otz, a labyrinthine goth coffee shop that serves an excellent cappuccino. The atmosphere is part of the experience. It comes from the architecture; the embrace of the huge live oaks overhanging the lanes; and the town's central metaphor, Mardi Gras, the multiday celebration during which the city throngs the streets to watch itself on parade.

It's also in the tuba, trumpet, and trombone that play heavily in the music scene. A tiny hole-in-the-wall in the French Quarter, the legendary Preservation Hall is dedicated to traditional New Orleans jazz and run by Ben Jaffe, a tuba player who followed in his father's footsteps after the latter ran the Hall for decades. In fact, brass instruments and marching bands are two motifs that permeate the city; you can see them in the obsessive band-formation drawings by Bruce Davenport, on display in Prospect 2, an exhibition that focuses on local artists, or in the pictures that line the walls at the legendary French-Creole restaurant Antoine's.

The city's bohemian frontiers, Bywater and Marigny, teem with new establishments. More and more galleries are appearing on St. Claude Avenue and Julia Street, showcasing talent both modern (Dale Chihuly's intricate glass sculptures at Arthur Roger Gallery) and historical (Mathew Brady and Timothy O'Sullivan's Civil War photography at Good Children Gallery). Restaurants are also proliferating, along with twentysomethings on bicycles toting laptops and vegan muffins from Satsuma Café. In nearby Lakeview, Mondo features a menu as eclectic as the city itself: a ceviche with fresh tortilla chips and guacamole; Thai shrimp-and-pork meatballs; pizza from a wood-burning oven; deviled eggs.

Yet despite this renewal, what persists is a landscape of gorgeous imperfection. In the French Quarter, the Garden District, and Uptown the handsome, the sublime, and the ruined intermingle in surprising ways. Among the carriage houses and wrought-iron balconies, an unassuming print and copy shop isn't your usual destination when exploring a city, but Laredo Printing—a museum of graphic design and music history covered in concert posters made by owner Fred Laredo for Chuck Berry, Bruce Springsteen, and the Neville Brothers—illustrates a point: in New Orleans, a lot of the oysters have pearls.

Mardi Gras performers in the Seventh Ward. Above: Pouring a Sazerac in an Uptown bar.

Locals hanging out at La Gloria.

SAN ANTONIO

REINING IN THE WILD WEST

THE LONE STAR STATE'S SECOND-LARGEST CITY WAS ONCE known for little more than the Alamo, which became a symbol of the Republic's independence from Mexico in 1836. But San Antonio is finally coming around to its myriad treasures, namely its prized riverside location.

The famous San Antonio River Walk, an eight-mile cobble- and flagstone path that connects much of downtown, hosts 5 million visitors a year. (City officials plan to extend the walkway to 15 miles by 2013.) Nature lovers might spot yellow-crowned night herons, barred owls, or red-eared slider turtles; fashionistas are equally at home in the trendy cafés, hotels, and shops along the cypress-lined banks. The Museum Reach section meanders past the San Antonio Museum of Art. The route, landscaped with native plants and small water cascades, features art installations— Donald Lipski sculptures and glow-in-the-dark murals by Mark Schlesinger—under every bridge.

Thirty minutes from downtown, the JW Marriott San Antonio Hill Country Resort & Spa makes a peaceful base, thanks to a 26,000-square-foot spa, two golf courses, a greenhouse, nature trails—even a water park. Closer to the action is the 27-room Hotel Havana, Liz Lambert's restored 1914 hacienda, where guests wake up to breakfast feasts of Cuban espresso and sweet Mexican pastries.

Chef Johnny Hernandez spent seven years in Mexico researching the country's street foods for La Gloria, in the Pearl Brewery District. Grab a patio seat and order a traditional *sope*, a crispy tortilla topped with spicy *chicharrones* (pork rinds), or chile-adobo-simmered skirt steak served in a *molcajete*. Down the street at Italian restaurant Il Sogno, industrial floor-to-ceiling windows offer views of the kitchen, where chef Andrew Weissman whips up house-made crostini and *pasta allo zafferano*—mussels, shrimp, and pancetta with saffron cream sauce. In the same building, cookbook author Melissa Guerra stocks hard-to-find housewares from Central and South America at her Tienda de Cocina. *Molinillos*, hand-carved milk frothers from Mexico, and Chilean earthenware pots make useful souvenirs for the gringos back home.

La Gloria's skirt steak, served in a *molcajete*. Above: A cushioned perch in the Grand Suite at Hotel Havana.

CONTINENTAL DIVIDE

A SCENIC DRIVE, NORTH TO SOUTH

Going-to-the-Sun Road,
near Glacier National
Park, in Montana.

THE ICONIC CROSS-COUNTRY ROAD TRIP IS USUALLY DRIVEN EAST TO WEST, always chasing the setting sun. But the invisible line that runs along the top of the Rocky Mountains, north to south, proves an even better guide. Along the Continental Divide, the glaciers of Montana give way to the mesas of New Mexico. The contest between the route before you and the glory all around, between close concentration and overpowering distraction, becomes your constant companion.

Montana is all copper and green—a honeypot of forest, open space, and fertile land. Only a few hours away from the start of your trip in Kalispell, Going-to-the-Sun Road isn't the highest one you'll travel, but it's sure to be the most spectacular. Built in the 1930's, the pike takes visitors into the heart of Glacier National Park, past Logan Pass to Triple Divide Peak—from whose flanks water flows in not two but three directions, adding the Arctic to the Atlantic and Pacific.

Continue through the Tetons of Wyoming and the burbling pits of Yellowstone to South Pass, where the Oregon, Mormon, and California trails converge with the old Pony Express route. At Mad Dog and the Pilgrim Booksellers, in sleepy Sweetwater Station, 60,000 antiquarian, out-of-print, and just plain curious volumes will derail your forward thrust like a mighty pine fallen across your path. While you're at it, pull into the Two-Bit Cowboy Saloon, at Miner's Delight Inn, set within a tiny former mining settlement in nearby Atlantic City, for the state's best single malts.

High-desert sagebrush yields to blue spruce, pickups to Subarus, cowboy hats to baseball caps in Aspen, Colorado, though the faces are still tan and weathered. Where once the major boomtown was Leadville, now it's here, the mining done over drinks and on the slopes. Linking the two towns is Independence Pass, which at 12,095 feet is the highest paved crossing of the Continental Divide. Settle into a cozy, fake-fur-trimmed lounge chair with a bourbon-spiked Aspen Slush at Sky Hotel, then sip a hot toddy at the Little Nell, a glossy après-ski hangout across the street.

Then you're on to New Mexico, where the mountains emerge shorn of their peaks, rising randomly across the desert floor like tables draped in gold and red. Stockpile your water before entering the swirling volcanic terrain of El Malpais National Monument. Later, cool the afterburn of green-chile cheeseburgers with iced tea at Largo Café, in Quemado. Silver City, a hilly town that sits almost directly on the Continental Divide, is your final stop, your journey along America's spine complete.

LAS VEGAS

A BIG, FAT EPICUREAN ADVENTURE

Nighttime on the Strip.

IN THE PAST, THE VEGAS FOOD SCENE WAS DEEMED TASTELESS in more ways than one—splashy casino-side dining rooms offering up leathery steaks and flavorless crab legs. But in recent years the parameters have expanded tenfold for food lovers. Today you can sample every kind of cuisine, on every size budget: Michelin-starred bistros; suburban pizzerias; chefs' haunts in Chinatown mini-malls. Settle in at the Mandarin Oriental—a haven of gimmick-free refinement at CityCenter—and between rounds of blackjack, go on a city-wide restaurant binge.

Near the Sahara hotel, Lotus of Siam, which some have proclaimed the best Thai restaurant in North America, serves Issan-style deep-fried beef jerky that will make your eyes well up—not so much from the heat (though it packs plenty) as from its sheer abundant goodness. At Archi's Thai Kitchen, a 15-minute drive away in a stucco hut across from a pet-grooming service, you'll find the ultimate chicken *satay*: tender thigh meat marinated overnight in curry powder, sugar, and garlic, then deep-fried and grilled to an ideal balance of juiciness and char. It's served with a sauce that isn't peanut-buttery sweet but rather spicy, dusky, demanding another dip. South of the airport, Bachi Burger specializes in pork buns and Asian-inflected burgers. The Neapolitan-style Settebello Pizzeria, in the suburb of Green Valley, is equipped with a 950-degree wood-fired oven for blistering the crust of a margherita pie just so.

Back on the Strip, chef Paul Bartolotta's coastal-Italian restaurant, Bartolotta Ristorante del Mare, is known for impeccably fresh and shockingly expensive fish. Your waiter rolls up a cart full of evidence: silver-flecked sea bream; spiny scorpion fish; glistening snapper. (For an extra $85, the kitchen will shave white truffles on it.) At last, you hit the MGM Grand for Joël Robuchon, the grandest restaurant in Vegas, from the man some call the world's greatest chef. The opening courses at his 50-seat dining room are standouts: a tin of osetra caviar hiding a layer of crabmeat and fennel cream; airy egg-yolk ravioli with chanterelles and spinach foam. Pairings are equally assured, such as the minerally white burgundy from Méo-Camuzet that drinks beautifully with roasted lobster and sea-urchin flan. Before you know it a *mignardises* cart appears, glittering like a jewel box—the last thing you remember before waking up the next day to do it all over again.

Bartolotta Ristorante del Mare's sautéed clams. Below: The dessert cart at Joël Robuchon.

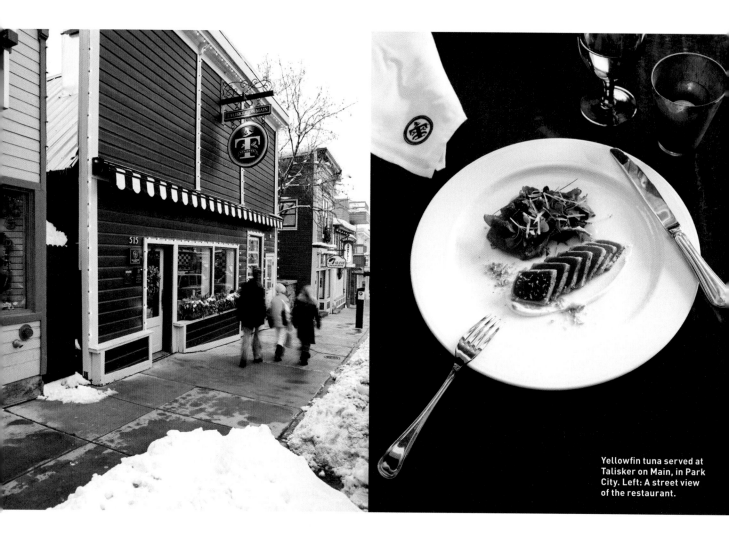

Yellowfin tuna served at Talisker on Main, in Park City. Left: A street view of the restaurant.

PARK CITY
HIGH-ALTITUDE ESCAPISM

THE 2002 WINTER OLYMPICS WAS A GAME-CHANGER, PUTTING this tiny Utah town on the map and prompting a building boom that is reaching its zenith today, resulting in several new high-end hotels. There's the Waldorf Astoria Park City, a ski-in property with a Golden Door spa; the St. Regis Deer Valley Resort, which has a fleet of butlers to cater to your every whim; and the Montage Deer Valley, with its deep soaking tubs and bowling-lane-lined gastropub.

But despite all the swank—and the annual Sundance Film Festival, which continues to lure movie-industry movers and shakers—this old silver-mining town has managed to retain its iconoclastic personality. Downtown is comprised of a single road—aptly named Main Street—

Main Street's Burns Cowboy Shop. Left: Two-time Olympic mogul skier Jillian Vogtli on the slopes.

with brightly painted buildings dating to the early 1900's and offbeat stores like the gunslinging, boot-selling Burns Cowboy Shop. Nearby, an old red trolley rumbles by and the triangular Egyptian Theater marquee announces shows like *Reefer Madness, the Musical.*

Of course you can't come to Park City without sampling the snow, which is phenomenal. Maybe that's why the town seems to have more Olympic residents than any other city in the country. Many of them work out year-round at a $22 million state-of-the-art training facility. Mere mortals spend their days blasting through the powder on Stein's Way, named for 1952 Norwegian Olympic champion Stein Eriksen, or riding the lifts to the expert Lady Morgan Bowl.

The restaurant scene has undergone a similar transformation, thanks to the opening of Jean-Georges Vongerichten's JG Grill at the St. Regis. The intimate bistro Talisker on Main, helmed by local star chef John Murcko, is the most significant boost to Park City's restaurant row, with short-rib shepherd's pie and roasted-corn bisque that will bolster you for a day on the slopes. The fireside Bar Bohème at the Sky Lodge and the historic High West Distillery are other options for whiling away the evening. Or do as the locals do and make a beeline to the No Name Saloon. A moose head presides over the proceedings, and the guy doing shots at the other end of the bar might just be the mayor.

Sweetbreads served over spaghetti at Le Pigeon. From near right: A street view of Clyde Common, in the Ace Hotel; Nong Poonsukwattana in her chicken-and-rice cart, Nong's Khao Man Gai.

PORTLAND

WHERE THE EATING IS EASY

IS PORTLAND, OREGON, THE MOST FOOD-OBSESSED PLACE IN the country? It sure feels like it, given the endless parade of back-to-the-land lettuce farmers, coffee micro-roasters, sandwich innovators, and food-cart proprietors on display. The city's enduring culinary obsessions may date to the 1960's, when a wave of idealists came to grow their own food and do their own canning, bringing an awareness of the politics of consumption that never went away. But current chefs have a more trenchant approach: they like meat, and they want to have a good time.

Take Beast, a two-woman, two-seating, six-course, set-menu show in which 20 or so satisfied-looking participants eat communally and leave no trace of boudin noir set in apple and duck-fat pastry, or sliced hanger steak with brown-butter béarnaise. At Le Pigeon, the celebrated Lower Burnside space that is half civilized bistro and half culinary crack den, your darkest desires (*foie gras torchon* with buttermilk pancakes; sweetbreads with blue cheese) are indulged. Ned Ludd, a pure-hearted restaurant with a wood-burning oven, offers up house-made charcuterie, slow-roasted chops, and flatbreads. Even the Ace Hotel—a fitting pad for a Portland stay—has a restaurant, Clyde Common, that takes tavern-style dishes to a new level.

For all the off-kilter sophistication of its restaurants, Portland also excels at more casual fare. After all, this is a town that takes civic pride in Voodoo Doughnut's bacon-maple-glazed variety. Innovative sandwich shops are packed. For pork-belly *cubanos* and meatball heros, try Bunk Sandwiches; for a flank-steak hoagie with blue cheese mayo or a BLB (bacon, lettuce, and golden beets), go to Meat Cheese Bread, in Southeast. The city's food trucks are as celebrated as any dining establishment. You'll find vanilla-bean *panna cotta* served with local strawberries at the Sugar Cube, and poached chicken and rice with soup at Nong's Khao Man Gai, which has a devoted following on Twitter. In Portland, the food nerds are the cool kids.

A plate of charcuterie at Beast. From far left: Le Pigeon's counter dining; the Sugar Cube.

BACK PACKING

The edgy inventory at Afterlife Boutique. From near right: Gravel & Gold's decorative housewares; the corner of 18th and Lapidge Streets.

A shady bench on Valencia Street. From far left: San Francisco's Golden Gate Bridge; tea sets at Gravel & Gold.

SAN FRANCISCO

STOCKING UP IN THE MISSION

THE SUNNY MISSION DISTRICT OF SAN FRANCISCO HAS LONG been a vibrant mash-up. The enclave's colorful Latino culture and artistic spirit comes courtesy of immigrants from South and Central America, who began migrating here in the 1970's, opening up tiny taquerias and painting larger-than-life Diego Rivera–inspired street murals for all to enjoy.

Unlike the throwback architecture, some of which dates to the mid 1800's, the music and arts scene has always been on the cutting edge—a launchpad for punk rockers and artists who've gone on to international renown. But lately the Mission is getting a reputation for something new: a spate of small, innovative boutiques that outfit the local hipster set. Quirky shops line both sides of Valencia Street, the main drag. Siblings Danielle and Luke Teller curate the Afterlife Boutique, which carries reconstructed antique jewelry and collectible rock-concert shirts priced from $45 to $1,000; don't miss the sweatshirt emblazoned with the phrase MICHAEL JACKSON FOR PRESIDENT in the red font from his *Thriller* album. Two blocks down, Paxton Gate specializes in taxidermy, but fashionistas flock to the store for its one-of-a-kind python-rib hoop earrings and sterling silver pieces inspired by nature. Also a draw: the extensive array of gardening accessories, from delicate glass cloches and terrariums to minimalist Japanese shears.

The streets around Valencia are also rife with offerings. Bibliophiles will want to seek out the books imported from the Caribbean and Latin America at Libros Latinos, on Mission Street. Nearby, the light-filled Gravel & Gold is a treasure hunter's dream, brimming with everything from Japanese paper goods to wool blankets made on Prince Edward Island. Union Square may have once had a lock on the Bay Area's shopping scene, but now the Mission is the most stylish place to be.

A character on Hollywood Boulevard. Right: The collectibles at Hollywood Movie Posters.

HOLLYWOOD

RETRO TREASURES RIPE FOR THE TAKING

FOR THOSE BESOTTED WITH THE GOLDEN AGE OF THE SILVER screen, a Hollywood film souvenir bears the ultimate provenance. Starstruck shoppers in search of movie memorabilia head to Tinseltown, of course—a trove of posters, props, and fashions that hark back to cinema's glory days.

Launch your hunt from the corner of Hollywood and Vine at the Redbury, one of the latest hotels in Sam Nazarian's club-centric SBE brand, where apartment-style suites provide plenty of space to stow your finds. Vintage prints and stills are on offer at Hollywood Movie Posters, which occupies a sunny lair in Artisan's Patio, a 1914 landmark that is now a charming retail passageway. Larry Edmunds

Vintage dresses at Decades. Right: The Bettie Page boutique.

Bookshop is another paper-crammed emporium, bursting with more than 20,000 entertainment-related books and mile-high stacks of yellowing fan magazines. At the vast Prop Store, in Chatsworth, you'll find such memorabilia as Angelina Jolie's speargun from *Lara Croft: Tomb Raider,* or 15-foot-high faux-Egyptian Horus statues from the sci-fi TV show *Stargate SG-1.*

But maybe it's not your walls that need the dressing. The consignment store It's a Wrap carries clothes that have been worn on (or at least purchased for) a set: faux-garnet bangle bracelets that graced someone's arm in the television show *The Starter Wife*; an olive-green gabardine suit with crystal detailing once donned by a diva on *All My Children.* At the Bettie Page boutique—a delightfully ridiculous shop devoted to the cheerfully sexy dominatrix—the mood is Midcentury and the full-skirted printed shirtwaist dresses are surprisingly demure, considering Page's line of work. Alas, in L.A., there is vintage and then there is *vintage.* Decades is the latter, a rarefied showroom where celebrities buy or borrow one-of-a-kind, high-end gowns for red-carpet galas. As you sit on a python-covered pouf atop a 1940's monkey fur rug, you might convince yourself that you really need that flower-strewn Mia Farrow–worthy Ossie Clark frock from the 1970's. Yes, you do.

WISHING WELL · SHAVE ICE THE ORIGINAL SINCE 1983

The Wishing Well shave ice truck, in Hanalei Bay.

The Napali Coast, on the northwestern side of Kauai. Below: Getting ready to surf on Hideaways Beach.

KAUAI

PARADISE FOUND

NATURE STILL CALLS THE SHOTS ON KAUAI, WHICH BUBBLED up from the ocean floor 5 million years ago to become the oldest and westernmost of the major Hawaiian islands.

On the Eden-like North Shore, waterfalls spill from jagged cliffs in deep green valleys; clouds hover and vaporize, altering the light. Anchoring this camera-ready nook is the St. Regis Princeville Resort, 251 rooms carved into the bluffs above the eastern tip of Hanalei Bay. The grounds roll down past the low-key pool to the beach and bay. The crescent-shaped swath is near perfect, but for the local version of paradise make your way to Pali Ke Kua Beach, also known as Hideaways, tucked under a canopy of false kamani trees surrounded by 30-foot-high black lava-rock walls. Green sea turtles occasionally lunge their way onto the sand there. Don't miss the shave ice at the Wishing Well truck nearby. A few miles further along the shore, the Kalalau Trail (Hawaii's most famous spot to hike) clings to the Napali Coast for 11 untamed miles of bamboo and ohia trees, switchbacks, waterfalls, killer ocean views, and vertigo-inducing drop-offs.

Past Kalaheo, the terrain becomes drier, the sun stronger, and the pace considerably slower. On the southwest side of the island, Waimea is everything you want in a Hawaiian town—a friendly, authentic local scene; a few decent restaurants; and a warm place to stay. The Waimea Plantation Cottages is pure old-school Hawaiian "*aloha*": 57 former sugar-field bungalows, refitted as guest accommodations and scattered around 27 acres of wide lawns, ironwood and coconut palms, empty hammocks, and massive banyan trees. The days begin to fly by unaccounted for—a hike up in Waimea Canyon State Park; a swim at a deserted stretch of beach in Polihale State Park; an evening spent watching the neighborhood kids play baseball. Before long, you find yourself on the porch at Wrangler's Steakhouse for an early dinner, just as you were the night before.

HONOLULU

UNCOVERING OAHU'S LOCAL HAUNTS

SWAYING PALM TREES AND WHITE-SAND BEACHES have endeared Honolulu to the tourist trade. But there are homegrown pleasures, too. Check in to the 353-room Modern Honolulu—designed by Yabu Pushelberg—then seek out the places where locals shop and eat.

The starting bell rings at 7:30 a.m. at the Saturday KCC Farmers' Market, where you can fuel up on aromatic Kona coffee and sliced papaya with a wedge of lime. If you're *akamai* ("smart," in Hawaiian), you'll arrive early to preorder tart apple bananas, aged honey, and fresh-baked breads. Orchid lovers in search of takeaway buds follow the winding road through Palolo Valley's residential Kaimuki neighborhood to Kawamoto Orchids, a kaleidoscopic three-acre nursery. More blooms are on hand at one of the lei makers in Chinatown: Lin's and Cindy's are two family-owned businesses whose fragrant pikake and plumeria garlands start at just $5. For 1950's-era kitsch such as silk Aloha shirts, hand-tinted postcards, and mahogany ukuleles, Tincan Mailman is a must. On the high end, evening gowns and clutches at Anne Namba's namesake shop are made with vintage Japanese kimono and obi fabrics; Hillary Clinton and Aretha Franklin are fans.

Queue up with the office crowd at Yama's Fish Market, a concrete-floored takeout joint specializing in Hawaiian plate lunches, including 14 types of *poke* (marinated raw fish). House-made noodles at the always crowded Jimbo, in the city center, have a cult following. Seasonal ingredients are front and center at Town, where the menu changes nightly. A few recent standouts: risotto with *pepeiao* (Hawaiian wood ear mushrooms) and a tender Big Island strip loin. But no trip to Honolulu is complete without a breakfast at Boots & Kimos. The macadamia-nut pancakes come smothered in a sugar-and-butter concoction and topped with macadamia shavings—the perfect start to a day spent canoeing against the waves near Lanikai Beach.

Canoeing off Honolulu's
Lanikai Beach.

FOGO ISLAND

AN UNEXPECTED ARTISTS' HAVEN

A SMALL FISHING VILLAGE OFF NEWFOUNDLAND'S COAST might just be the most unlikely place for an artistic awakening. But this tiny community—on an island of craggy shores and miles of blissful nothingness in northeastern Canada, reachable only by ferry—is fast becoming a cultural destination.

It's all thanks to residents Elísabet Gunnarsdóttir and Zita Cobb and Newfoundland-born architect Todd Saunders. The creative trio is behind Fogo Island Arts Corporation, a series of boldly geometric structures, many of which are on stilts, that are inspired in part by the wooden fishing stages that dot the seaside. Built to pay homage to the island's original arts and crafts traditions, the studios host workshops, art projects, and exhibitions that lure international contemporary artists to this secluded setting. The Saunders-designed, 29-room Fogo Island Inn is scheduled to open in 2012, but for now visitors can stay at Foley's Place, a bed-and-breakfast in a clapboard house that dates back a century.

Nature's artistry is also on display throughout the island. Trek along the 5½-mile Turpin's Trail, which leads you from a sandy beach through a wildflower-edged forest and rocky shores. Go on a berry-picking expedition (partridgeberries, blueberries, and marshberries grow in abundance here). Then organize an outing with nature writer Roy Dwyer, who will take you out on his boat and recount tales from Fogo's colonial past.

A traditional Irish-style structure on Fogo Island.

Outdoor dining on a
pedestrian-friendly
corner of Vieux-Montréal.

MONTREAL

A MULTICULTURAL MELTING POT

FORGET EVERYTHING YOU'VE HEARD ABOUT MONTREAL—
that it's a kind of toy-size Paris on the St. Lawrence. Its true identity
is more nuanced than that. Both Canadian and Québécois, part
anglophone and part francophone, Montreal is a city that defies
easy categorization, a patchwork of ethnic enclaves that looks and
feels like nowhere else on the planet.

Grab a set of wheels from Bixi, the public bike system that offers
24-hour service at 400 different docks, and explore the elegant
fieldstone buildings and tight alleys of the historic Vieux-Montréal.
At day's end, the quietly chic Le Petit Hôtel makes an ideal resting
point. North of downtown, the tree-lined Plateau Ward has rows of
dainty pink, purple, and green Victorian houses. Casa Bianca, a
boutique B&B, is nestled within a white Renaissance Revival
building and the bistro La Salle à Manger serves house-cured
charcuterie: shredded *jambon persillé*; headcheese with sweet
carrots; rabbit pâté in a jar. Around Rue Rachel, there are Portuguese
bakeries—try *natas*, yellow custard-filled pastries—and rotisserie
shops that sell smoky chicken and addictive fries.

Mile End is a hip residential district with shops (Style Labo for
vintage housewares; Les Touilleurs for kitchen items) and
restaurants such as the landmark deli Wilensky's Light Lunch.
Slightly northwest is Little Italy and Marché Jean-Talon, the largest
outdoor farmers' market in North America. Older gentlemen sit at
tables outside Caffè San-Simeon, on Rue Dante, speaking Italian
and smoking cigarettes; soppressata and mortadella sandwiches
are on the menu. To the west is the Middle Eastern quarter of Ville
St.-Laurent. You'll recognize Abu Elias, a Lebanese grill joint, not
by the name painted on the window but by the triple-parked cars
in the lot. Drivers wait on orders of *kafta, shish taouk*, and
sandwiches made with *sujuk*, a dry sausage that's grilled, slicked
with garlicky aioli, and wrapped in charred flatbread. The
combination is deeply flavorful, oddly earthy, and—like the city
itself—more complex than you could have imagined.

Eating ice cream
in Vieux-Montréal.
Below: The Mile
End antiques store
Style Labo.

Dusk settling in on the beach at Vancouver Island's Sooke Harbour House. Left: A farm truck in the Cowichan Valley.

COWICHAN VALLEY

AN OFF-THE-RADAR CULINARY JOURNEY

IF YOU LIVE ANYWHERE SOUTH OR EAST OF, SAY, VANCOUVER, you've probably never heard of the Cowichan Valley. This bucolic corner of Vancouver Island purposely keeps a low profile, its residents preferring to let the area's food and wine do the talking for them. But its simple delights are slowly being discovered. The Mediterranean-like microclimate sustains an impressive range of small farms, vineyards, and artisanal producers, whose bounty is increasingly sought after by British Columbia chefs and keyed-in travelers making culinary pilgrimages. To experience all that's on offer in the region—a homespun, affordable alternative to

Napa—we've mapped out the perfect two-day drive.

Start in Victoria, a 30-minute flight or 1½-hour ferry ride from Vancouver. With its prim flower gardens and mahogany-trimmed pubs, B.C.'s capital feels like a prosperous English city circa 1950. The waterfront gastropub Spinnakers is the place for creamy Fanny Bay oysters, rich seafood chowder, and the pub's own ESB cask ale, all served on a deck overlooking the harbor. From there, head north through the forested Malahat range into Cowichan Valley proper. At the end of one especially rutted drive is Fairburn Farmstay & Guesthouse. The 1896 farmhouse sits on 130 acres,

A beekeeper tending to one of the hives at Tugwell Creek Honey Farm & Meadery, in Sooke. Left: Sooke Harbour House's Thunderbird Room.

home to a herd of water buffalo that is the source of Fairburn's fresh mozzarella.

On day two, drive six miles north to sample local products at the Duncan Farmers' Market, in the valley's workaday hub. Stop in for a pint at the convivial Craig Street Brew Pub, whose Shawnigan Irish Ale is the best of several house-made beers. Other musts in your culinary wanderings: True Grain Bread & Mill, in Cowichan Bay, for crusty organic loaves and German pretzels; Merridale Ciderworks, seven miles south, where Rick Pipes and Janet Docherty make heirloom-apple cider; and, back over the mountains on the blustery southwest coast, Tugwell Creek Honey Farm & Meadery, to taste house-harvested honey and mead.

Last stop: Sooke Harbour House. Tucked away on a semiprivate peninsula, the 28-room inn has the isle's finest restaurant, which showcases Dungeness crabs and sweet Weathervane scallops caught nearby as well as produce from an expansive garden—all overseen by charismatic co-owners Sinclair Philip and his wife, Frederique. Toast them with a glass of smoky-sweet Brandenburg No. 3, an amber dessert wine from Cowichan's own Venturi-Schulze. Then it's off to bed, as the waves lap the rugged shore below.

Diving into the cliffside pool at the Golden Rock Inn, on Nevis.

CARIBBEAN

ERTO RICO JAMAICA DOMINICAN REPUBLIC BARBADOS NEVIS
RTIN ANGUILLA MARTINIQUE PUERTO RICO JAMAICA DOMINIC
PUBLIC BARBADOS NEVIS ST. MARTIN ANGUILLA MARTINIQUE
CO JAMAICA DOMINICAN REPUBLIC BARBADOS NEVIS ST. MART
GUILLA MARTINIQUE PUERTO RICO JAMAICA DOMINICAN REPU
RBADOS NEVIS ST. MARTIN ANGUILLA MARTINIQUE PUERTO RI
MAICA DOMINICAN REPUBLIC BARBADOS NEVIS ST. MARTIN AN
RTINIQUE PUERTO RICO JAMAICA DOMINICAN REPUBLIC BARB
VIS ST. MARTIN ANGUILLA MARTINIQUE PUERTO RICO JAMAICA

PUERTO RICO

FEASTING ON A TROPICAL BOUNTY

LET OTHER PEOPLE COME TO PUERTO RICO FOR ITS BEACHES, its rain forest, its salsa and reggaeton dance halls. You'll want to get to know it through your taste buds. And why not? Like Puerto Ricans themselves, the island's cuisine is friendly and approachable, with robust flavors and strong traditions.

Pork shows up everywhere: roasted on a spit in the stalls along the Ruta del Lechón, a winding mountain pass 30 minutes from San Juan, or in the house-made *longaniza* sausage at José Enrique, a restaurant near San Juan's lively market square, La Placita. Refinement comes by way of Condado, San Juan's community of hip restaurants and renovated resorts fronting the Atlantic. At chef Wilo Benet's Pikayo, in the Conrad Condado Plaza Hotel & Casino, the menu alludes to Italy and Asia but maintains plenty of native touches (foie gras with ripe plantain; griddled shrimp in a guanabana beurre blanc). Indeed, island favorites pair well with international flavors. At Budatai, a sexy Latin-Asian fusion restaurant, egg rolls are stuffed with local *butifarra* sausage. And there's the just-caught snapper in a kombu broth with shaved truffles at L'Auxerre, in the historic town of San Germán, a 1½-hour drive from the capital.

Much of the indigenous cuisine is based on relatively bland ingredients, such as rice and tubers. But in the right hands, even Puerto Rico's most humble food can be extraordinary. *Fondas*—modest restaurants serving home-style specialties like *mofongo*, the ubiquitous mound of fried plantains mashed with garlic and cracklings—verge on the revelatory. Drive a few minutes out of San Juan to the seaside village of Piñones, where all the kiosks are promisingly dilapidated; the tastiest *alcapurrias* (torpedo-shaped yuca fritters filled with meat or seafood) come from Tropical Heat and are best washed down with the juice of a freshly scalped coconut. This is the ultimate beach food—the Caribbean's answer to a Coney Island hot dog. Back near La Placita, as plate after plate of appetizers arrives at José Enrique, it can be hard to stop: delicately fried *empanadillas*, chile-spiked *escabeche* of black cod, thinly sliced octopus with a fragrant peanut sauce. All too often, the best meal you have in Puerto Rico is the one you shouldn't be eating, throwing caution—and your dinner plans—to the wind.

Mango and papaya *batidas* served in La Placita, in San Juan. Opposite: Conrad Condado Plaza Hotel & Casino's seaside terrace.

Bayside, the Asian-inspired restaurant at Couples Tower Isle. Left: Sandals Royal Plantation's colonial-style entrance.

OCHO RIOS

REINVENTING THE ALL-INCLUSIVE

SWAPPING BRACELET BEADS FOR DRINKS, LINING UP FOR SOGGY burgers, chasing breakfast with a few margaritas—the hallmarks of the classic all-inclusive getaway have left style-seekers with much to be desired. Thankfully, a new generation of resorts in Jamaica's tony Ocho Rios is giving the genre a fresh image.

Couples Tower Isle began life as a magnet for the 1950's Hollywood jet set, attracting guests such as Eva Gabor, Debbie Reynolds, and Noël Coward. Today, the resort is as glamorous as ever courtesy of a $30 million makeover: minimalist pastel-hued rooms look out to the azure Caribbean Sea; buffets are displaced by six restaurants; and activities such as scuba, catamaran cruises, golf, and waterfall tours have replaced sing-alongs and talent nights. There's also a golden beach, where access to the resort's

free Wi-Fi means you don't have to choose between plugging in and tuning out.

Five minutes down the coast, the Royal Plantation, one of Sandals' newest properties, is more traditional, but the spirit is much the same. In each of the plantation-style suites you'll find candles and conch shells arranged on a coffee table, dark-wood four-poster beds, and a telescope stationed on the balcony (rooms face either the ocean or the mountains). Butlers deliver canapés of smoked salmon and shrimp cocktail twice a day, and will freshly press your laundry as you need it. The bartender offers 12-year-old rum and a champagne-and-caviar menu. Would you like a second helping of steamed lobster on the terrace? Like most everything else at the resort, it comes at no extra charge.

An airy beach *palapa* at Balcones del Atlántico, on the Samaná Peninsula.

SAMANÁ PENINSULA

LUXURY GOES OFF THE MAP

AWAY FROM THE THRUM OF PUNTA CANA, THE 35-MILE-LONG Samaná Peninsula has long been the getaway that in-the-know Europeans and Dominicans reserved for themselves. Just a 90-minute drive from the capital city of Santo Domingo, the hilly region has pristine cove beaches, cafés in former fishing shacks, and world-class scuba diving and kite surfing. With the addition of several plush hotels, those sunbathers are going to have to share the sand.

In 2008, the secluded natural beauty of the peninsula prompted French transplants Cary Guy and Marie-Claude Thiebault to do something few high-end hoteliers in the Dominican Republic have dared: think small and out-of-the-way. The Peninsula House, their gracious, gingerbread-trimmed Victorian, tops out at 12 guests and is set on a bluff overlooking the Atlantic Ocean. Since then, the area has continued to attract new hotels to its laid-back shores. The 86 villas at RockResorts' Balcones del Atlántico, which lie on a protected half-mile-long crescent of coast, feature Viking appliances and oversize balconies. Its competition is the marina-side Bannister Luxury Condominium Hotel, a resort within a residential complex that includes an equestrian center and two tennis courts.

And there's more on the horizon. In 2013, Auberge Resorts will unveil Casa Tropicalia, with 37 beach bungalows and an open-air spa on Samaná Bay. Meanwhile, about 60 miles northwest of the peninsula—and within driving distance of each of these hotels—the quiet beach town and coastal nature reserve of Playa Grande will welcome the world's first Aman golf resort.

BARBADOS

THE NEW HOT SPOTS

Unusual table accessories
at St. Nicholas Abbey.
Opposite: A stretch of
rugged shoreline on
Barbados's eastern side.

Fishing boats off the coast near the Atlantis hotel. Clockwise from left: Sandy Lane hotel; a suite balcony at Atlantis; Nishi's salmon with shoestring potatoes.

POLO MATCHES NEXT TO SUGARCANE FIELDS, AFTERNOON tea at pastel-colored plantation houses, stone windmills turning in the breeze: Daydreams about Barbados often involve the remnants of the former colony's high-society heyday under British rule. You can still find pockets of that lifestyle in the opulent resorts that line the Caribbean Sea–facing Platinum Coast, but these days the West Indies' easternmost isle is buzzing with newfound energy.

The Barbados food scene has long been hailed as one of the region's finest, and restaurants are finding fresh inspiration in global influences. The chosen retreat of the silk-cravat and shih-tzu-in-a-satchel set, the legendary Sandy Lane hotel is now home to Bajan Blue, a beachfront dining room that puts a modern spin on flavors from the West Indies, Polynesia, and Southeast Asia. You can also see what the fuss is about nearby at Briton Paul Edwards's Japanese restaurant, Nishi, which highlights barracuda and roe of flying fish—the native catch.

To explore the island's remote interior, stay at Lush Life Nature Resort, with 10 spacious cottages made from indigenous courbaril wood and set along a secluded hilltop fringed by rain forest. Pounded by the Atlantic, Barbados's eastern shore is even wilder and more unspoiled, a panorama of steep cliffs and huge waves, wide fields and verdant forests. The Atlantis was the first hotel built here; now the 10 airy suites feature large canopy beds with mosquito netting and bright accents.

Sample homegrown Mount Gay and other brands of rum at one of the 1,600 cheerily painted stands where Barbadians meet to sit and sip; for a more formal setting, seek out the distillery in St. Nicholas Abbey, an 18th-century Jacobean mansion on the edge of St. Peter. A five-minute drive away, the Morgan Lewis sugar mill is one of only two working sugar windmills in the world. Then head to the Old Pharmacy Gallery & Star Bar, housed in an early-20th-century apothecary and showcasing local and international talent such as self-taught Rastafarian artist Ras Ishi. Afterward, wander over to the tiny, wood-framed beach bar across the street for the weekly movie under the stars, screened on the seaside terrace.

Bajan Blue, Sandy Lane's Asian-influenced restaurant. Below: The 18th-century Morgan Lewis sugar mill.

The Sugar Mill Suite, at
Golden Rock Inn. Opposite:
Boats on Paradise Beach.

NEVIS

HAUTE HIDEAWAY IN THE MAKING

Golden Rock's outdoor restaurant, the Rocks. From near right: Coconut-crusted tuna salad at Mango, in the Four Seasons Resort Nevis; two of the hotel's spa cottages.

UNTIL YOU'VE SLEPT IN ANNA WINTOUR'S BED YOU CAN'T imagine how good she has it. You start to get an idea as you lay in an immense mahogany four-poster the size of a trampoline at the Golden Rock Inn, six pastel cottages tucked into the sides of a green hill in Nevis, where the legendary *Vogue* editor spent the holidays in 2010. It's no wonder Wintour chose this island. Drowsy, clean, and unspoiled, Nevis is experiencing a wave of silent colonization by philanthropist millionaires, artists, and media moguls who come for the old Caribbean atmosphere, and have established it as the new, pre-paparazzi St. Bart's.

Over the past 20 years, a roster of high-end properties has sprung up to accommodate them. The first to set down roots was the Four Seasons Resort Nevis. Fitted out with the requisite tennis courts (there are 10 of them), biomorphic pools, a golf course, and a spa, it occupies an unblemished stretch of white-sand beach on the leeward side of the island. Next came the photogenic, Anglocentric Nisbet Plantation Beach Club, a gingerbread-style resort on a 30-acre former sugar plantation. Most recently, after experiencing Nevis's immunity to the commercialism and glitz that characterize much of the Caribbean, artists Helen and Brice Marden became unlikely hoteliers, opening the Golden Rock Inn. The hotel—which was designed by Ed Tuttle, the Paris-based architect who gave the Amanresorts chain its signature Zen restraint—is built within a series of old sugar mill buildings and nestled in a lush tropical garden that is home to monkeys, goats, lizards, birds, and butterflies.

Though the comforts of such resorts make it nearly impossible to leave them, do try. Up the rain-forested slopes of Nevis Peak, the woods are dense and filled with flamboyant trees, elephant ear, hibiscus, kapok, and soapberry. Ancient but newly discovered sulfur springs bubble away in unexpected places. You can also visit the childhood home of Alexander Hamilton, who lived on the island until the age of 10, sip a Killer Bee rum cocktail at Sunshine's Beach Bar & Grill, on Pinney Beach, or simply spend the afternoon drifting to sleep under a stand of coconut palms along the dappled turquoise sea. In Nevis, the quiet is always preferred.

On a boat at the Nisbet Plantation Beach Club. Left: Sunshine's Beach Bar & Grill, on Pinney Beach. Right: Local schoolchildren.

The island's Caribbean coast. Right: The Rainbow Café, in Grand Case.

ST. MARTIN

TWICE THE CHARACTER

TRAVELERS WHO ALIGHT ON THIS WISHBONE-SHAPED ISLAND will discover a place in the throes of a cheerful identity crisis. There's the slow-paced French side to the north, and to the south, the perky, happy-hour-friendly Dutch part. But the two halves of this pleasantly bifurcated land have more in common than you might think: picturesque seaside hamlets, foodie finds, and sun-kissed beaches.

At the open-air market in Marigot, the French capital, stock up on spices from neighboring Guadeloupe and tamarind- and pineapple-inflected chili sauces, sold in colorful hand-painted bottles. Epicureans flock to the northwestern village of Grand

Dockside in Marigot, the French capital. Right: A nook in the Love Hotel's lobby.

Case for the upscale cuisine (sea bass stuffed with fennel and tomato; pan-fried duck foie gras served on house-made bread) and impressive wine cellar at L'Escapade. Nearby, Caribbean flavors find their way onto the menu at the Rainbow Café in the form of curries and chutneys. Check in to the Love Hotel, seven whitewashed rooms owned by a charming Gallic couple who sell glasses of house-infused banana-vanilla rum at the beachfront bar. At sunset, an otherworldly sense of calm descends as you peer out over the horizon and the white sands that envelop the hotel. If you look closely, you can spot the island of Anguilla glimmering in the distance.

There's plenty to do on the other side of the island. Try your luck with the slots at the Princess Port de Plaisance casino, in Cole Bay; weekend floor shows feature dancers in feathered and bejeweled headdresses. Some of the best shopping can be found on Front Street, overlooking the cruise ships anchored in Philipsburg, the lively Dutch capital. For a taste of the local flavor, stop by the Guavaberry Emporium, where the native fruit is doused in rum and muddled with sugar to create a tasty, bittersweet liqueur. What's more satisfying than a dip in the clear waters at Great Bay beach, right off the city's boardwalk? A refreshing rum sundowner enjoyed along its wooden planks.

ANGUILLA

A CAREFREE GETAWAY

A dish of grilled local crayfish
at the Straw Hat Restaurant.

Cap Juluca's domed lobby. Right: Horseback riding on the beach at Maunday Bay.

THE BRITISH WEST INDIAN ISLAND OF ANGUILLA, A FERRY RIDE away from St. Martin, has been fortunate: it frequently ducks the brutal hurricanes that plague the Caribbean. Another big draw is its English-speaking residents, who are as unpretentious and fun-loving as ever. They call themselves "belongers," and one visit to this 16-mile-long, calypso-beating paradise will convince you to join them.

Drop your bags at Cap Juluca, a haven of Frette sheets and Moroccan-style rugs on 179 leafy acres along Maunday Bay, then borrow a bike and pedal to one of Anguilla's beaches—there are 33 of them, with sand that ranges in color from pink to vanilla. Bring fins and a mask to gin-colored Crocus Bay to snorkel among the angelfish. Down the shore you'll find designer Fabiana Liburd's boutique Why Knot; ask her to show you how to tie her signature cover-up in the local style. The rest of the day is yours to while away with a Pyrat rum piña colada at Dune Preserve, a driftwood bar owned by Anguilla-born reggae artist and raconteur Bankie Banx.

On an island with dozens of roadside grill stands, dinner is never far off. The standout is B&D's Barbecue for its smoky pork ribs to go. Nearby, try the famed Anguillan crayfish at the open-air Straw Hat Restaurant. If you'd rather eat traditional West Indian dishes (Creole conch stew with fried plantains; goat curry), grab a table at E's Oven, where chef Vernon Hughes cooks on the former site of his mother's stone furnace. But don't leave Anguilla without dining at KoalKeel. Set in a limestone cottage built in the 18th century by Dutch sugarcane planters, the restaurant features chef Gwendolyn Smith's crayfish ravioli, pigeon-pea soup, lamb medallions with pumpkin gratin, and—for a sweet finale—a rum-truffle tower. Later, follow the line of belongers to Pumphouse, a bar that brings in crowds for its rum punches, reggae bands, and Thursday calypso night.

Breakfast the next morning is a similarly raucous affair. French expat Geraud Lavest oversees the kitchen at Geraud's Patisserie, where the café au lait is straight out of Paris but the mango-topped French toast is all Anguilla. In October, you'll find Lavest bottling jars of house-made peach-ginger marmalade that pack neatly into your suitcase.

MARTINIQUE

TOURING A MULTICULTURAL PARADISE

Le Petibonum, a beachside
shack in Le Carbet. Opposite:
The ferry dock at L'Ilet Oscar.

A street in the town of Les Anses d'Arlet. Clockwise from below: Boating around L'Ilet Oscar; grilled red snapper at Chez Tante Arlette, in Grand-Rivière; a roadside chapel.

THE PASTRIES ARE FRENCH, THE FABRICS INDIAN, THE MUSIC rumba-esque, and the vibe is pure Creole. Geographically, Martinique is sandwiched between St. Lucia and Dominica, but it has far more in common with Haiti and Trinidad. Local traditions and a patois have evolved as Carib Amerindians, British and French colonists, African slaves and Tamils, and Chinese field laborers made the volcanic island their home. As a result, Creole manifests itself not only in the cuisine but also in the flair with which residents conduct their daily affairs. Market vendors in towns like Les Anses d'Arlet pair Chanel accessories with *corsage en broderie anglaise* blouses and madras skirts; zouk dance music blares from Mercedes taxis idling next to mango-juice stalls; and dapper postmen delivering letters wear the woven-palm *bakoua* hats once worn by cane cutters.

Play castaway at L'Ilet Oscar, an antiques-filled plantation house on a private island along the eastern coast. For a bona fide taste of life in the Antilles, visit the market on Rue Isambert, in Fort-de-France, where you can find freshly picked pineapples, pure cacao, and searing sauces made with Scotch bonnet chiles. Seek refreshment at low-key Le Petibonum, in the row of barbecue shacks that lines the town of Le Carbet's shore. Owner Guy Ferdinand is a wizard with seafood: his grilled local albacore is paired with a creamy sesame aioli and accompanied by a ti' punch of lime juice, sugarcane syrup, and white rum. If you prefer something a little more formal, you can have crab farci and chilled Provençal rosé at Grand-Rivière's Chez Tante Arlette, or head to chef Jean-Charles Brédas' haute-Creole restaurant, Le Brédas, for conch gratin with spring onions, nutmeg, and garlic smothered in bubbling Emmental cheese.

Fight the temptation to linger over lunch. Now comes the adventure. It takes intrepid driving on rough roads edged by untrimmed vegetation—past wild-pig-crossing signs—and then a sweaty hike under a rain-forest canopy to reach the hidden beach of Anse Couleuvre. All that effort seems counterintuitive given the island's easy-going atmosphere, but it's worth it to see the blue Caribbean Sea kiss black sand.

Local kids in Les Anses d'Arlet. Above: A guest room at L'Ilet Oscar.

A view of Puerto Marqués Bay from the Hotel Encanto, in Acapulco, Mexico.

MEXICO & CENTRAL & SOUTH AMERICA

EXICO CITY ACAPULCO SAN MIGUEL DE ALLENDE VERACRUZ NI
LIZE LIMA SACRED VALLEY PATAGONIAN LAKES REGION EASTE
ENOS AIRES IGUAZU FALLS URUGUAY SAO PAULO MEXICO CITY
APULCO SAN MIGUEL DE ALLENDE VERACRUZ NICARAGUA BE
CRED VALLEY PATAGONIAN LAKES REGION EASTER ISLAND BU
RES IGUAZU FALLS URUGUAY SAO PAULO MEXICO CITY ACAPUL
GUEL DE ALLENDE VERACRUZ NICARAGUA BELIZE LIMA SACRE
TAGONIAN LAKES REGION EASTER ISLAND BUENOS AIRES IGU
LLS URUGUAY SAO PAULO MEXICO CITY ACAPULCO SAN MIGUE

Mexico City's Museo
Universitario del Chopo.
Opposite: The sculpture
outside the Palacio de
Bellas Artes.

MEXICO CITY

SOUTH-OF-THE-BORDER STYLE

The foyer at Condesa DF hotel.
Below: The Museo Universitario
Arte Contemporáneo.

VERSITARIO ARTE CONTEMPORÁNEO

IT'S EASY TO FORGET THAT MEXICO CITY IS AN ARTISTIC epicenter. But the Distrito Federal has become a contemporary hub, full of buzzy restaurants, design-driven hotels, and pioneering museums and galleries, prompting visitors to view the city in a new light.

The latest accommodations underscore this sleek transformation. On the Paseo de la Reforma, a grand boulevard that channels the Champs-Élysées, the Yabu Pushelberg–designed St. Regis Mexico City features floor-to-ceiling windows with views of the city center. Condesa DF, in chic, leafy Condesa, has become one of the city's most fashionable addresses, thanks to its vintage-inspired interiors and popular Japanese-Mexican fusion restaurant. Amid the luxe shops of the Polanco district is Las Alcobas (also designed by Yabu Pushelberg): soundproofed walls and an earthy palette create a cocooning effect on busy Avenida Presidente Masaryk.

In the historic center, the Neoclassical Palacio de Bellas Artes may be the town's top cultural draw. For experimental mixed media and performance art, check out the Museo Universitario del Chopo, housed in an early-20th-century building recently redesigned by star architect Enrique Norten. In Chapultepec Park, Museo Tamayo presents 20th-century masterpieces by the likes of Picasso, Miró, and Rothko. To see up-and-coming talent, head to a trio of galleries: Kurimanzutto, OMR, and Proyectos Monclova. And for avant-garde works, visit the Museo Universitario Arte Contemporáneo, a soaring, light-filled structure. Frida and Diego would be proud.

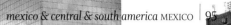

Kurimanzutto gallery's gift shop. Clockwise from right: Looking out from the St. Regis Mexico City; one of the hotel's guest rooms; mounted police near the Palacio de Bellas Artes.

ACAPULCO

A RAT PACK–WORTHY REVIVAL

The bean-shaped pool
at Hotel Boca Chica.

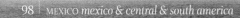

The beach near Hotel Boca Chica. Clockwise from above: A cliff diver at La Quebrada; boating on the bay; El Fuerte de San Diego, in Acapulco's Traditional Zone.

THE HISTORY OF ACAPULCO READS LIKE A CAUTIONARY TALE. Mexico City elite "discovered" it; Frank Sinatra crooned about it; spring breakers invaded it. Still, the essential elements of Acapulco's appeal remain—great physical beauty and weather as excellent as one could imagine. And with an influx of investment and interest in cutting-edge infrastructure, a renaissance is on the horizon.

Just south of the Grand Hotel Acapulco, Avenida Costera Miguel Alemán becomes Carretera Escénica, a corniche with sweeping views of emerald hills and the Pacific. It's here, on the road to the emerging Diamond Zone, where the resort town is beginning to shine anew. The playful Zibu, one of the area's best restaurants, evokes the daredevil energy of the city's famous cliff divers at La Quebrada. Up the road, the spotlight-stealing Becco al Mare provides a movie-star photo op for its stylish young diners. Nearby, the $310 million Mundo Imperial complex is a popular gathering spot thanks to its forum-style theater; along with the high-end La Isla shopping center next door, it's a Mexican version of South Beach at a fraction of the price.

The latest hotels embody the scope of Acapulco's new ambitions. With three restaurants, a world-class spa, and infinity pools in every villa, the Asian-style Banyan Tree Cabo Marqués has transformed the empty peninsula on the south side of Puerto Marqués Bay into a see-and-be-seen destination. On the opposite shore you'll find Hotel Encanto, an all-white ode to the sea. And in the center of the Traditional Zone, Hotel Boca Chica is a haute structure restored to its Rat Pack glory with sixties furniture and Pop-tropical details—proof that Acapulco is swinging once again.

A minimalist hallway at Hotel Encanto. Above: The view from Banyan Tree Cabo Marqués.

El Jardín park, with La Parroquia beyond. Right: A guest room at Rosewood San Miguel de Allende.

SAN MIGUEL DE ALLENDE

BALANCING THE OLD AND THE NEW

WITH ITS NARROW COBBLESTONED LANES AND COLONIAL architecture, the central Mexican city of San Miguel de Allende is a model of historic preservation. Brightly colored stucco buildings double as banks, museums, and bookstores, and the iconic rose-tinted spires of the Gothic-styled La Parroquia church dominate the horizon. Look closely at the streets of this UNESCO-protected town, however, and you'll find a spate of innovation and creativity that's lending a vibrant, modern edge to this atmospheric enclave.

A covered walkway in El Jardín. Left: Art at Fábrica La Aurora.

The most telling sign of its evolution: the Rosewood San Miguel de Allende, a luxury resort set on four palm-studded acres near El Jardín, the plaza at the center of public life. Arcaded walkways and courtyards call to mind a traditional hacienda; inside, guest rooms— some of which have verandas facing La Parroquia—feature hand-carved furniture from Guadalajara. At bustling lunch spot Café Rama, international dishes (Indian butter chicken; Thai yellow curry) are made with indigenous ingredients such as nopal (prickly pear), *verdolagas* (purslane), and chayote (a mild tropical squash).

Design aficionados will fall for Fábrica La Aurora, a 1902 factory turned art center that's a 10-minute stroll from downtown, with more than three dozen contemporary galleries and boutiques. Stop in at Superficies for colorful tiles made in nearby Dolores Hidalgo, famous for its decorative pottery. After dark, follow the fashionable crowd to the terrace bar La Azotea for a cactus martini—a tequila-and-vodka concoction that's as potent as it is delicious.

A quiet corner of Xalapa.
Below: The city's
mountainous surroundings.

VERACRUZ

ON THE TRAIL OF A CONQUEROR

IN MEXICO, IT SEEMS, YOU'RE ALWAYS TREADING IN THE footsteps of historical giants. Hernán Cortés is one example: the Spanish conquistador, whose 1519 invasion led to the fall of the Aztec Empire, cut a swath from the Gulf of Mexico into the tropical interior on his way to Tenochtitlán (now Mexico City). You can more or less trace his route today, a journey that takes you through charming villages and archaeological sites.

The port town of Veracruz is near one of Cortés's first landing points. Check in to the Emporio Veracruz, a modern hotel near the Malecón and the colonial lighthouse, Faro Venustiano Carranza. From there, drive 30 minutes north through Cardel—the main crossroads of this trip—with a stop at the impressive sand dunes on the beach at Chachalacas. Fifteen minutes away, the landscape is remarkably different in Zempoala, a lush oasis of tropical trees with a clear view to the Totonac Templo Mayor. Break for lunch at Tomy, a restaurant in nearby Paso del Bobo that serves specialties such as garlic *acamayas* (a prawn-like delicacy) and *minilla* (a fish stew made with tomatoes and chiles). Finish your meal with a *torito*, a coffee drink infused with brandy, milk, and peanuts. Then continue 20 minutes north to Quiahuiztlán, the ruins of an ancient cemetery set on a hill that looks out to the Gulf, before returning to Veracruz.

The next day, head north, stopping first in the provincial capital of Xalapa, home to some of Mexico's richest ecological preserves. There's Parque Juárez, a terraced green space overlooking the Sierra Madre Oriental; Los Berros, where locals go for morning runs; and Los Tecajetes, filled with native plants found in the country's cloud forests. Twelve miles away, Xico is a small village with outsize flavor thanks to its star product, mole sauce. Sampling the gastronomic treasures at the restaurant El Acamalín—from house-made tamales to the cured, dried beef known as *cecina*—it's no wonder Cortés set his sights on this fertile land. The real question is why he ever left.

A pool at the Emporio Veracruz hotel.

Swimming in the pool at the
Jicaro Island Ecolodge.

A suite at the Jicaro Island Ecolodge. Below: Lounging in one of the hotel's casitas.

JICARO ISLAND

ECO GOES LUXE

COGNITIVE DISSONANCE: THAT'S THE DOMINANT SENSATION you feel upon arrival at Jicaro Island. Before you are palm trees, thatched roofs, blue skies, even a volcano in the distance—but the air has none of the tropical tang you'd expect, and there are no waves or powdery shores. That's because Jicaro, 10 minutes by boat from the southwestern colonial town of Granada, is located on Lake Nicaragua. And the surprises don't end there.

The island's single acre is devoted to Jicaro Island Ecolodge, a hotel as sensitive to the environment as it is easy on the eyes. Its nine casitas, with their slatted façades and mosquito-netted beds, are crafted entirely from Nicaraguan timber salvaged from storm-felled trees. The food is all organic and locally sourced, solar power heats the water for your shower, and a freshwater infinity pool is adjacent to the wellness center. Hotel staff can arrange a number of adventures: hiking around the cloud forest on the Mombacho volcano, learning to cast nets with fishermen along the lake's *isletas*, and viewing pre-Columbian petroglyphs on the island of Ometepe. Sipping on a passion-fruit-banana cocktail back at Jicaro and watching cormorants dive into the lake, you're likely to feel a little smug. Your under-the-radar travel discovery is an unqualified success.

A signpost in downtown Caye Caulker. Right: Local children on the beach.

CAYE CAULKER

TREASURES UNDER THE SEA

THERE'S NOT A TRAFFIC LIGHT IN SIGHT ON THE MANGROVE island of Caye Caulker, a five-mile, three-street strip of land located a 15-minute flight from Belize's main airport. In its former life, it was said to be a pit stop for travel-weary sailors and pirates who sought out its freshwater reserves; these days, Caulker is the ideal spot for underwater aficionados, as well as those in search of some serious hammock time.

The atmosphere everywhere is delightfully unassuming ("No shirt, no shoes, no problem" seems to be the motto of choice). Drop your bags at colorful Seaside Cabanas, where each of the 10 rooms and six cabins comes with its own roof terrace facing the Caribbean. Then head out to the reef—the second-largest in the world and a UNESCO World Heritage site—on a speedboat trip arranged by the hotel. In Hol Chan Marine Reserve, a protected sanctuary, you can snorkel amid nurse sharks and

stingrays in the aptly named Shark Ray Alley. Experienced divers can plumb the depths of the legendary Blue Hole, a network of underwater caves that make up one of the wonders of the natural world.

There are more leisurely pursuits to enjoy back above sea level. Your post-adventure indulgence: a platter of curried lobster and coconut rice at Jolly Roger's Grill & Restaurant, where the cheerful picnic tables spill onto the sand. The shacklike spot may look basic, but its freshly caught seafood delivers on all counts. Or take the 30-minute launch to the upscale shops and restaurants on neighboring isle Ambergris Cay. The perfect end to the day: Retire to one of the teak chaises on your hotel's pool deck with a cold Belikin beer and marvel at how seamlessly the island's *other* motto—"Go slow"—has become your own.

A view of Islas Ballestas. Left: The lobby at Hotel Paracas.

LIMA

AN INSIDER'S LOOK

LIMEÑOS ADORE THEIR TOWN—AND WHY SHOULDN'T THEY? Centuries-old buildings nod to the past, while striking new architecture heralds the future; inventive restaurants serve up fresh twists on local favorites; and high-concept shops merge traditional techniques with a modern aesthetic. To tap into the city's palpable energy, seek out the places residents prefer.

The best way to understand Lima is to start at the beginning. See pre-Columbian artifacts at the Museo Larco, a renovated 18th-century mansion built atop the remains of a seventh-century pyramid. The Museo Enrico Poli spotlights ancient Peruvian gold and silver; for woven textiles from the coast, visit Fundación Museo Amano. You can take home your own contemporary crafts from Dédalo Arte y Artesanía, which specializes in flatware and jewelry, or Indigo Arte y Artesanía, known for its alpaca-wool clothing.

The city is also an epicurean wonderland. In the Miraflores neighborhood, chef Virgilio Martínez Véliz—a former disciple of star chef Gastón Acurio—helms Central restaurant, renowned for its tasting menus of updated Peruvian dishes (don't miss the braised baby-goat leg seasoned with herbs from his rooftop garden). Far simpler is the ceviche served with *cancha serrana* (toasted corn) at nearby Pescados Capitales.

On weekends, do as the natives do and head out of town. A three-hour drive south, Paracas is known as Lima's version of the Hamptons. Stay at the sleek Arquitectonica-designed Hotel Paracas, whose rooms pay homage to the sand and sea with bamboo-lined walls, Peruvian cotton sheets, and cerulean linen throws. Board the hotel's yacht to the untouched Islas Ballestas and San Gallán. The only sounds you hear are crashing waves and the calls of pelicans, penguins, and sea lions as your boat draws close to shore.

A dancer wearing traditional dress. Above: Strolling in Cuzco's main square.

SACRED VALLEY

AT THE TOP OF THE WORLD

INCAN SETTLEMENTS ARE A DIME A DOZEN IN PERU'S SACRED Valley—a fact that neither deters the throngs of visitors nor diminishes the impact of the sites here. As you wind your way along the Inca Trail, part of the road system forged by pre-Columbian tribes, what's striking is that most of the ruins hardly seem ruined at all.

The journey begins in Cuzco, which, at 11,000 feet above sea level, is one of the highest cities in the world. At the Hotel Monasterio, a former 16th-century seminary, rooms are pumped with oxygen to ward off *soroche* (altitude sickness), and guests are greeted with *mate de coca* (an age-old Incan remedy for whatever ails you). A few blocks away, in a minimalist glass box located in the courtyard of the Museo de Arte Precolombino, the Map Café serves Nouveau Andean specialties, including a surprisingly delicious guinea pig confit. In the Plaza de Armas, Kuna sells hats, shawls, and ponchos made from llama, baby alpaca, and vicuña wool.

Outside the city center, Ollantaytambo is one of the country's most important archaeological complexes—a spiritual crossing where priests and astrologers gathered to bury the ashes of the dead. Today, it provides easy access to the Inca Trail, which begins in Pisac to the south and ends in Machu Picchu. On the way, visit the town of Chinchero, where artisans weave and paint floral patterns into wool; on Sundays, they join vendors from 14 neighboring communities to sell their wares at a mountaintop market nearby. A 20-minute train ride takes you from Cuzco to the village of Aguas Calientes, from which a bus zigzags up to Machu Picchu. Sure, you've seen it pictured in guidebooks too many times to count, but these vistas are immune to overexposure. Even amid the crowds, the prevailing sentiment is peace.

An aerial view of the Incan city of Machu Picchu and the Urubamba River.

The lobby at Castro's Palafito
1326 Hotel Boutique.

PATAGONIAN LAKES REGION

ROADS LESS TRAVELED

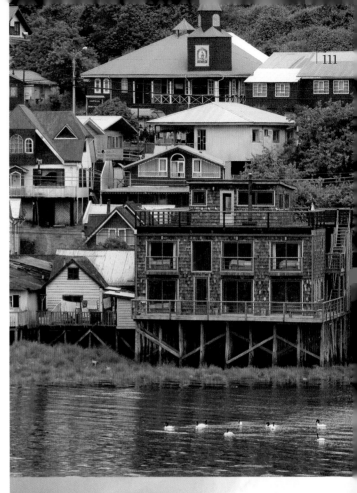

Saltos del Petrohué, in Vicente Pérez Rosales National Park. Above: *Palafitos* in Castro.

PICTURE THE HILLS OF SCOTLAND AND THE BRIGHT FISHING hamlets of Scandinavia—transported to the South American continent. That might be the best way to explain Chile's Lakes Region. A three-day drive reveals authentic discoveries framed by a pristine landscape.

From El Tepual Airport, in Puerto Montt, on Chile's mainland, navigate the dirt roads to Mercado Angelmó, an open-air market where vendors hawk garlic, eggs, and freshly caught salmon, and strolling musicians serenade visitors on their 25-string *guitarrones chilenos*. Follow the Pan-American Highway north to Puerto Varas and check in at the rustic Quincho Country Home hotel, overlooking Lake Llanquihue. If you have the time, set aside an afternoon to explore Vicente Pérez Rosales National Park (waterfalls at Saltos del Petrohué; the black-sand beach at Todos los Santos Lake), then drive up the Osorno volcano for views of the snowcapped peaks.

Before leaving Puerto Varas the next morning, stock up on provisions along Calle Walker Martínez, where bushels of wild black cherries are sold on sidewalk corners. Fifty miles south, in Pargua, a 40-minute car ferry takes you to the little-known isle of Chiloé. Once on the island, head to the coastal town of Puñihuil for a chance to spot otters, sea lions, and penguins on the beach. A hearty lunch awaits at Restaurant Quetelmahue, which serves Chiloé's signature *curanto al hoyo*—shellfish, sausage, chicken, and potatoes, cooked underground for hours in a pit. Afterward, drive south on Route 5 to the village of Castro, famous for its rows of colorful *palafitos* (houses built on stilts). The Palafito 1326 Hotel Boutique is a 12-room gem facing Castro Bay.

On your last day, tour the waterfront Mercado Artesanal de Castro and indulge in an unusual-yet-appetizing breakfast of salmon ceviche with red peppers. Contemporary-art lovers can detour toward MAM-Museo de Arte Moderno Chiloé, a shingled farmhouse that displays works by Chilote artists. Farther south, see blue whales in Quellón's Corcovado Gulf before arriving at Espejo de Luna, a quirky eight-room hotel and restaurant with a main lodge built in the shape of a shipwreck. After dinner, a funicular takes you to a viewing platform high above the myrtle forest to gaze upon the galaxies as you've never seen them before.

The curvaceous exterior of Explora's Posada de Mike Rapu. Below: A guest room at the hotel.

EASTER ISLAND

UNLOCKING AGE-OLD SECRETS

IT'S 2,237 MILES TO THE NEAREST POINT IN CHILE AND 1,243 miles to the closest inhabited area, the Pitcairn Islands. You'd be hard-pressed to find a place on earth more isolated than Easter Island, the setting for one of the world's most mysterious marvels on a surreal speck of land that appears like a waking dream. Easter Island's claim to fame has long been its *moai*, colossal statues that were each carved from a single stone. Weighing up to 20 tons and sometimes reaching heights of 30 feet, the monoliths are a fiercely guarded treasure among the native Rapanui, a tribe that makes up more than half of the island's population. The statues' origin remains an enigma.

Your best bet at uncovering the island's secrets: a stay at Explora's Posada de Mike Rapu, a LEED-certified lodge with Pacific Ocean views and 30 pine-and-concrete rooms designed to maximize privacy and relaxation. Each afternoon, a guide helps you choose the next day's activities: hiking, biking, fishing, snorkeling. But the star itineraries are those that bring you to see the *moai*. In Ahu Tongariki, 15 of them stand atop a ceremonial platform with their backs to the sea. The Rano Raraku volcano, whose crater harbors a freshwater lake covered by thickets of totora reeds, is surrounded by *moai* in varying stages of completion. And Ahu Akivi is where you'll find the isle's seven sole ocean-facing statues. For a 360-degree panorama of the land, climb to the top of Maunga Terevaka before taking a breather on the white sands of Anakena.

Back at the lodge, weary adventurers indulge in creature comforts—a soak in the solar-powered Jacuzzi; a hot-stone rub in the Hare Taheta massage room; a dinner of *cracra* fish roasted in taro leaves. End the night as any modern-day explorer would—over a pisco sour at the bar, exchanging stories with fellow wanderers.

A row of *moai* at Ahu
Tongariki, on Easter Island.

The geometric Puente de la Mujer. Left: Inside Pick Market.

BUENOS AIRES

A MODERN-DAY REVIVAL

IT'S OFTEN SAID THAT BUENOS AIRES HAS MORE IN COMMON with Europe than with its South American neighbors. Thanks to its antiques galleries and Art Deco mansions, the so-called Paris of the Pampas is flourishing despite its recent economic upheavals. Check in to the Algodon Mansion, whose 10 suites are synonymous with discreet luxury, or the Palacio Duhau-Park Hyatt Buenos Aires, where the crystal chandeliers and ornate plasterwork are offset by contemporary furniture. Then set forth to discover the latest hot spots favored by style-obsessed Porteños.

The food scene revolves around *puertas cerradas*, or closed-door restaurants, where chefs open their houses to a handful of patrons a few nights a week. Palermo-based Casa Coupage is one of the movement's founding institutions; the sommelier-owners

Fabrics at Arte Étnico Argentino. Right: Chez Nous, the restaurant in Algodon Mansion.

pair mineral-rich Chardonnays and dense Argentinean Malbecs with dishes such as skirt steak served alongside quinoa and portobello mushrooms. An unmarked doorway in Villa Crespo conceals Almacén Secreto, the private kingdom of chef Abigail Machicado, who prepares dishes from Argentina's north (*charquisillo*, a stew made with cured meat), center (oven-baked Paraná River fish), and south (venison *raviolones*).

Shopping, of course, is one activity at which Buenos Aires residents excel. Amid San Telmo's antiques galleries, Arte Pampa sells tribal-style dolls, llama-motif mirrors, and lacquered paper lampshades, all handcrafted in the central province of La Pampa. Nearby, master silversmith Marcelo Toledo creates pewter-lined gourds meant for sipping maté, Argentina's national drink. In Palermo, Arte Étnico Argentino sells rustic, hand-finished furniture crafted in Argentina's northwest; look for the cupboards made of naturally felled chanar wood. And Recoleta's airy new food hall, the comprehensive Pick Market, is the perfect place to while away an afternoon.

Besides tango shows and *fútbol* matches, there are plenty of ways to access the country's rich traditions. The labyrinth of dwellings, cisterns, creeks, and courtyards below San Telmo at El Zanjón reveals centuries of urban living dating back to the city's founding in the 1500's. And at La Peña del Colorado, Palermo's popular music hall, leading folk musicians stamp out complex rhythms—a sound track as invigorating as Buenos Aires itself.

IGUAZÚ FALLS

INTO THE WHITE ABYSS

YOU'D EXPECT A PLACE KNOWN AS LA GARGANTA DEL DIABLO (Devil's Throat) to be dark, fiery, and foreboding. In fact, it's the opposite: bright, open, even spiritual. Straddling the border between Argentina and Brazil, the rocky, U-shaped terrain and the waters that rush through it make up the largest cataract in Iguazú Falls, a massive natural wonder that's second only to Niagara in terms of flow—a white gash in the lush vegetation of the surrounding rain forest.

A one-hour-and-45-minute flight from Buenos Aires brings you to the gateway town of Puerto Iguazú, in Argentina's northern Misiones province. From there it's just 11 miles to Iguazú National Park, a UNESCO World Heritage site where a puma might amble languidly across your path and playful capuchin monkeys frolic in the trees above you. The only hotel on the Argentinean side of the park is the Sheraton Iguazú Resort & Spa, where rooms have balconies with views of the falls (keep your sliding door closed when you leave or risk finding monkeys in your bed). Ask the resort to arrange a guided horseback ride through the forest, a moonlight sailing expedition down the river, or a visit to native Guaraní settlements. The spa specializes in treatments utilizing maté, which is said to soothe and stimulate muscles.

The falls themselves are thrilling. Elevated walkways and platforms take you along the Iguazú River, past the smaller cascades of Salto Mbigua and Salto San Martín. In lower Iguazú Canyon, clouds of pulverized water created by the force of the deluge at Mosqueteros render your glasses useless; breathing freely is near impossible. Dense gusts of mist signal your last approach: the thundering La Garganta del Diablo. A bridge guardrail just above the falls is virtually aligned with the torrent. The hum is incessant, primordial, threatening, entirely captivating.

The waterfalls at Iguazú National Park.

A local boy with his pet parakeet. Right: A street in Colonia del Sacramento.

COLONIA

A QUIET BOLT-HOLE FOR THE JET SET

FIRST THERE WAS SEXY PUNTA DEL ESTE. THEN CAME ITS boho-chic neighbor, José Ignacio. Now Uruguay's southern region of Colonia is poised to lure the country's socialite crowd from its traditional stomping grounds. For the moment, however, the area remains South America's best-kept secret.

A one-hour ferry ride across the Río de la Plata takes you from Buenos Aires to the 17th-century former Portuguese stronghold of Colonia del Sacramento. From the Barrio Histórico, head to Iglesia Matriz, Uruguay's oldest church, and a whitewashed lighthouse that offers a bird's-eye view of the town. Linger over drinks at El Drugstore, a tapas restaurant filled with brightly painted chairs and bold paintings (snag a seat in the black 1929 Ford, one of two vintage cars parked out front). Shoppers can stock up on merino-wool sweaters and shawls at designer Silvia Sarti's Oveja Negra; Almacén la Carlota sells handmade zinc bowls. Canopies of flowering jacaranda trees in cobblestoned alleys provide a shaded respite.

Fifty miles north, the town of Carmelo is known for its gaucho legends and vineyard-laden landscapes. Stay in one of 20 bungalows— some with views of the river—at the Four Seasons Resort Carmelo and ask a concierge to arrange a horseback tour of your surroundings. Savor the earthy charm of the brick-walled Bodega y Granja Narbona restaurant, where the pasta is house-made and the Parmesan cheese comes from the owner's dairy farm six miles away. At the restored 1909 cellar, taste honey grappa and the country's rustic Tannat wines; come in March and April when the grapes are harvested—just don't tell anyone else about it.

Overlooking the Río de la Plata at the Four Seasons Resort Carmelo.

The skyline of São Paulo at dusk.

SÃO PAULO

THE FUTURE OF BRAZILIAN CUISINE

SUBTROPICAL WARMTH, HIGH-ENERGY URBANISM, CHEFS with a taste for the experimental—São Paulo has all the makings of an international food destination. In its best restaurants, avant-garde European techniques are executed using native ingredients to create a distinctly original cuisine.

Updates on grandmotherly favorites once relegated to cheap rice-and-beans joints are on order across town. At the adobe-hued Dalva e Dito, you can sample coconutty *moqueca baiana*, a seafood stew from the Afro-Brazilian state of Bahia; *porco na lata*, pork confit cooked in a tin can; and sorbets suffused with tropical flavors such as *caju* (cashew nut) and *graviola* (soursop). The legendary Saturday *feijoada* (pork-and-black-bean casserole) buffet at A Figueira Rubaiyat takes place in the shade of a 100-year-old fig tree. Nearby, Maní delivers its own post-molecular variation on the country's national dish. Husband-and-wife chefs Helena Rizzo and Daniel Redondo spherify black beans into an intense liquid; the pearls arrive on the plate dotted with linguica and oranges and topped with julienned fried kale. Restaurants don't get more Brazilian than Mocotó, in the working-class Vila Medeiros district an hour outside the city center, where specialties include *mocafava*, a cow's-hoof soup mixed with favas, linguica, shredded beef, and cilantro; and *carne de sol*, salted air-dried beef cooked *sous vide* for 24 hours then smothered with roasted garlic—all washed down with a glass of artisanal cachaça.

You can't take a bite out of the food scene without dipping into its melting pot of identities. The perfect Paulista Sunday follows a *futebol* match with the upscale, ultra-cheesy pizza at Bráz; try the wood-fired chard-and-pine-nut pie with a side of Calabrian sausage bread. Bar Original honors Brazil's German heritage with a *chopp*, a diminutive pull of ice-cold, house-made draft beer. And the city's 1.5-million-strong Nikkei population—the biggest Japanese community outside Japan—finds comfort in white-hot Kinoshita's hybrid cuisine. Who knew that *umeboshi* plum sauce was such a perfect foil for grilled *pupunha* (a type of palm heart)? It's at once exotic and familiar—and pure São Paulo.

Chef Helena Rizzo of Maní restaurant. Below: Cured *bottarga* with daikon and *mitsuba* at Kinoshita.

Melange and chocolate cake at Café Bräunerhof, in Vienna.

EUROPE

ELAND DUBLIN SCOTLAND LONDON EAST SUSSEX PORTUGAL
TURIAS PARIS BEAUNE CAP FERRET THE ALPS GHENT ITALIAN
LENTO FLORENCE COPENHAGEN VIENNA SKOPELOS GOZO IST
PETERSBURG ICELAND DUBLIN SCOTLAND LONDON EAST S
RTUGAL ASTURIAS PARIS BEAUNE CAP FERRET THE ALPS GHE
LIAN LAKES SALENTO FLORENCE COPENHAGEN VIENNA SKOP
ZO ISTANBUL ST. PETERSBURG ICELAND DUBLIN SCOTLAND
ST SUSSEX PORTUGAL ASTURIAS PARIS BEAUNE CAP FERRET
PS GHENT ITALIAN LAKES SALENTO FLORENCE COPENHAGEN

ICELAND

A NEW BREED OF NORDIC CUISINE

The Snæfellsnes Peninsula.
Opposite: A coffeehouse in Reykjavík.

Farm workers on Vallanes, in Eglisstaðir. Clockwise from left: A map of Iceland on the wall of a Reykjavík coffee-house; the dining room at Dill, in Reykjavík's Nordic House; the Gufufoss waterfall.

Locals in Reykjavík. Below:
Hótel Buðir's puffin with stout
crackers and parsley oil.

IN A COUNTRY OF VIKING DESCENDANTS AND MODERN foragers, it's fitting that the culinary aesthetic remains wild at heart. So it is in Iceland, where the stark, primeval landscape of volcanoes and glaciers has bred an influential new kind of Nordic cuisine. Summer may be fleeting on the cusp of the Arctic Circle, but plenty still grows here: mushrooms, berries, moss. And during this brief but bountiful season, a locavore-minded traveler can easily discover how short the journey is from field to table.

On the outskirts of Reykjavík, the capital, a minimalist building is the setting for Dill, one of the most compelling dining destinations in all of Europe. By day, the restaurant serves as museum cafeteria for the Alvar Aalto–designed Nordic House; after hours, chef Gunnar Karl Gíslason and his sommelier, Ólafur Örn ("Oli") Ólaffson, produce poetry from an experimental kitchen the approximate size of a bread box. What winds up on Dill's 10 tables is often extraordinary: cubes of salt-preserved wild salmon with capelin roe and smoked-rapeseed mayonnaise; a loin of Icelandic beef cooked rare and dusted with incinerated leeks. Ingredients, from birch oil to pickled wild green strawberries, have the capacity to surprise. Even the humble potatoes are highly prized, hailing from an organic farm in eastern Iceland called Vallanes, not far from the Gufufoss waterfall.

The drive from Reykjavík to Hótel Buðir, Iceland's finest country hotel, usually takes about 2½ hours on a scenic byway that winds around fjords in the Snæfellsnes Peninsula. But for foragers scanning the road in search of fragrant thyme or stalks of seeding angelica, the leisurely trip can take most of a day. Buðir's owner and chef, Petur Thordarson, sources much of his menu from the surrounding countryside, and his kitchen will gladly provide guests with plastic buckets to go forth and gather their own wild bounty. In the height of summer, when berries are ripe for the picking, this love of gathering becomes a national obsession. For an Icelander, a good berry patch is a closely guarded secret: a seasonal delight, all the more precious for being so short-lived.

The O'Connell Bridge, over the river Liffey. Right: Sheridans Cheesemongers' Irish farmhouse varieties.

DUBLIN

JOINING THE CONVERSATION

DUBLIN IS A STORYTELLER'S PARADISE. WALK INTO A RANDOM pub and you'll meet many a born raconteur; hop into any taxi, it seems, and an interview with an author (perhaps from Antony Farrell's Irish-centric roster at Lilliput Press) will be on the radio. Writers loom large, literally—a bronze figure of James Joyce stands on North Earl Street, and a monument to Oscar Wilde resides in a park facing his former abode at No. 1 Merrion Square. Conversation is the main commodity, and even in trying economic times, this town is thriving.

Much of the discourse takes place over pints of Guinness, the drink of choice at the long and narrow Cobblestone pub, in Smithfield. At Buswell's, near St. Stephen's Green, vast leather

Lilliput Press's Antony Farrell, in his Dublin apartment. Left: Hake with mussel-and-clam stew and Dublin Bay prawns at the Winding Stair.

armchairs surround a bar of deep red brocade and mahogany. The Stag's Head, one of the oldest taverns in town, is located just outside the din of the Temple Bar neighborhood; on Saturday nights the streets flow with liquor and the sidewalks sway with revelers, upholding Dublin's reputation as a city of drink. The food scene, on the other hand, has taken a turn toward the healthy, organic, and local. Passing South Anne Street, sample the varieties at Sheridans Cheesemongers, including the St. Tola, an organic, raw goat, and the Gubbeen, a washed-rind semisoft. Or you can dine on a delicate white-turnip-and-tarragon soup at the Cake Café, in the Portobello neighborhood, or on a fresh char-grilled mackerel at the Winding Stair, a charming restaurant and bookstore steps from the river Liffey.

Fittingly, the literary life of the country represents one of the town's greatest attractions. Stroll through the Trinity College campus to reach the Long Room library, where 200,000 rare books fill an expanse of shelves from floor to ceiling. Lesser-known Marsh's Library, right behind St. Patrick's Cathedral, opened to the public in 1701. But the ultimate bibliophile's destination may be the Dublin Writers Museum, a Georgian town house that's home to manuscripts and memorabilia from the likes of Beckett and Joyce. Gaze at the first edition of Bram Stoker's *Dracula* or at Beckett's telephone, and one thing is clear: In Dublin, the promise of a good story is never far off.

COLONSAY

LEAVING THE MAINLAND BEHIND

SHEEP OUTNUMBER PEOPLE ON THE HEBRIDEAN ISLE OF Colonsay, a 2¼-hour ferry ride across the Atlantic from the west coast of Scotland. Its rugged landscape is marked by a series of extremes: mighty winds, rocky terrain, and plenty of thorns, thistles, and burrs. But the natural beauty is endless. Jagged outcroppings along the shore give way to some of Britain's best beaches, which yield in turn to a verdant, fertile interior. Add ancient ruins and a woodland garden, and you've got a remote getaway worthy of a Romantic poet.

Indeed, those who have made the wildflower-carpeted island home are the sort of characters you'd find in a Robert Burns classic. There's aspiring naturalist Kevin Byrne, who can take you on walks across the mile-long sands of Kiloran Bay and name every buzzard flying overhead. Then there's General Store proprietor Mike McNicholl, who will tell you about the dolphins he saw that morning before selling you a bottle of Laphroaig single-malt scotch. You can meet most of the locals at the village hall during Saturday's weekly ceilidh, a Gaelic folk dance that's as authentic a celebration as you'll find in the British Isles.

Mysterious stone circles and ancient forts attest to the island's long history, which dates back to 7000 B.C. Colonsay House has a comparatively recent lineage—built in 1750, the private residence is surrounded by 20 acres of gardens that welcome visitors. (Go during May to see the finest rhododendrons in Scotland.) Alex and Jane Howard, Colonsay House's owners, also run the island's only formal lodgings, the whitewashed Colonsay Hotel, located on the estate. The nine guest rooms are simply yet comfortably furnished; the restaurant features produce from the garden and seafood from surrounding waters; and a hearth provides the perfect spot to gather after dinner. As is typical of the island, the atmosphere is homey, not grand. This is the true definition of unspoiled.

Colonsay's cliffs, overlooking
the Atlantic Ocean.

A typical evening outside the Dove Freehouse pub, in Bethnal Green.

LONDON

A RENAISSANCE IN THE EAST END

THE ROUGH-AND-TUMBLE HISTORY OF LONDON'S EAST END indelibly colors its contemporary identity. The area is profoundly ingrained in Londoners' minds as a working-class district, whether English or immigrant. But call it *new energy* or *gentrification*—change has come to the neighborhood's hardscrabble corridors, as blue-chip creative talents, from hoteliers to designers, work their way into the fabric of daily life. Now the scene is an intersection of commerce and community, one that's dynamic and downright chic.

A walk down Redchurch Street, in busy Shoreditch, manifests this transition in its most concentrated state. Art exhibition spaces (such as the Gallery at Redchurch Street) are set alongside shops built in former warehouses. Fashionable apothecary Aesop sells boutique fragrances in slick surroundings, while the merchandise at menswear store Hostem appeals to both hedge fund managers and hipsters. The creative class congregates at the rooftop bar and brasserie at Prescott & Conran's Boundary, on the western end of Redchurch Street. From there you can see the terrace of Shoreditch House, the Soho House group's eastern outpost, which has a strictly enforced no-suits-or-ties dress code.

A few blocks to the south is Brick Lane, a cacophonous artery known for its Indian-food scene and now the stage of a thriving independent fashion movement. Visit the Old Truman Brewery, not for pints of ale, but rather for the almost 200 homegrown businesses that enjoy a fiercely local following. It is connected to the lane by Dray Walk, a small pedestrian alley of shops such as the playful Folk. In and around Brick Lane, multiple markets flourish, including the storied one in adjacent Spitalfields (Thursday, not Sunday, is the connoisseur's day for antiques).

Less than a mile north, Bethnal Green's Columbia Road stands in contrast to Redchurch Street's sleek gentility and Brick Lane's hurly-burly edge. You can bargain for Dutch tulips and Kenyan lisianthus at London's top flower market; its Dickensian atmosphere comes courtesy of vendors' semi-ironic cockney accents. If it is Saturday, stroll down Goldsmith's Row to Broadway Market, where you'll find the most interesting people-watching in town. Equal parts farmers' market and urban style show, it's a microcosm of the East End as a whole: critical mass at its best.

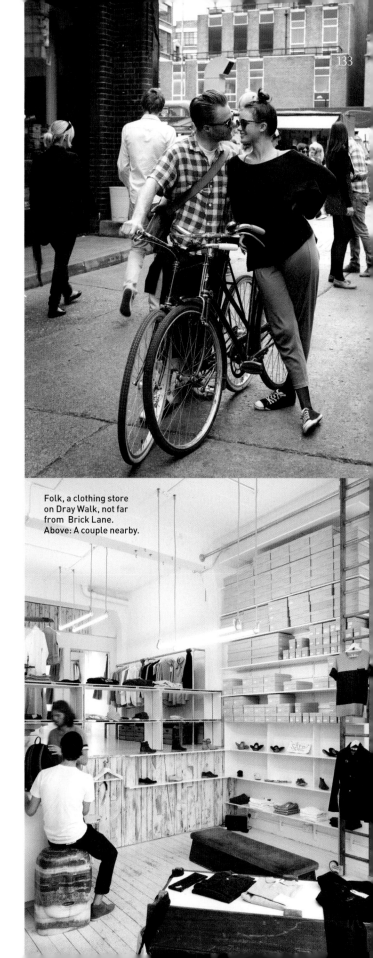

Folk, a clothing store on Dray Walk, not far from Brick Lane. Above: A couple nearby.

The 15th-century main house at Great Dixter Gardens. Left: Lupines in the Long Border.

EAST SUSSEX

TRADITION AND CREATIVITY COLLIDE AT GREAT DIXTER GARDENS

ONE OF ENGLAND'S MOST BEAUTIFUL AND BELOVED GREEN spaces, Great Dixter Gardens represents the seamless expression of a fascinating sensibility. Time seems suspended; to see it is to enter a landscape where tradition inspires creativity and studious technique yields glorious results.

At Dixter, house and garden are equally impressive. Both were designed in 1910 by the renowned architect Edwin Lutyens, in collaboration with garden designer Gertrude Jekyll. But it was the legendary horticulturalist and writer Christopher Lloyd who truly brought them to splendor in the mid 20th century. After his death in 2006, management of Dixter went to his closest friend, Fergus Garrett, who now serves as the talented and charismatic head gardener. Garrett oversees a series of intensive gardening courses that are open to the public throughout the year; they serve not only as a splendid introduction to a beautiful place but

also as a way to learn from an undisputed master in his field.

Tuition for the weeklong stay includes most meals, as well as lodging at a nearby country inn. Amid lectures ("The Basics of Soil Composition," "Tools of the Trade") and tasks such as pruning shrubs and dividing root balls, life in the house follows the same patterns laid down decades ago. Cocktails feature Lloyd's favorite 12-year-old Scotch. Dinner is prepared by the genial manager of house and garden, who uses the same handwritten recipes favored by Dixter's owners a hundred years back. Field trips might include a visit to the world's preeminent breeder of hamamelis (witch hazel) or an afternoon at Sissinghurst Castle and its famous white flower beds. But the real magic happens outdoors: crouching over patches of flowers; preparing the soil for a new burst of growth. Dixter shows you how the garden can be the work of a lifetime, and how a lifetime can be transformed by flowing with the rhythms of the seasons.

The grand entrance to Sintra's Hotel Tivoli Palácio de Seteais.

SINTRA

PORTUGAL'S MOUNTAIN HIDEAWAY

LESS THAN AN HOUR NORTH OF LISBON, THE ANCIENT HILLS of Sintra have been lauded in literature, romanticized by royals, and occupied by invaders from the Romans to the Moors. The enclave's allure is all about dipping into a decorated past: in the 18th and 19th centuries, foreign and domestic monarchs built over-the-top estates such as Quinta da Regaleira (now a museum and concert venue) and Pena Palace, a medieval monastery transformed by Portugal's King Ferdinand II into a blend of Gothic, Moorish, and Renaissance styles. Both of these visitor-friendly landmarks are surrounded by elaborate gardens that are worth a visit in themselves. Portuguese monarchs may have abandoned their summer homes here, but the ancient village—with its exotic architecture and forested parkland for hiking and biking—has never been more popular for day-tripping Lisboans and visitors.

Envelop yourself in the city's old-world atmosphere with a stay at the legendary Hotel Tivoli Palácio de Seteais, Sintra's grande-dame property. Originally the 18th-century residence of the Dutch consul, the Neoclassical building opened as a hotel in the 1950's, and has played host to celebrities such as Catherine Deneuve and John Malkovich. A meticulous restoration of its frescoed rooms and period furnishings has revived its fabled opulence, while also adding era-appropriate details like a maze of hedges that overlooks the valley below. Hotel staff will happily arrange your choice of area activities, from wine tasting and dining in the 19th-century Monserrate Palace nearby to a sail down the Estoril coast to see the Manuelin Tower of Belém, in a picturesque city along the Tagus River. The most memorable way to see the sights? A tour of the UNESCO-designated town center in the hotel's 1930's-replica sidecar.

ASTURIAS

A LOW-KEY FOODIE CAPITAL

NESTLED IN THE CANTABRIAN MOUNTAINS, THE NORTHERN Spanish province of Asturias, a tranquil, under-the-radar region on the Bay of Biscay two hours west of Bilbao (and the homeland of chef José Andrés), is a place for people with prodigious appetites. Come hungry, and you'll find everything from seafood feasts to 20-course lunches and some of the greatest cheeses in the world.

From Oviedo, the province's cosmopolitan capital, it's a 20-minute drive to Prendes and the Michelin-starred Casa Gerardo. The father-son team of Pedro and Marcos Morán puts a warmer, more accessible spin on *vanguardista* cooking: red mullet with potato emulsion; sea urchin with tahini; razor clams in almond butter. The climax is an ethereal *fabada*, a stew of beans simmered with sausage and slabs of pork fat that is Asturias's best-known dish. Wash it down with lukewarm cider, the local libation, which comes from the apple orchards that dot surrounding hillsides. Farther east in the cobblestoned fishing village of Tazones, the ramshackle Bar Rompeolas turns out fried calamari, glorious egg-battered monkfish, and basketball-size crabs cooked to perfection. At wood-paneled La Huertona, in Ribadesella, where the dining room looks out over the Picos de Europa national park, the food is traditional and spectacular—baby eels sizzling in garlic; a classic *fabada*. End your tour of the coast viewing edgy art in Llanes, a town of tidy clapboard houses.

Inland Asturias consists of a chain of ancient towns hidden between the Cantabrian Mountains; make Cangas de Onís's La Cepada, a quirky hotel with a panoramic view, your base to see them all. No food lover's tour of Asturias is complete without a stop at the village of Arenas de Cabrales, home to the famed cheese. The best varieties are blended from equal parts cow's, sheep's, and goat's milk, then aged six months in one of the region's ubiquitous mountain caves. Order a *ración* at a bar, and it arrives crumbly and veined with blue. The taste is nothing less than a revelation: fruity and nutty, faintly spicy, and completely irresistible.

La Huertona's octopus and chips. From near right: The view from La Cepada hotel's terrace; a waitress at Bar Rompeolas.

An installation by artist Agustín Ibbarola, in Llanes. From far left: Calle Pelayo, in Oviedo; chef José Andrés.

A rainy day on Avenue Junot, in Paris's 18th Arrondissement. Right: The library at Hôtel Jules.

PARIS

HIDDEN JOYS IN AN ICONIC CITY

YOU CAN'T VISIT PARIS WITHOUT SEEING THE SIGHTS: THE Eiffel Tower, the Champs-Élysées, the Arc de Triomphe. But the farther-flung corners of the city, the neighborhoods less explored by outsiders, have an allure all their own. Relaxed, friendly, and pleasantly cacophonous, they offer a candid glimpse of what makes Paris one of the most authentically charming places on earth.

The best place to stay is in the Ninth Arrondissement, where accommodations rank high on idiosyncratic appeal. Hôtel Amour shook up the district with its boldface-name patrons, cheeky décor, and hourly-rate policy when it opened in 2006. A few blocks away, newcomer Hôtel Joyce has immaculate, affordable rooms with superb beds and lots of light. To the southeast lies boutique property Hôtel Jules, whose lobby resembles a space-age library.

The reception desk at Hôtel Joyce. Right: Pain de Sucre's raspberry tart and house-made marshmallows.

These quartiers are home to some of the best examples of "bistronomy," a back-to-basics movement that dispenses with the grumpy, bow-tied waiters and confusing array of silverware and usually involves under-$50 prix fixe menus, small-batch ingredients, and young chefs who cut their teeth in haute establishments. In the 11th, the down-at-the-heels interior of Astier belies the fine French cooking—pressed beef cheek with a deviled egg, or braised pig with beets and honeyed turnip. At Le Bouchon et l'Assiette, in the 17th, the food is painstakingly sourced, with flashes of globalism. Scallops are served in a wispy ginger bouillon; a velouté of garbanzo beans arrives with *sobrasada* sausage. Somehow the shock of eating so well for such little money never wears off.

Paris is also a paradise for the acquisitive. But some of the best boutiques are found in neighborhoods that don't scream "Shopping!" In the Abbesses enclave, in the 18th, Spree offers European and Asian fashion labels casually laid out over Midcentury Modern furniture. Across the street, the art and furniture gallery Papiers Peints is set in a former wallpaper store designed by Le Corbusier. Anyone who wishes to brave the bustling *grands magasins* will find sugary sustenance at À la Mère de Famille, a traditional confiserie in the Ninth, full of froufrou offerings at every turn. The knockout punch, however, comes at Pain de Sucre, in a quiet corner of the Third, where the raspberry tart is akin to fine art and the *pirouette pomme* features caramelized apples arranged atop pistachio-and-lime cream. One bite will have you feeling like you belong here.

Cucumber salad at Le Jardin des Remparts restaurant.

A seating area at Le Jardin des Remparts. Left: The view from the Maison Joseph Drouhin.

BEAUNE

AN OENOPHILE'S DELIGHT

THE PACE OF CHANGE IS SLOW IN BEAUNE, AT THE CENTER OF Burgundy's wine industry. History suffuses the streets, from the 15th-century stone ramparts to the working grape press built in 1571. The main square is fashioned as precisely as a movie set. Shops selling mundane items are impossibly beautiful. An idealized rendering of a French medieval town adapted for modern existence, Beaune is surprisingly full of authentic discoveries—if you know where to look.

Off busy Place Carnot, Fromagerie Hess displays its artisanal cheeses—crumbly, creamy, aged—behind a crowded counter. Taste your way through the varieties while the passionate shop owner offers commentary like a painter describing his various works. On Rue Monge, the unremarkable storefront at Charcuterie Raillard offers no

clue to the delights within, including the *jambon persillé* (a simple slice of cold ham with parsley) and a spring terrine that conjures flavors from somewhere deep in the Gallic soil.

The wines, of course, are some of the most extraordinary in the world. Camera-carrying oenophiles race to Richebourg, Romanée Conti, or La Tâche. Right in town, the cool, tranquil cellar at Maison Joseph Drouhin was constructed in the Middle Ages and leads to tunnels that extend below the city. At Le Jardin des Remparts, Beaune's most ambitious restaurant, the vintage to order is Drouhin's 2002 Les Petits Monts, with a hue that resembles a drop of water on the skin of a wild cherry. Weightless in your mouth, intoxicatingly aromatic, it proves that there is no wine as enjoyable as Burgundy at its best.

CAP FERRET

FRANCE'S HIDDEN COAST

Carcans plage

Maubuisson · Carcans

Lacanau ocean

Lacanau

Le Porge

le Crohot

Ares

Claouey

Andernos

G. Piquey

Taussat

le Canon

Lanton

l' Herbe

Audenge

ARCACHON

Le Teich

La Nune

Les ... illes

Factur

Les ...rieau

La Teste

CAP. FERRE

Pyla/mer

Cazaux

A map of Cap Ferret, on
view at the Hôtel des Pins.
Opposite: On a sand dune
looking out to the Atlantic.

Oysters at Chez Boulan.
Clockwise from above:
The entrance to
La Maison du Bassin;
La Co(o)rniche's salmon
carpaccio; kite surfing
at Plage de l'Horizon.

Anchored in the Bassin d'Arcachon. Below: Colorful shirts for sale.

MENTION CAP FERRET AND YOU MIGHT GET A RESPONSE THAT smacks of pop legends, Ferraris, and leathery men. But the Atlantic enclave has more in common with salty Cape Cod—pine forests; oyster shacks; rough waves—than the phonetically similar town on the Côte d'Azur it's often mistaken for (that would be Cap *Ferrat*). Even in the height of summer, the shoreline offers many pockets of privacy. Kids on bicycles are as plentiful as hydrangeas. And bargain-priced oysters are hauled out of the ice-blue waters straight onto your plate. Compared with the fussiness of Paris, a three-hour TGV ride and 90-minute drive away, this skinny peninsula on France's northwestern coast—along the diamond-shaped estuary of Bassin d'Arcachon—is nothing if not laid-back.

Hotels are a scarce commodity in Cap Ferret; the best one, La Maison du Bassin, is often booked months in advance. Its crisp interiors, nautical antiques, and sisal rugs doused with orange-flower water remain true to the area's shabby-chic spirit—as does the rustic, country-Deco Hôtel des Pins. A notch or two up on the city-slicker barometer, the recently opened Côté Sable has modern deck furniture and a Clarins spa. And a ferry ride across the bay, in Pyla-sur-Mer, Philippe Starck's whimsical new La Co(o)rniche is set in a split-timber former hunting lodge, complete with the requisite scene-y restaurant and a poolside terrace.

In Cap Ferret, it's all backyard barbecues and oysters—the theory being that such casual perfection needs little help. A cluster of mismatched furniture on a lawn makes up Chez Boulan, where platters of the briny bivalves are served with lemon wedges and white wine. A few blocks away, Le Père Ouvrard is popular for its fish-based tapas (succulent grilled prawns; sardines *à la planche*). The toughest reservation in town is the scruffy Chez Hortense, with long wooden tables and garlicky, bacon-strewn mussels that are as good as the regulars say they are. Afterward, the bottle-service set heads to Sail Fish, a simple beach bar turned stylish bistro. Single portions of grilled Argentinean entrecôte and chocolate mousse could each feed three, but diners manage to dance regardless—among the tables, in the large front bar, or out on the patio. At midnight, the strains of *Off the Wall*–vintage Michael Jackson stream out the door and mingle with the sound of surf just over the dunes.

Hotel Therme Vals's thermal bath. Left: A rustic stable in Vals.

THE ALPS

A ROAD TRIP THROUGH SWITZERLAND AND AUSTRIA

CRISSCROSSING SWITZERLAND AND AUSTRIA'S BYWAYS yields mountain highs of every kind: old-world artisans, stellar food, and low-key architectural marvels.

In St. Gallen, 90 minutes east of Zurich, the coffee and *Galler Biber*, a gingerbread-style confection with almond filling, perk up the weary at Confiserie Roggwiller. Don't miss the eighth-century Abbey of St. Gall, and its 2,100 antiquarian manuscripts. Drive 20 miles northwest toward Rorschach—a wooden bathhouse just outside town is perfect for a restorative dip—before crossing into Bregenz, Austria. Contemporary art museum Kunsthaus Bregenz is set in a glass-and-steel building designed by Swiss architect Peter Zumthor. From there, it's 23 miles to Bezau and the Hotel Post, a country inn with modern flair (staffers dressed in dirndls; rooms furnished with white leather sofas). Dine on Austrian classics at local favorite Engel.

The next morning, pick up a pair of handmade wooden clogs at Devich, before you hit the road again. Minimalist cheese co-op Kasekeller is a must in blink-and-you'll-miss-it Lingenau. Nearby, stock up on cool schnapps glasses at Schwarzenberg's Textil Hirschbül. Drive 32 miles to Feldkirch and check in to the Hotel Alpenrose. It's a short walk to medieval Schattenburg Castle, where residents feast on what are said to be Austria's largest schnitzels.

On your last day, head south through Maienfeld (home of the fictional Heidi) and stop in Kunz-Keller, a store selling bottles of the area's little-known Pinot Noir. Hike the pine-studded paths in Flims, or catch a paddleboat tour at Lake Cauma Park. Then it's on to Surcasti, where Swiss chef Reto Derungs serves whatever's fresh at Ustria Casa da Luzi. End your journey at the modernist spa Hotel Therme Vals, also designed by Zumthor. A soak in its stunning architectural baths is worth the trip alone.

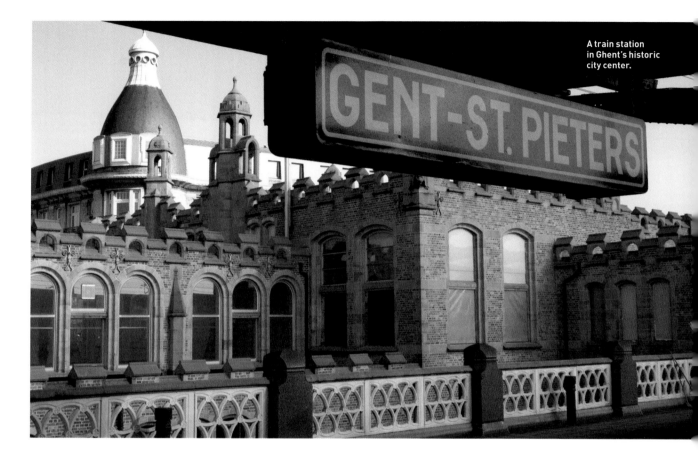

A train station in Ghent's historic city center.

GHENT

AN OLD-WORLD ENCLAVE GOES MODERN

ONCE THE CROWN JEWEL OF MEDIEVAL EUROPE, GHENT HAS long been overshadowed as a travel destination by its better-known Flemish sisters Antwerp and Bruges. But the town, 30 miles northwest of Brussels, has the best of both worlds: cutting-edge boutiques and design museums that rival Antwerp's, and centuries-old cobblestoned streets similar to those in Bruges.

Ghent's heritage is visible everywhere you look: on the Graslei, an old merchants' street of guild houses along the Leie River, or in the Gothic spires of St. Bavo Cathedral, the town's most recognizable landmark. (The church's 15th-century altarpiece, *The Adoration of the Mystic Lamb*, painted by Jan van Eyck, is one of the treasures of the Renaissance.) Contemporary art, including works by Joseph Beuys and Luc Tuymans, is on display at the Stedelijk Museum voor Actuele Kunst (S.M.A.K.). Farther north, the Design Museum Gent is a building in two parts. Walk through the 18th-century mansion,

with its tableaus of domestic life from that era, then tour the newer extension and its permanent collection of 20th-century furniture.

Art and design aren't the city's only strengths. In the Middle Ages, Ghent grew rich on wool cloth (after Paris, it was Europe's biggest town north of the Alps). Today, the narrow shopping strip of Vlaanderenstraat capitalizes on that legacy. Eva Bos makes custom apparel such as Audrey Hepburn–inspired evening dresses. A short walk away, Het Oorcussen carries pieces by avant-garde Belgian designers, including Ann Demeulemeester and Dries Van Noten. Around the corner, Obius stocks Martin Margiela sweaters and Veronique Branquinho heels. The style factor extends to the hotel scene, thanks to an influx of chic inns. Our favorite: the affordable Chambreplus, where the husband-and-wife owners run a cooking school in the cellar and guests learn to make—what else?—Belgian chocolate.

The patio at Relais
Regina Teodolinda,
overlooking Lake Como.

ITALIAN LAKES

LIVING THE GLAMOROUS LIFE

STATELY GARDEN VILLAS, ARTISANAL FOOD SHOPS, ALFRESCO restaurants: what's not to love about Italy's lake region? Stretching from Piedmont to Lombardy and the Veneto, the area has had a mythic quality since ancient Roman writers such as Pliny the Younger wrote lovingly about its shady plane-tree walks and flowery banks. Today its beauty continues to captivate—just ask George Clooney. A scenic drive is the best way to take it all in.

Celeb quotient notwithstanding, Como embodies low-key glamour. The 30-mile-long western shoreline runs from the miniature sailing port of Cernobbio (home to the fabled Villa d'Este, a favorite of the international jet set) to Menaggio. In Laglio, the Relais Regina Teodolinda has six stylish suites in an 1800's villa with a 200-year-old garden. More gardens are on hand in the old fishing villages of Bellano and Varenna, along with medieval castles; at the restaurant Navedano, a former 19th-century windmill in the town of Como, you can feast on a vast seafood platter on a veranda surrounded by roses, orchids, and lemon trees.

Set along the southern banks of the Alps, Maggiore—Italy's second-largest lake—is the busiest. Most visitors head to Cannobio near the Swiss border, a labyrinth of cobblestoned streets and medieval palazzi. Lake Orta lies less than 10 miles west of Maggiore; in its main village, Orta San Giulio, rooms at the turreted Villa Crespi have four-poster beds and damask draperies. The real draw, however, is the hotel's Michelin-starred restaurant, where chef-owner Antonino Cannavacciuolo whips up such creative dishes as buffalo mozzarella ice cream with tomato sauce and basil granita.

Garda, straddling Lombardy and the Veneto, is the balmiest of the lakes. Sailors and windsurfers come for its breezy waters, while foodies are lured by the award-winning wines and olive oils. In Gargnano, the Grand Hotel a Villa Feltrinelli was once a 19th-century aristocrat's mansion, then the World War II residence of Benito Mussolini. In Salò, the Villa Arcadio Hotel & Resort, a former 13th-century convent, has a jasmine-covered terrace looking out over palm-studded shores. Stock up on dark chocolate–dipped candied orange peel in Salò's Vassalli Pasticcerie, and taste superlative olive oil from family-run Comincioli, in Puegnago del Garda. Don't miss Guerrieri Rizzardi Azienda Agricola: the 550-year-old estate's wine production is personally overseen by Countess Maria Cristina Rizzardi. In summer, tastings of Bardolino and Chiaretto are held in the kitchen garden of her lakeside family villa—an experience that sums up what *la bella vita* is all about.

One of Lake Orta's motor-taxi captains. Above: A chandelier at Villa Crespi.

SALENTO

UNCHANGED FOR THE BETTER

A courtyard at Lecce's Awaiting Table Cookery School. Opposite: The beach at Gallipoli, in the Salento region of Puglia.

Fried vegetables at Alle due Corti, in Lecce. Above: The Awaiting Table Cookery School.

FLANKED BY THE ADRIATIC TO THE EAST AND THE IONIAN SEA to the west, the Salento—the province in the heel of the boot at the tip of the Italian peninsula—is the best expression of the Puglian character. It has the cleanest water, the friendliest locals, the most delicious food. It's an Italy of 30, 40 years ago: remote; behind, in the best sense; not trampled by tourists.

The Salentine Peninsula is made for driving—so long as you stick to the pretty, secondary roads. You can make it from sea to sea in less than two hours, although each town will entice you along the way with its own sleepy sort of rhythm. Head south from Bari, past dense olive groves, vineyards, and flat earth the color of cinnamon, to Lecce for a lesson at the Awaiting Table Cookery School. You can learn to make fresh *burrata* in an 18th-century castle, owned by a baron whose family reigned over the city in bygone centuries. Or glean the finer points of baking bread from American-born Silvestro Silvestori, whose grandmother was Leccese and who has run the school since 2003. After a day spent kneading pasta dough and picking lemons for house-made *limoncello,* your bed for the night awaits around the corner at Suite 68, a chic B&B in a private palazzo. But don't skip town before having lunch at the family-run Alle due Corti restaurant and swinging by Claudio Riso's papier-mâché workshop.

Eighteen miles southwest in Nardò, the seven-suite Masseria Bernardini was built by a Milanese architect and gallery owner, who installed modern kitchens and gardens fragrant with rosemary and lavender. You'll find earthenware dishes and woven straw totes at the nearby Terrarossa Arte Salentina, a well-curated crafts shop. The town center is full of Baroque churches where women fan themselves in the pews; the men, meanwhile, gather in barbershops or in *circolι* (social clubs), playing cards and drinking beer.

Down the coast in Gallipoli, stop at the fish market for more clams and mussels than you could eat in a lifetime. From there, it's an easy 20-mile drive to the *entroterra,* the region's interior, a secret world within the blue-green border of coastal Salento. In the town of Maglie, stop at Antica Pasticceria G. Portaluri for almond-flavored *ricciarelli* cookies and the ladyfinger-like *savoiardi.* Farther on, the 11 villages of the Grecia Salentina seem closed-off and mysterious, with Greek roots that may go back as far as the eighth century.

Twenty-five miles away, at the very edge of Italy, Santa Maria di Leuca makes a dramatic conclusion. Survey the meeting of the seas from a promontory that was once home to a temple of Minerva and a guidepost for ancient sailors. In the empty, windswept piazza, a sign points out—as if, surrounded by infinite water, you needed reminding—that you have finally reached the ends of the earth.

Piazza Salandra, in Nardò. Clockwise from below: The breakfast room at Lecce's Suite 68 hotel; Claudio Riso's shop in Lecce; pastries from Maglie's Antica Pasticceria G. Portaluri.

The Lounge at J.K. Place Firenze. Left: A view of Il Duomo, over the Piazza della Signoria.

FLORENCE

ART'S CUTTING EDGE

THE BIRTHPLACE OF THE ITALIAN RENAISSANCE HAS BECOME a hot spot for contemporary creativity—no small feat, given Florence's artistic record. Dozens of galleries have opened in the past decade, uncovering fresh Florentine and international virtuosos and building a new identity for the city along the way. The Tuscan capital provides an ideal context for comprehending the present while relating to the past.

Within walking distance of the emerging art district of Diladdarno, the J.K. Place Firenze is an inspiring work in itself, designed by architect Michele Bonan and overlooking the church of Santa Maria Novella. Stop by the sprawling FOR Gallery, a photography and video showroom, then walk five minutes northwest to Poggiali e Forconi to see rotating shows by the likes of Patti Smith and David LaChapelle. At Galleria Biagiotti, American owner and director Carole Biagiotti presents Italian artists, such as street painter Ericailcane, known for his whimsical fauna-themed drawings.

In a former church, Museo Marino Marini houses 183 sculptures by the mid-20th-century Tuscan artist, famous for his stylized equestrian pieces. Meanwhile, in the basement of a Renaissance palazzo, La Strozzina showcases themed exhibits by young talent on the rise. The Sangallo Art Station, a gallery and café, features both the well-known (1970's Pop artist Mario Schifano) and the up-and-coming. Next to the Ponte Vecchio, Isabella Brancolini oversees the exhibits at Brancolini Grimaldi and selects what's on show at nearby Gallery Hotel Art. The best way to end a visually packed day: over a caipirinha and popcorn at the tiny Art Bar, a favorite with the city's bohemian set.

Inside Tivoli Gardens'
Concert Hall Rotunda.
Left: Cured red char
with rye bread and
pickled cucumber at
Nimb Brasserie.

COPENHAGEN

TIVOLI GARDENS' 21ST-CENTURY TRANSFORMATION

THEME PARKS ARE, BY DEFINITION, LIGHTWEIGHTS WHEN IT comes to style. The exception: Copenhagen's Tivoli Gardens. Thanks to a starchitect-led growth spurt, this petite magic kingdom, in the center of the Danish capital, is aiming to become a bona-fide cultural destination for the 21st century.

Since the park's inception, in 1843, serious design has been at the heart of its appeal. You can trace certain Danish Modern motifs to details created by great architects and designers—from Poul Henningsen's iconic spiral streetlights (1949) to Frits Schlegel's sinuous concert hall (1956). Successive generations of avant-garde Danes also put their stamp on the place. But the real changes began in 2008 with the opening of the Nimb complex— the renovation of an iconic 1909 building that resembles a Moorish Taj Mahal. Its new incarnation, by Italian architect

Matteo Thun, includes a 13-room hotel with oiled-oak floors, silver wallpaper, and Philippe Starck bathtubs; a Michelin-starred restaurant, Herman; the chic Nimb Brasserie; and Andersen Bakery, a Japanese shop selling Danish pastries and named after Hans Christian himself. In 2012 you'll be able to stroll along Tivoli Edge, a glass-walled arcade filled with stores and cafés.

The park's influence has even spread to downtown Copenhagen. A shuttle bus can take you across the Bernstorffsgade to the site of the old rail yard at Kalvebod. There you'll find the park-affiliated, 402-room Tivoli Hotel & Congress Center. Conceived by Kim Utzon, arguably Denmark's greatest living architect, the hotel incorporates elements of Tivoli style, from headboards with thick circus stripes to staffers in harlequin attire. It's part kitsch, part high design—and wholly in keeping with the Tivoli Gardens tradition.

VIENNA

PRESERVING A WAY OF LIFE

THE VIENNESE SPEAK OF COFFEEHOUSES AS HAVING SOULS, often resisting even the slightest change to the 300-year-old institution. Cultural standbys like Old Town's Café Korb, with its marble-topped tables, bentwood chairs, and waiters formally clad in jackets and bow ties, seem practically untouched since the early 20th century, when luminaries such as Gustav Klimt and Sigmund Freud made the city's café scene legendary. Today, residents remain justly proud of this fact, but in an age of higher real estate costs and global competition, even the beloved *Kaffeehaus* must adapt to an uncertain future.

The good news is that despite the arrival of Starbucks (nine and counting in the Austrian capital), many of these fabled meeting places are flourishing. The fashionable Café Landtmann, whose wood-paneled interior is lit by ornate brass chandeliers, has added a glass-enclosed winter garden designed by cutting-edge Austrian firm Wehdorn Architects. Café Museum, designed in 1899 by Adolf Loos and a favorite of artist Egon Schiele, was resurrected in October 2010 after a year's closure. And stalwarts such as Café Central, Café Ritter, and Café Weimar still bustle with all-day activity. Vienna's coffeehouses are as much a part of the city's self-image as opera and the waltz, and they remain map-marked stops for tourists and residents. They're not going anywhere.

Viennese *melange* and Landtmann's *feine Torte* at Café Museum. Opposite: The newspaper rack at Café Landtmann.

The Adrina Beach Hotel, on the Aegean coast. Right: Strolling the Old Town of Skopelos.

SKOPELOS

A CLASSIC GREEK IDYLL

HOLLYWOOD SCOUTS WERE ON TO SOMETHING WHEN THEY skipped over Mykonos and chose sleepy Skopelos, in the western Aegean, as the location for the 2008 film *Mamma Mia!* The setting, with its hidden coves, lush forests, and blue-roofed tavernas, stoked the travel fantasies of moviegoers everywhere. Even after such mainstream exposure, Skopelos has managed to stay under the radar. A one-hour ferry ride from the island of Skiathos, in the Sporades, the 37-square-mile island still feels like a discovery.

At the recently renovated Adrina Beach Hotel, the 49 pastel rooms face a pine tree–covered coastline. The property and its newer sibling, Adrina Resort & Spa, are located on a quiet stretch of sand where daybeds beckon. Those with more ambitious agendas will find that Skopelos Town was made for walking; from the cobbled streets that hug the curved harbor, a tangle of paths ascends the hillside to the ruins of a 13th-century Venetian fortress, passing dozens of whitewashed churches that peek above terra-cotta rooftops.

Rent a bike in town and explore bucolic roads lined with almond orchards and olive groves. Charter a boat to circle the island's perimeter and spend the afternoon on adjacent Alonissos, where you might spot dolphins or an endangered Mediterranean monk seal. After a day on the water, a simple feast awaits at one of Old Town's tavernas; you can dine on grilled lamb in the garden at Perivoli, then walk to open-air Mercurius Bar & Café for live *rebetika* music. A steep climb up the hillside, Ouzeri Anatoli is run by musician Giorgios Xindaris, who often performs with his sons. The ouzo flows freely, and screenwriters couldn't have scripted the atmosphere better.

A view of Victoria, Gozo's capital, as seen from the city's hilltop citadel.

GOZO

UNWINDING BY THE SEA

THE TINY MALTESE ISLAND OF GOZO IS SUPPOSEDLY WHERE Odysseus was "held captive" by Calypso after the Trojan War. One look at the landscape—inky water, dramatic cliffs, pristine beaches—and it's no wonder he stayed for seven years. This Mediterranean haven is steeped in history, with Bronze Age ruins, crumbling castles, and elaborate churches dotting the rolling hills.

An ancient citadel crowns the capital town of Victoria, with three monasteries housed inside its walls. You can spend the night in the atmospheric St. Augustine Convent, which peers over mazelike streets lined with Baroque town houses. On St. Francis Square, Tapie's Bar is known for its people-watching and its excellent *pastizzi* (ricotta-filled pastries). Just outside town, the restaurant Ta' Frenc occupies an old farmhouse, with tables set in a fragrant herb garden; the menu consists of seasonal French and Maltese specialties, including *fenkata* (rabbit sautéed in a white-wine-and-pea sauce) and duck glazed with local prickly pear liqueur.

In the quiet town of Sannat, Hotel Ta' Cenc & Spa is located within a 370-acre nature preserve. The sprawling property features a 17th-century palazzo and 85 stone bungalows, many with patios or terraces overlooking a private beach. From there it's a short drive to Dwejra Bay, where you can snorkel amid octopuses and starfish or take a boat to see the natural rock formation known as the Azure Window. Along the water's edge, the dramatic Ta' Cenc cliffs are a breeding ground for rare birds. At sunset the scene is especially unforgettable, the only sound the songs of warblers echoing against the rocks.

ISTANBUL

ANCIENT FLAVORS COME TO LIFE

Waterfront tables at Zarifi
restaurant, on the Asian
coast of the Bosporus.

A waiter at Cercis Murat Konaği. Above: The Blue Mosque.

THE TAVERNA FARE OF ISTANBUL IS ONE OF THE WORLD'S tastiest cuisines—mezes, kebabs, and fresh fish, best washed down with raki and preferably in sight of the Bosporus. But what most travelers don't realize is that this is just one interpretation of Turkish food. Lately, a handful of restaurants have resurrected ancient recipes that draw on the city's past as the capital of the Ottoman Empire.

Strong, heavy food was what sultans loved best, and it's showcased on the extensive menu at Asitane. The soft, garlicky *has pacasi tiritli* (lamb's trotter) and the beefy *fodula* stew may be the ultimate comfort dishes, but more delicate offerings round out the repertoire, including dolmas stuffed with minced lamb, rice, and pignoli served atop sweet melon. At Zarifi, just off main pedestrian thoroughfare Istiklal Street, owner Fehmi Yaşar pays tribute to the old Ottoman minorities of the neighborhood—Armenians, Greeks, Sephardic Jews, and others. Order the Hungarian honey eggplant, which has a memorable sweet-savory flavor. Right next to tourist favorite Galata Tower, Kiva Han specializes in ethnic Anatolian food: *fellah köfte,* meatless bulgur dumplings steeped in tomato broth, and sherbets so authentic that they come topped with snow shipped from mountain caves.

A 35-minute ferry ride from central Beşiktaş—the Blue Mosque glowing in the distance—brings you to Bostanci, on Istanbul's Asian side, where you can walk along the water to Cercis Murat Konaği. Inside, well-heeled Turks feast on a fusion of Turco-Arabic dishes from the southeastern city of Mardin. A spicy pink *muhammara* dip is served with atomized bread crumbs and goat cheese; the steamed *kubbes,* dumplings stuffed with minced beef and pignoli, surely began life in Shanghai and traveled to Turkey via the Silk Road. Also on the Asian side, past the Kadiköy fish-and-produce market, lies Çiya Sofrasi, a no-nonsense counter that's become a pilgrimage site for global foodies. Owner Musa Dağdeviren has an anthropological fetish for ingredients—witness the *kaya koruğu,* fresh local bush-greens found in river silt, or the syrupy, deeply comforting dessert made of olives. Each dish is painstakingly recovered from old folk memory and worth savoring.

Probka restaurant
in St. Petersburg.
Right: A young local
on Nevsky Prospekt. 96

ST. PETERSBURG

RUSSIA'S SECOND CITY STEPS INTO THE SPOTLIGHT

Culture clash at a bus stop. Below: The Grand Hotel Europe's lobby bar.

EDGY LITTLE SISTER TO BIG-MONEY MOSCOW, ST. PETERSBURG has always worn its number-two status with style, thanks to the independent spirit that thrives behind its colorful Neoclassical façades, a legacy of its enlightened founder, Peter the Great. Russia's Soviet years were hard on the city, but it has bounced back with new museums and sophisticated shops—proof that it remains the country's cultural heart.

In central St. Petersburg, a hidden stairwell leads to the multi-functional art center known as Loft Project Etagi, a former bread factory turned industrial-chic exhibition space. Contemporary works are the focus of two recently opened institutions on Vasilevsky Island: Erarta, a columned 20th-century building that showcases up-and-coming Russian talent, and Novy Museum, which specializes in paintings and sculptures from genre-defining artists (including Sots-Art duo Komar & Melamid). For a similar aesthetic back on the mainland, visit eclectic gallery Rosphoto. To see classical music's emerging stars, there may be no more evocative place in the world than the Concert Hall at the Mariinsky Theatre, a mainstay of the White Nights festival held in St. Petersburg each summer.

Cutting-edge boutiques also embody the current zeitgeist. At LowFat Studio, a workshop and showroom for the eco-friendly fashion line of Merya and Vera Dmitrieva, a refrigerator is stocked with seasonal snacks for shoppers, from gooseberries in spring to ice cream bars in summer (but save room for the groundbreaking Italian cuisine at Probka, a favorite of the Russian cognoscenti). Quilted leather jackets and avant-garde frocks fill the racks at Lyyk Design Market, a white-on-white space in a courtyard off the Griboyedova Canal. Across town, Generator Nastroenia (the name translates to "mood generator") sells merchandise guaranteed to lift spirits, such as leather journals embossed with cheeky Russian-language jokes or propaganda-themed covers. As souvenirs go, they're a worthwhile alternative to the ubiquitous matryoshka dolls—and a playful homage to St. Petersburg's Soviet roots. If a fresh take on czarist glamour seems like a better fit, visit the lobby bar at the 1875 landmark Grand Hotel Europe and order your vodka neat—the way the locals do.

Performing tricks in front
of the Hermitage.

A corner of the lobby at the Royal Mansour Marrakech, in Morocco.

AFRICA &
THE MIDDLE EAST

MARRAKESH

SAVORING A DESERT OASIS

Al Baraka's chicken *tagine*.
Opposite: Looking out
from the Royal Mansour
Marrakech to the Kutubīyah
mosque's minaret.

Tea time at Café de France.
Clockwise from left: Inside
the spa at the Royal Mansour
Marrakech; the Hassan
counter in Jamaā El Fna
square; a local patisserie.

MARRAKESH WALLOPS THE SENSES WITH A RIOT OF COLORS, sounds, and tastes. Whether in the souks of the walled medina or the modern district of Guéliz, there is no better place to revel in the diversity of North African cuisine—lamb, couscous, eggplant, all redolent of cumin, saffron, and the chili paste *harissa*—than this ancient crossroads.

In the medina, the former *riad* of French designer Pierre Balmain serves as the setting for Dar Moha, which bills its cuisine as *nouvelle marocaine*, though celebrity chef-owner Moha Fedal takes an *ancien* approach to couscous. Compare earthy Berber barley pellets with the more familiar durum wheat, here as light and fluffy as snowflakes. Nearby you'll find Haj Mostapha N'Guyer, the local emperor of *mechoui* (roasted lamb), in robe and skullcap, at his Haj Mostapha stand. Seek out his alter ego at Guéliz's Chez Lamine, where the vendor speaks French and sports a business suit. The lamb is spectacular at both locations: roasted until meltingly tender (request the flavorful neck and rib meat) and served on butcher paper with cumin salt; your flatbread serves as plate, utensil, and napkin for all that rich, fatty goodness.

The roof-terrace tables at Café de France offer the best vantage point for watching the sun set over the legendary Jamaâ El Fna square and the Kutubīyah's minaret beyond. Tasting your way through the square itself can be challenging: the tablecloth stalls are filled with tourists; the authentic ones often require a stomach of steel. Thankfully, Hassan comes through with slender, juicy *merguez* sausages served at a tin counter thronged by big families.

A short walk from the boisterous souks, the extravagant Royal Mansour Marrakech is the walled-off personal project of his Royal Highness Mohammed VI, King of Morocco. Parisian chef Yannick Alléno of Michelin-three-starred Le Meurice oversees its trio of restaurants, including La Grande Table Marocaine. Chandeliers glitter above filigreed metal tables under a coffered ceiling; waitresses in white caftans proffer platters of *seffa medfouna*, a complex veal-and-apricot stew buried in a mound of vermicelli ornamented with almonds and cinnamon. Your meal complete, amble past lavishly tiled public spaces to the soft patter of courtyard fountains.

A 20-minute hop from town along the old Fez route brings you to the informal restaurant Al Baraka, its cheery outdoor tables an agreeable distance from the on-site gas station. Don't let the pumps deter you from trying the flatbread—as blistered and chewy as Rome's best *pizza bianca*—served at a window where Berber ladies slap dough into a wood-fueled oven. Before you leave, stop at the *tagine* counter for blackened pots of whole country chicken, pungent with preserved lemons and olives, and beef shank fragrant with cloves and sweet, smoky prunes.

Traditional Moroccan cooking ingredients. Above: Jamaâ El Fna's food stalls.

Masai watchmen near Lamu
Island's Kizingoni Beach.

LAMU
A FAR-FLUNG SEASIDE OUTPOST

FOR MORE THAN A THOUSAND YEARS, EAST AFRICA WAS AT THE center of the world trade map, drawing a steady influx of Africans, Arabs, Indians, and Europeans. Though more recently discovered by a coterie of the latter with a penchant for campaign-inspired furniture, the four islands that make up the Lamu archipelago, on Kenya's northeastern coast, still feel blissfully remote.

Board a motor launch from the mainland to the vehicle-free Old Town of Lamu, a UNESCO World Heritage site. Beyond a crumbling pier crowded with handcarts bearing sacks of basmati rice, high-walled, jasmine-scented lanes guard stately houses of whitewashed coral stone—the residences of wealthy traders' descendants. Bed down at Lamu House, which has 10 guest rooms in two adjacent buildings. Then wander through the backstreets for a glimpse of daily life: women peddling live chickens in woven baskets; vendors setting up impromptu stands to sell fruit cups and coffee; young girls in head scarves carrying home yellow plastic jugs of water. Small shops along the main thoroughfare stock everything from Zanzibar peppercorns and chewing tobacco to disposable cell phones and marine-engine parts.

On the promenade at the modest restaurant Olympic, a lady named Mama Fatuma makes addictive coconut rice infused with cinnamon, clove, and cumin seeds. Or you can snack continuously from charcoal braziers set up in the alleys rather than sit down in any one place for a meal; graze on roasted cashews, lentil-and-potato *bhajia,* and chili-dusted cassava chips. As the day fades quench your thirst at the waterside Petley's Inn, where voyeurs mingle with locals at the convivial rooftop bar.

Three miles south of Old Town is Shela Village, or "Little Europe," where wealthy expats and Nairobi elite have built their villas. The Peponi Hotel is the place for a sundowner—cool off with an Old Pal, a refresher of vodka, lime, and bitters, before enjoying a dinner of grilled giant prawns in a searing *piri-piri* chili sauce served in the breezy dining room.

Charter a small powerboat to traverse deeper into the archipelago, past clusters of mangrove along Manda Bay and dhows plying in the opposite direction, toward the dry hills of Kiwayu, the northernmost island. Clear skies, gentle waves, and a vanilla-sand beach lull you from the confines of your own restless world.

Applying henna in Old Town. From right: Cruising past mangrove forests on Manda; a courtyard and plunge pool at the Lamu House hotel.

Lamu's Old Town.
Left: A private
airstrip on Manda
island. Right: Playing
a horn made from a
conch shell on a
traditional dhow.

NAIROBI

AFRICA'S NEW STYLE SCENE

A playful resident
at the David Sheldrick
Elephant Sanctuary.

A suite at Hogmead, in Karen. Above: KikoRomeo's locally made dresses.

TRAVELERS ONCE CONSIDERED THE KENYAN CAPITAL A MERE pit stop en route to a safari. Now stylish hotels, trendy boutiques, and cutting-edge galleries are transforming the city formerly nicknamed Nairobbery. "There's been a burst of creativity—Kenyans are coming together in everything from fashion to the arts," says Shamim Ehsani, co-owner of Tribe Hotel. In the heart of the Diplomatic District, it attracts a mix of hipsters and dignitaries with its W-on-expedition design (Masai sculptures in the lobby; African-print throws in the rooms). Close to the genteel suburb of Karen—named for *Out of Africa* author Karen Blixen—Hogmead has patrician country house touches such as wood-paneled soaking tubs and leather club chairs. Nearby, you can go on safari without leaving town: the eco-chic Nairobi Tented Camp offers wildlife drives and overnight stays in luxury tents at Nairobi National Park. If you have a soft spot for pachyderms in particular, visit the David Sheldrick Elephant Sanctuary, half an hour away.

Modern retail centers are also popping up. Open-air Village Market is a one-stop shop for groceries, local crafts, and authentic African fashions. Across town, the sleek Yaya Centre looks like something you'd find in L.A.; be sure to pick up one of the tribal-themed dresses at KikoRomeo.

On the art front, the Loft, One Off Gallery carries a variety of pieces, from Peterson Kamwathi's politically charged drawings to James Mbuthia's recycled-bottle mobiles. You'll see artists at work at the Banana Hill Art Studio Gallery, which represents more than 50 up-and-coming African painters and sculptors.

Nairobi's chefs are marrying indigenous ingredients with flavors from around the globe. Cracked chili crab, slow-cooked in roasted red pepper and coriander pesto, is on the menu at Seven Seafood & Grill, in Westlands. At gastropub Talisman, in a 1920's bungalow in Karen, the signature dish is butter-poached duck with tree-tomato coulis. Also on the horizon: a Talisman hotel. Perhaps you should book an extended stay.

ZAMBIA

INTO THE WILD

THE THUNDEROUS RUSH OF VICTORIA FALLS IS REASON enough to visit Zambia, in south-central Africa. Add the game-rich nation's colossal lakes, whitecapped rivers, grassy savannas, and a portion of the Kalahari Desert, and you have to wonder: *Why haven't I been here before?* You're not the only one. Now a handful of safari operators and lodges are helping Zambia become the next great African destination.

In 2011, Sanctuary Retreats opened Sanctuary Zebra Plains, four luxe tents on South Luangwa National Park's eponymous river. With vintage campaign furniture and an open-air library stocked with travel books and literature, it has the kind of old-world aesthetic usually found in East African properties—plus elephant,

The pool at Sanctuary Sussi & Chuma. Opposite: A view of South Luangwa National Park from Sanctuary Zebra Plains.

leopard, and giraffe sightings to match. The smaller Bushcamp Company, which pioneered South Luangwa walking tours, has six renovated park camps, including Zungulila, four thatched-roof dwellings with canopy beds and plunge pools facing the antelope-filled plain. For an authentic bush experience that's reminiscent of a private homestay, consider the lodges of Remote Africa Safaris, owned by John Coppinger, a former guide who has worked in the region for more than 20 years, and his wife, Carol. Our favorite: the Chikoko Trails camps, which are situated near Africa's most populous hippopotamus habitat.

Other new properties and tours have cropped up farther west along the Zambezi River, whose rapids provide the ultimate adventure aboard a canoe. You can cross white rhinos and wildebeests off your wildlife checklist at Toka Leya, where ecotourism operator Wilderness Safaris has set up camp in the shade of two ancient baobab trees overlooking the river. South African pine walkways link the 12 canvas tents; a bar and an infinity pool offer cool comfort. The last three days of Austin-Lehman Adventures' Zambezi to Victoria Falls family program are dedicated to cruising on a 30-foot-long houseboat as you cast for the region's legendary piranha-like tiger fish. And at Sanctuary Sussi & Chuma, just a few miles away from Victoria Falls, 12 luxurious stilted villas and a main pavilion are built into a stand of ebony trees lining the river bank. Off the beaten track never looked so good.

JOHANNESBURG

A CREATIVE HUB EMERGES

Attic restaurant, in the
Parkhurst neighborhood.
Opposite: A corridor at
Circa on Jellicoe gallery.

Colin Davids in his 44 Stanley shop, Vintage Cowboys. Clockwise from left: A Casper government vehicle at the Apartheid Museum; Moemas restaurant's broccoli, eggplant, and potato salads; the exterior of Circa on Jellicoe.

The shopping and
gallery complex
Arts on Main. Above:
Attic restaurant.

THOUGH JOHANNESBURG FAMOUSLY IMPLODED IN THE
1990's, the city has reemerged from the cloud of its dark past with a
thriving arts and culture scene, thanks to smart designers and
developers who are leading a surprising revivification.

From the airport, board the Gautrain; in 15 minutes, the new
mass-transit train will bring you to the all-suite Saxon Boutique
Hotel, Villas & Spa, set on six acres of landscaped gardens. Here,
Nelson Mandela finished writing *Long Walk to Freedom* following
his release from prison. Five minutes away by car is Moemas, a
pocket-size café and bakery in upscale Parktown North that
specializes in inventive salads, such as broccoli, tomato, and *halloumi*
with mustard-seed dressing and eggplant with herbed yogurt, basil,
and pistachios. Photo-ready sweets like raspberry-coulis meringues
and bread-and-butter pudding round out the ever-evolving offerings.
Or visit Parkhurst's restaurant row, where the fare ranges from sushi
to rustic Italian. Antiques-filled Attic serves an eclectic menu
(French guinea fowl risotto; Namibian mussels; Scottish salmon)
inspired by the travels of its globe-trotting owners.

In Parkhurst's burgeoning gallery district, head to design studio
Maker to view furniture and ceramics by homegrown product
designers, and Gallery 2, where Western Cape native Joshua Miles
displays his colorful woodblock prints. In neighboring Rosebank,
Circa on Jellicoe is best known for contemporary South African art
and the 400 striking, 30-foot-tall aluminum "fins" that surround the
space. Shopping is the main draw at Milpark's 44 Stanley complex—
be sure to check out Tiaan Nagel's sophisticated dresses and the
retro furnishings at Vintage Cowboys. The stylish Arts on Main
one-ups them all, combining both retail and gallery space on the
newly revitalized eastern edge of the Central Business District.

To truly understand Johannesburg, visit the Apartheid Museum.
It's an invaluable primer on the city's longstanding race divisions, as
well as the 19th-century gold rush that brought prospectors from
around the world. And it's a powerful reminder of just how far the
city has come.

CAPE WINELANDS

A FARM-TO-TABLE MOVEMENT ROOTED IN THE PAST

The garden at Babylonstoren, in the Franschhoek Valley.

Delaire Graff Lodges &
Spa's reception area.
Left: Babel restaurant, at
the Babylonstoren farm.

NOT LONG AGO, THE IDEA THAT A CHIC SOUTH AFRICAN HOTEL could be a celebration of Afrikaner style and culture would have been unthinkable. But a generation since the end of apartheid, a wave of creative locals are reclaiming their ancestors' achievements—and forging a fresh identity in the process.

In the Franschhoek Valley, La Motte is a tribute to the Afrikaner way of life. The 420-acre property recently unveiled both an art museum and a restaurant that specializes in historic *Boerekos* (Boer recipes that date back 350 years) with a modern twist. Chef Chris Erasmus sifted through settlers' letters, diaries, and cookbooks to create a menu that serves as a culinary archive of a people. Saffron fish curry recalls food of the Malay slaves shipped to the Cape, while meaty dishes such as pomegranate-glazed pork belly reflect the Dutch, German, and Flemish roots of the region.

Less than 10 miles away, Babylonstoren is a testament to the tribe's almost mythic love for the land. The working guest farm combines no-frills earthiness with a contemporary aesthetic, and its vegetable garden is at the center of all the fecundity. Scented beds of rosemary and wild garlic yield to an orchard of *naartjies* (a citrus fruit similar to a tangerine) and nectarines and an apiary for honey. In the gabled manor

house, the reception area resembles a traditional farm store, with computers hidden behind mounds of fresh-picked beets and lettuce. Stay in one of the 14 thatched-roof *landhuisies* (cottages), which combine the austerity of a Boer residence with the cool minimalism of Philippe Starck: white sofas and rugs; claw-foot tubs; sleek kitchens. If you prefer to let someone else cook for you, amble down the road to the on-site restaurant, Babel, set in a former cattle kraal.

Outside the valley, on a soaring mountain traverse that links Franschhoek with the more commercial wine region of Stellenbosch, is Delaire Graff Lodges & Spa, owned by Laurence Graff. The billionaire British diamond jeweler spent six years building Delaire, hiring famed London designer David Collins to do the interiors. Walk the dimpled floor in the main restaurant and you'll find it's made of peach pips and red resin, a current take on the treatments once used in Cape Dutch houses. Diners feast on Winelands fowl, Cape oysters and mussels, and vegetables from the lodge's own garden against the backdrop of paintings by South African artists. At first glance, it seems like a cosmopolitan mash-up, but at its heart, the estate is as grounded in the Winelands as those earthy Afrikaner properties in the valley below.

Outside the Gordon Hotel. Right: A section of Design Museum Holon's undulating façade.

TEL AVIV

HIGH DESIGN TAKES HOLD

JERUSALEM MAY BE ISRAEL'S POLITICAL AND RELIGIOUS CAPITAL, but Tel Aviv is the nation's creative heart—an aspirational nexus of culture, finance, and media along the lines of New York City. In this UNESCO World Heritage site, you'll also find the largest concentration of Bauhaus architecture in the world, design being an overriding theme since the city's inception in 1909. And amid glittering new residential and commercial towers conceived by Philippe Starck, I. M. Pei, and Richard Meier are high-concept industrial shops, single-artist showrooms, and expertly curated furniture boutiques that are upping the landscape's style quotient.

A light display at Aqua Creations Showroom. Right: Retro TLV's vintage furniture.

Check in to the Gordon Hotel & Lounge, a streamlined waterfront boutique cast in white, then set out to explore the city. If you're a vintage hunter, you'll swoon over the restored furniture by Eames, Nelson, and Aalto at Retro TLV. Other worthy finds: 1950's-era Israeli items, from Hebrew-language typewriters to kibbutz-style chairs. For contemporary lighting and accessories by young up-and-coming Israelis, head to Talents Design, down Yehuda HaLevy Street. Ayala Serfaty's Aqua Creations Showrooms carries a selection of bubble- and pouf-shaped ottomans and chairs covered in velvet and Lycra. And housed in a former train station nearby, Made in TLV stocks a range of design books, tabletop pieces, and photographs.

The outskirts of town are providing fertile ground for expanding Tel Aviv's artistic legacy as well. The curvaceous Design Museum Holon, the brainchild of Tel Aviv–born Ron Arad, opened to rave reviews in 2010. Farther north, in the emerging Noga district, pick up some of Rose & Bloom's funky housewares, including signature "lamp dresses"—lights covered in Mondrian-inspired Mylar paper shells. At the end of the day, only one question remains: How to get it all home?

RODRIGUES

SERENITY BY THE SEA

An aerial view of islets
off the southeast
coast of Rodrigues.

LOCKED IN A SHALLOW LAGOON in the middle of the Indian Ocean, about 350 miles from Mauritius proper, the fish-shaped isle of Rodrigues was virtually unknown until Prince William chose it as a paparazzi-free bolt-hole before the days of Kate. He's in good company. With its verdant valleys and hidden islets, the island is a haven for quiet-seeking hikers, snorkelers, and kite-surfers, too.

The waterfront Creole-style Mourouk Ebony Hotel is the place from which to take it all in; splurge on a waterfront villa, which gives you access to your own personal chef. If you tire of sitting seaside in a chaise longue, suit up for a visit to the hotel's Bouba Diving Center, which organizes excursions to check out the sea anemones and tropical fish that live in the protected barrier reef across the lagoon. Back on land, venture to the François Leguat Tortoise & Cave Reserve nearby to spy on Aldabra tortoises, brought to the island at Charles Darwin's recommendation after indigenous turtles became extinct in the 1800's.

Coralie la Diffe'rence is a must for freshly caught seafood down the road from the hotel. Prefer to stay put? Mourouk Ebony's restaurant serves Mauritian specialties (tangy chutneys; hearty curried stews) in a gingerbread-style dining room; vegetables come from a tidy on-site garden, fish from the ocean in front of you. Get to the open-air bar early on Wednesday and Friday evenings to catch a traditional *sega tambour* performance, a frenzied, erotically charged dance in which sarong-clad women shuffle and clap to accordion melodies and up-tempo drumbeats. The next morning, the landscape happily returns to its usual state of somnolence.

A monk in the Goddess of Mercy Temple, in Penang, Malaysia.

ASIA

KYO HONG KONG SHANGHAI HANGZHOU BEIJING SINGAPORE E
DERABAD MUMBAI PUDUCHERRY GOBI DESERT TIBET PENANG
LI INDONESIA KOH SAMUI TOKYO HONG KONG SHANGHAI HANG
IGAPORE BANGKOK CAMBODIA HYDERABAD MUMBAI PUDUCHE
ET PENANG CON DAO VIETNAM BALI INDONESIA KOH SAMUI TO
ANGHAI HANGZHOU BEIJING SINGAPORE BANGKOK CAMBODIA
JMBAI PUDUCHERRY GOBI DESERT TIBET PENANG CON DAO VIE
JONESIA KOH SAMUI TOKYO HONG KONG SHANGHAI HANGZHOI
NGKOK CAMBODIA HYDERABAD MUMBAI PUDUCHERRY GOBI DE

TOKYO

SEARCHING FOR A CULINARY EPIPHANY

Tokyo's Ginza
shopping district.

Kondo, a tempura restaurant in the Ginza. Clockwise from below: A sushi platter at Sushi Takumi Okabe; roasting bonito over rice straw at Owan; Restaurant Kinoshita's duck offal.

Tempura at Kondo.
Below: Owan's
chef-owner,
Kuniatsu Kondo.

TOKYO'S OBSESSIVE DEVOTION TO FOOD MAKES IT ONE OF THE best places in the world to experience culinary thrills—at least according to Michelin, which has awarded its restaurants 320 stars, more than either Paris and New York. The quest for gastronomic nirvana encompasses an astonishing range of dining, from the exclusive and obscure to the raffish and humble.

The odyssey begins on a high note at Sushi Takumi Okabe, in the Asakusa neighborhood. Chef Kaichiro Okabe (a mentor of Masa Takayama, whose $450 *omakase* menus are the toast of Manhattan sushi cognoscenti) produces Edo-era masterpieces at an unprepossessing nine-seat counter. Squid comes stuffed with a chopped egg, crab roe is laced with pungent seaweed, and thin slices of needlefish are dabbed with a red-pepper-and-sesame sauce.

In Tokyo, specialization verges on the maniacal—there are restaurants that serve just eel or blowfish, noodle shops solely for udon or soba. Tempura becomes a revelation at Kondo, a 15-seat spot atop one of Ginza's needle-like towers. Nearby at Rokukakutei, the only items on the menu are *kushiage:* fried morsels on skewers (shiitake and salmon; beef wrapped around a string bean). On the opposite end of the spectrum is the vast food hall at the department store Takashimaya, in neighboring Nihonbashi, where locals go for *gyoza* (pork dumplings) right off the griddle and Japanese pickles sold by the gram. The $60-a-pound green tea sells briskly; the $100 melons, displayed in ruffled tissue like Fabergé eggs, less so.

At the modest Owan, down an alley in Ikejiri, the gently priced *omakase*—just $50 per person—shows an artful attention to detail you'd expect in the most affluent of settings. A gossamer opener of freshly made tofu arrives with special salts. Scallops, oysters, and broccoli rabe stud a soft steamed dumpling floating in a dashi broth. Throughout the meal, an assistant behind the 12-seat counter carves ice into specific shapes the chef requires.

Your last stop is the unlikeliest of all. French food in Tokyo, you might ask? But food lovers in the know flock to the 32-seat Restaurant Kinoshita for owner Kazuhiko Kinoshita's inspired Francophile cooking. The six-course tasting menu features more than a few memorable moments—a lush seafood bisque; a tender venison fillet served rare; a dessert of tangerine segments on a shallow island of crème brûlée. Pretty amazing, considering the chef has never even been to France.

Forest Bird, a boutique and café. Right: Moustache's ready-to-wear creations.

HONG KONG

A SHOPPER'S DREAM

THE CENTRAL DISTRICT HAS ALWAYS BEEN HONG KONG'S nerve center, but in recent years tastemakers have begun to migrate west to Sheung Wan and SoHo. Popular with merchants since the 1800's, these residential neighborhoods are full of traditional stores selling medicine, paper lanterns, and antique pottery. Now they're joined by fashionable boutiques and stylish spots for creative types to unwind.

A mix of homegrown and expat design talent fills the area's best shops. In Sheung Wan, pick up 1960's-inspired knit sweaters and piped pajamas made with Japanese fabrics at Moustache, where the bespoke men's wear is designed by New York City transplants Ellis

Hullett House Hotel's Stanley Suite. Left: A view of Victoria Harbour from Nanhai No. 1.

Kreuger and Alex Daye. A 10-minute walk away, Fiona Kotur Marin—whose fans include Renée Zellweger and Tory Burch—showcases her snakeskin, shell, and silk brocade clutches at Kotur. In SoHo, Forest Bird displays a selection of clothes and handmade jewelry from small European and Japanese labels. Refuel over espresso and *macarons* at the boutique's tiny café, then hit Gough Street in burgeoning NoHo, where Homeless sells ceiling lights inspired by brass cooking pots. Afterward, grab a cocktail at Sugar, an alfresco bar on the 32nd floor of the East Hotel.

Board the 10-minute Star Ferry to Kowloon, where environmentally minded Ecols carries colorful dinner platters made from recycled wine bottles. For a bird's-eye view of the ground you've just covered, head to Kowloon's Nanhai No. 1, a contemporary Cantonese restaurant that serves tea-smoked chicken and barbecued pork belly in a sleek, harbor-facing dining room. Skyline views are also a key attraction at Hullet House Hotel, 10 suites in an 1881 building that was formerly the headquarters of the maritime police. Design literally reaches new heights with the arrival of the Ritz-Carlton, Hong Kong—at 1,600 feet the tallest hotel in the world. On its top floor, the Ozone bar faces Victoria Harbour and is *the* place to take it all in.

SHANGHAI

A TALE OF TWO CITIES

The view from Flair bar, on the 58th floor of the Ritz-Carlton Shanghai, Pudong.

Shanghai's cityscape along the Huangpu River. Clockwise from above: The courtyard in the Waterhouse at South Bund hotel; one of Shouning Road's market vendors; a lane in the French Concession.

SHANGHAI SHUTTLES BETWEEN TWO ABSTRACTIONS. THERE'S the street-level reality of close crowds, beeping motorbikes, and laundry hanging in the lanes; above are the gleaming high-rises, a silent meditation on hypermodernity. Spending time in both worlds reveals the many layers that make this city unusually hard to get to know.

In the Huangpu district, Shouning Road is boisterous, with vendors shucking oysters at food carts and selling roast duck at street-side grills to a happy throng of late-night snackers. Venture into the open-air food court to order grilled clams with garlic sauce, skewered duck tongues, charred rice cakes, and cold, crunchy pigs' ears. For the city's famous soup-filled dumplings, *xiao long bao,* the place to go is the cafeteria-style Jia Jia Tang Bao, also in Huangpu. The fresh-crabmeat version, at a relative splurge of $15 per dozen, is superb—thin-skinned and served in a deep, sweet, crabby broth.

The atmosphere couldn't be more different at the Park Hyatt Shanghai, on the Pudong side of town. Few cityscapes are as thrilling as the one viewed from your window, but the outside world ceases to matter once you're in this serene cloud city, a cocoon of whispered well-being. Nearby, atop Cesar Pelli's Shanghai IFC complex, the Ritz-Carlton Shanghai, Pudong, sets the standard in modern swank, with freestanding copper-clad bathtubs and a ski-lodge-in-the-sky bar. In contrast, the quirky design of Waterhouse at the Bund makes for a cool stay. The lobby soars with steel beams and unfinished concrete, and glass shaftways in guest rooms bring out voyeuristic tendencies (you can look down into part of the room below you—as in a traditional lane house).

Shanghai sometimes feels like an overproduced musical. The beauty lies in finding the unrehearsed numbers: a morning walk in the neighborhood known as the French Concession, where locals shop for the day's food (and sip drinks by night at trendy bars like El Cóctel); an impromptu conversation with a stranger that transcends language itself. In the midst of Shanghai's shifting perspectives, a moment of quiet human connection may be the biggest surprise of all.

Shouning Road at night. Above: A table at El Cóctel bar.

HANGZHOU

A NEW TWIST ON TRADITION

EIGHT CENTURIES AGO, MARCO POLO ANOINTED HANGZHOU "the most splendid city in the world." It is still one of China's best-preserved destinations, thanks to the careful stewardship of its pagodas, pavilions, and terraced tea plantations. A trio of luxury hotels is now giving this ancient capital appeal both old and new.

The 45-minute express train ride from Shanghai is like a trip back in time. Stroll pedestrianized Hefang Road, a collection of Qing dynasty houses and shops near the station, and stop at the 137-year-old Huqingyu Tang medicine shop to see pharmacists fill prescriptions with traditional remedies. Then head toward the mountain-fringed banks of West Lake, one of the city's most popular attractions. The Four Seasons Hotel Hangzhou at West Lake makes an ideal base, with its sloping pagodas and graceful green spaces (it's close to the Hangzhou Botanical Gardens). Fifteen minutes away, the 42 suites at Amanresorts's Amanfayun are housed in brick-and-timber dwellings surrounded by bamboo groves and forest. At the Banyan Tree Hangzhou, abutting the 2,800-acre Xixi National Wetland Park, villas are decorated with Chinese antiques (porcelain snuff bottles; calligraphy brushes) and positioned near arched bridges and a lagoon.

Picturesque landscapes aren't Hangzhou's only draw. The region is synonymous with *longjing*, a green tea prized for its light, sweet taste and aroma. Visit Guo's Villa, whose low, tiled wall encloses a courtyard where locals gather for tea and gossip. At the Old Dragon Well Imperial Tea Garden, you can still see the 18 bushes that were once the exclusive property of Qing dynasty emperor Qianlong. Nearby in Longjing village, numerous tea farmers peddle their wares; look for the hospitable Qi family, who will pour you a cup before you buy. The emerald hue and distinctive fragrance of this timeless elixir are as heady as Hangzhou itself.

The Lingyin Buddist temple, in Hangzhou. Opposite: West Lake at dusk.

Charly, the mixologist at Atmosphere lounge. Left: Xiu, in the Park Hyatt Beijing.

BEIJING

CHINA'S NIGHTLIFE-LOVING CAPITAL

IN THE YEARS SINCE THE OLYMPIC GAMES, BEIJING HAS become one of the Far East's most exciting nocturnal playgrounds. The city continues to evolve at full tilt, with new bars and hotel lounges popping up across town. From an under-the-radar whiskey club to a rooftop watering hole in a sleek skyscraper, the latest after-hours offerings are giving glittery Shanghai a run for its money.

The heart of expat nightlife is centrally located Sanlitun Village, where newcomer Apothecary is shaking up local cocktail culture with creative concoctions and house-made mixers. (Try the "secret Earl Grey": Beefeater gin finished off with pomelo-lavender bitters.) A five-minute stroll south leads you to D. Lounge, a brick-walled gallery that morphs into a nighttime gathering spot for fashion designers and media fixtures. Across town in the Central Business District, well-heeled urbanites take in live music while indulging in

crisp soft-shell crab fritters and spicy Sichuan-style chicken wings, Cohiba cigars, and Moët at Park Hyatt Beijing's rooftop Xiu. The bar's five interconnected pavilions are inspired by Song dynasty architecture. Ichikura is a more subdued option; the 12-seat Japanese whiskey den is stocked with a selection of rare aged varieties.

The China World Summit Wing resides in the top 18 floors of Beijing's tallest building. At its exclusive Atmosphere cocktail lounge, mixologist Serhan Kusaksizoglu—regulars know him as Charly—crafts a sophisticated menu of bourbons, rye whiskeys, and single-malts, all of which go down just a little too smoothly. True denizens of the night would be well advised to book at Sanlitun's Opposite House, where the subterranean lounge, Punk, has hosted art-world notables including David LaChapelle and Ai Weiwei. After a soak in your deep oak tub, the next morning won't seem quite so harsh.

Outside the Asian Civilisations Museum. Right: Checking in at Marina Bay Sands hotel.

SINGAPORE

BRIGHT LIGHTS, COOL CITY

IN SHINY, HAPPY SINGAPORE, SUPERLATIVES COME AT YOU with the subtlety of a sledgehammer. For the better part of the 20th century, the government spent billions transforming this island nation from a scruffy, licentious port into a squeaky-clean economic heavyweight. But behind the gleaming towers and air-conditioned malls, other Singaporean realities lie hidden in plain sight.

Once you escape the dead zone of the banking district, it's easy to slip into the embrace of old Singapura: on Serangoon Road in Little India, where Brahman priests perform time-honored devotions to the destroyer goddess Kali, or along the former cart paths off Pagoda Street—a center of 19th-century vice. As you wander through the city's botanical garden, banyans rise from buttressed roots and frangipani trees scatter their sweet-smelling blossoms, lending the place an air of floral dishabille.

The island's fusion of heritages is on display at the Peranakan Museum and the jewel-box Asian Civilisations Museum, set in a riverside colonial-era structure. A revamped National Art Gallery will open in 2015. Even resorts are getting in on the cultural act: Inside the supersize Marina Bay Sands hotel, you'll find floating art installations and a gigantic basin called *Rain Oculus,* by sculptor Ned Khan, cascading water onto the retail center below.

Locals eat passionately here, with a concentration that borders on reverence. At the Lavender Street Hawker Centre, you'll devour fish-ball noodles and oyster omelettes in the company of diners whose only remark might be a request to pass the chili sauce. Finish with a bowl of *assam laksa,* a classic noodle dish that's sometimes spiked with tamarind paste. There's something quintessentially Singaporean about the meal—full of sweet and bitter contradictions.

Gaeng hang lay (Burmese-style pork curry) at Soul Food Mahanakorn. Left: Sra Bua by Kiin Kiin.

BANGKOK

DISHING UP HISTORIC FLAVORS

RESIDENTS AND VISITORS AGREE: THE BEST FOOD IN BANGKOK has traditionally come from the streets. The varied regional cooking styles reflect the city's migrant history and are becoming an increasing influence on Bangkok's top chefs, who are bringing those diverse flavors to haute tables around town.

In the Thonglor neighborhood, Soul Food Mahanakorn uses free-range meat and organic produce in dishes such as *khao mok gai,* Thai Muslim–style chicken biryani served with a mint-cilantro-ginger sauce. A few blocks away, Phuket Town focuses on the fiery cooking of southern Thailand. (One standout: fat rice noodles with yellow crab curry.) For a sampling of the north's more subtle, herb-scented cuisine, head to Gedhawa, where rough-hewn wooden tables set the stage for Chiang Mai classics, including *khao soi* (egg noodles with chicken curry) and *sai ooua* (pork sausage).

Experimental interpretations can also be found. For molecular gastronomy with a Danish twist, visit Sra Bua by Kiin Kiin, in the Siam Shopping District. Chefs Henrik Yde-Andersen and Lertchai Treetawatchaiwong use liquid nitrogen to craft a frozen red-curry with lobster; seafood-flavored jellies star in a deconstructed *tom yum* soup. At the equally inventive Gaggan, near Lumpini Park, Ferran Adrià disciple Gaggan Anand spherifies cumin-spiked yogurt and blankets oysters with citrus-black-salt foam.

After such conceptual finery, it's refreshing to go back to the basics. At night, vendors along Chinatown's Yaowarat Road prepare Sino-Thai specialties such as roast duck and sweet black-sesame-seed dumplings, which diners ferry from griddle to communal table with infinite care. Hire a taxi to take you to Or Tor Kor market, where you can haggle at the stalls for custard apples and snakeskin pears and sample variations on green curry and sticky rice. You'll soon understand why this cacophonous center casts a spell on everyone.

Tented bungalows at the
4 Rivers Floating Lodge.

KOH KONG

A CAMBODIAN ECO-ADVENTURE

KOH KONG PROVINCE, AT THE BASE OF CAMBODIA'S CARDAMOM Mountains, is as isolated a spot as you're likely to find. Formerly the territory of Khmer Rouge insurgents, the region was long cut off from even the simplest kinds of development. But ecotourism has come to this corner of the continent, bringing with it an astonishing range of accommodations for travelers seeking true immersion.

From Phnom Penh, a 45-minute drive or two-hour boat ride takes you to the village of Chi Phat, a model of community-based tourism set up by an environmental group called the Wildlife Alliance. Local families open their residences to visitors, who spend days exploring the world's oldest rain forest, boating in the Preak Piphot River, and trekking to crystal-clear waterfalls. Rooms are bare-bones (a bed, a mosquito net, a flashlight), but clean and comfortable. You rise with the rooster's crow at 5 a.m. and turn in for the day at 11 p.m., when the village's generator shuts down.

An hour's drive west of Chi Phat, the 4 Rivers Floating Lodge is an entirely different experience. An escapist fantasy, the hotel is made up of a series of white tents that float on decks of recycled wood along a bend in the Tatai River. Rooms come equipped with king-size beds, rain showers, and outdoor sitting areas with ladders to the water. Each night, a three-course tasting menu is served at the restaurant; look for Cambodia's famous fish *amok*, wrapped in a banana leaf and steamed with coconut milk.

In the forest just upstream, the Rainbow Lodge strikes the perfect balance between comfort and adventure. The seven-room retreat is made up of solar-powered thatched-roof bungalows, each with a terrace and a hammock, and an open-air pavilion where guests gather for communal feasts. At dusk, a kayak trip along the glassy river is a near-silent experience, the sky streaked with gold and lavender. There's nowhere else in the world you'd rather be.

A puppeteer at Ramoji
Film City. Opposite:
The view from the
Charminar, or the Mosque
of the Four Minarets.

HYDERABAD

THRIVING ONCE AGAIN

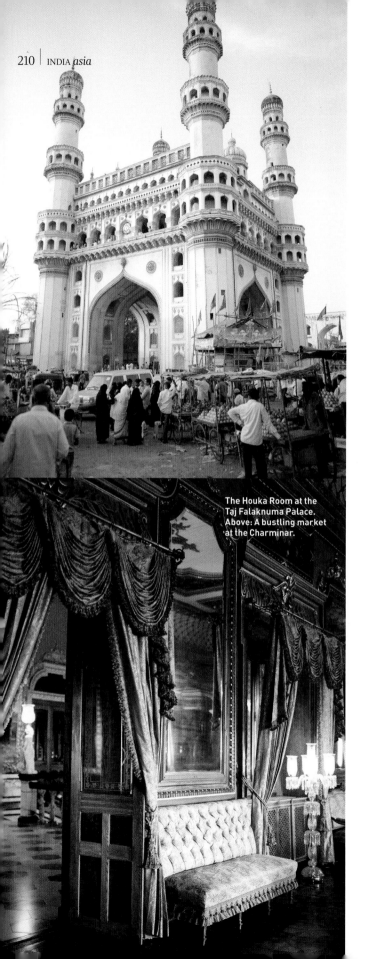

The Houka Room at the Taj Falaknuma Palace. Above: A bustling market at the Charminar.

PART BRIGADOON, PART EPCOT, HYDERABAD IMMEDIATELY pulls you into its hallucinatory past. Once an independent kingdom the size of France, the city was known as a place of mythic grandeur before the riches of its former ruler, the nizam, were mismanaged and eventually diminished. Now it's the hub of the country's high-tech industry—a boomtown with new hotels and renovated palaces, where history continues to be made.

What remains of the lost kingdom is magical. Walk the tangle of streets near the Charminar, or the Mosque of the Four Minarets, to find colorful street carts and restaurants where you can taste the local specialty, biryani. In the old days, the nizams possessed multiple palaces and hoards of priceless gems; some of that vanished splendor is on display at the refurbished Chowmahalla Palace, with its distinctive Moorish-style domes. More recently, however, the city's wealth has been concentrated in the nearby enclave known as Cyberabad, where Google, Microsoft, and Oracle have offices. At night, the sleek geeks meet for cocktails at the Aqua Bar in the Park, Hyderabad, hotel, which overlooks the lake in the center of town. An hour outside Hyderabad, Ramoji Film City, the largest moviemaking facility in the world, supplies the area with a contemporary dose of glamour.

Ten minutes from the shopping and business districts, the 122-room Taj Banjara looks out onto a lake of its own. But the Taj hotel group's crown jewel is the newly restored Taj Falaknuma Palace, the nizam's former residence, set on a hill south of town. The decade-long renovation was the dream of the current nizam's former wife, Turkish socialite Princess Esra, who oversaw every detail with autocratic zeal. The library, modeled on the one at Windsor Castle, has been restocked with nearly 6,000 rare books and manuscripts; the studies feature opulent Venetian glass chandeliers and ornate European furniture; and the Rajasthani and Asian gardens are in full bloom. In a city of long-lost treasures, the hotel is a harbinger of fortunes to come.

A carriage driver at the Taj Falaknuma Palace. Clockwise from below: Local children; biryani, Hyderabad's signature dish; bangles for sale at a street vendor.

At the restaurant Koh by Ian Kittichai. Left: Artist Srinivasa Prasad's *Tailor Mama* installation at Gallery BMB.

MUMBAI

A NEW FOCUS ON ART AND CULTURE

MUMBAI HAS LONG BEEN AT THE CENTER OF INDIA'S commercial success. In its current incarnation, the city is also asserting its reputation as a formidable destination for art, style, and design. The new cultural powerhouses may not be quite as glitzy as a Bollywood dance number, but they're no less exciting.

Modern art spaces have brought sophistication to southern Mumbai. The Fort district's Gallery BMB, which includes a cozy café and bookshop, focuses on burgeoning Indian painters and sculptors. In the street-stall-filled Colaba district, the cavernous Gallery Maskara packs a former warehouse with groundbreaking installations by local and international artists. Nearby, on the seafront, Volte specializes in new media installations.

For equally artistic threads, head to Bungalow 8, which made a name for itself almost a decade ago selling contemporary furnishings. Now it showcases sleek men's wear with a cutting-edge twist on Indian style, designed by Yves Saint Laurent vet Mathieu Gugumus-Leguillon. Snatch up handmade linens and elaborately embellished bedding—some of which can take more than 40 days to create—at Bandit Queen, a home-goods emporium near the center of town. Don't overlook fashion boutique Neemrana, which stocks cotton and georgette saris and hand-embroidered blouses.

Mumbai's elite gather for dinner at Koh by Ian Kittichai, the contemporary Thai restaurant in the InterContinental Marine Drive hotel. Signature dishes include green curry with slow-roasted chicken and Garota Bay scallops topped with pomelo salad. Book a room at the Taj Mahal Palace's restored Palace Wing. It took 21 months, 2,000 craftsmen, and $38 million to pull off the renovation—and the results, from the rosewood floors to the glass-walled bathrooms, are a comeback story all their own.

A quiet street in Puducherry. Right: The courtyard at Hotel de l'Orient.

PUDUCHERRY

THE FRENCH CONNECTION

FOR MORE THAN 300 YEARS, THE PORT CITY OF PONDICHERRY served as the capital of French India. The French left in 1954, but the atmosphere in Pondy, as locals affectionately call their coastal town—though the official name is now Puducherry—is still markedly different from the country's other urban centers. An unmistakable joie de vivre permeates the salty breezes drifting off the Bay of Bengal.

The city's French Quarter, which runs for almost a mile along the beach, is made up of pastel-hued residential villas with high garden walls, elaborate gateways, and arched windows and doors. The preservation of these graceful buildings has been the decade-long mission of the Indian National Trust for Art & Cultural Heritage. One of its most successful projects is the 16-room Hotel de l'Orient, an 18th-century mansion with a peach-pink façade and a central courtyard where guests linger over afternoon tea. Another hotel, Le Dupleix—named for the French governor who once lived there—has been painstakingly reconstructed, its exterior refinished with a traditional plaster made from egg white, powdered seashells, and yogurt. The two-story town hall, Hôtel de Ville, is a future candidate for restoration.

In fact, the trust has left its mark all over the quarter, from the recently revived Le Café (whose corridors feature sepia-toned photographs of local buildings from the 1930's) to the newly built, colonialesque Citibank at the corner of Rue Suffern and Rue Bussy, and the Notre Dame des Anges Church, one of the oldest in Puducherry. Enter the periwinkle-and-salmon structure and look into the neighboring courtyard to see an age-old symbol of France—a statue of Joan of Arc—with the glittering sea behind her.

A caravan en route
to Flaming Cliffs,
in the Gobi Desert.

GOBI DESERT

TRAVELS BACK IN TIME

FOR MILLENNIA, IT HAS BEEN A PLACE FEW WILLINGLY ENTER. The Gobi Desert, a fabled expanse of sand and rock under a scorching sun, once served as a natural barrier between Mongol hordes and dynastic China. In recent decades, the stark beauty of this landscape has lured growing numbers of travelers eager for an eye-opening experience away from the modern world. The journey, however, is not for the faint of heart. From the capital city of Ulaanbaatar, it's a three-day drive to the South Gobi province and its treasures; within 20 minutes of leaving the city, the road becomes a dirt trail, and frequent hard braking is required to cross sudden dips in the ground.

The South Gobi has three major sights. In Gurvan Saikhan National Park, Yolyn Am is a narrow gorge famous for its glacier-like layers of snow and ice, shielded by cliff walls from the punishing Gobi sun. Also in the park, the giant sand formations of Hongoryn

Els are known as the Singing Dunes, thanks to the humming sound heard as innumerable grains of sand shift in the wind. Sunrise and sunset are the best times to visit them; tour companies can arrange for overnight stays at a *ger*, or traditional nomad tent, with a panoramic view. More upscale accommodations lie just outside the park at the eco-friendly Three Camels Lodge. Many of the 40 *gers* are heated by wood-burning stoves and come with private bathrooms and toiletries made from camel's milk.

The last of the region's big tourist draws is Bayanzag, where in 1922 an American expedition team came upon a wealth of dinosaur fossils at a site they named Flaming Cliffs. Subsequent expeditions have turned up other prehistoric treasures, and today travelers can join a caravan on camelback to help unearth dinosaur remnants in the rock. In this territory of natural wonders, it's the most fantastical discovery of all: evidence of visitors from 60 million years ago.

Barkhor Square,
near Lhasa's
Jokhang Temple.

LHASA

WHERE TO GO NEXT

FEW PLACES FEEL SO REMOTE AS LHASA: SURROUNDED BY THE Himalayas, cloaked in Tibetan Buddhism, and—at 11,975 feet— one of the world's highest cities. It has been easier to get here since the debut of a railway line in 2006, a breathtaking train ride past snowcapped peaks, though until recently, mostly backpackers and robed pilgrims walked Lhasa's medieval streets. But now this mystical destination is welcoming a new set of adventurers.

You don't have to forsake comfort for enlightenment at the St. Regis Lhasa Resort. The hotel pays homage to local architecture with sloping white façades and long, narrow windows. Many of the 162 guest rooms face Potala Palace, the former residence of the Dalai Lama. The Iridium Spa promises to melt away any altitude-related malaise with a nutmeg-and-butter massage, while the Si Zi Kang restaurant serves *shamdey* (yak-and-potato stew) and *pag* (barley cakes).

Lhasa's charms are easily accessible. Ask your concierge to arrange for lunch at nearby Norbulingka, the Dalai Lama's traditional summer palace, or visit the seventh-century Jokhang Temple, Tibetan Buddhism's holiest site. A few steps east, market stalls display handmade turquoise earrings and silk *thangka* paintings. For the most skillfully made artisanal goods, visit Lhasa Villages Handicraft Center, a nonprofit shop selling scarves made of soft yak hair and embroidered door curtains—said to ward off both cold drafts and evil spirits.

Excursions outside Lhasa are equally unforgettable. Drive 30 miles to the Ganden Monastery, a 15th-century complex erected around the tomb of its founding monk. Travel 15,000 feet above sea level to Namtso Lake, a longtime spiritual retreat for pilgrims who trek across its frozen waters. As you gaze over its shimmering surface, the "roof of the world" seems almost within reach.

PENANG

AWASH IN AUTHENTICITY

SRI NADARAJAR SIVAGAMI

A devotional stop along
Jalan Masjid Kapitan
Keling, or Harmony Street,
in Georgetown. Opposite:
Busy Air Itam Road.

A guest room at Clove Hall hotel. Clockwise from below: Joss sticks and incense cones at the Goddess of Mercy Temple; the pool at the Eastern & Oriental Hotel; RELA officers at Chew Jetty.

AFTER A PROLONGED POSTCOLONIAL SLUMBER, TURTLE-shaped Penang, an island off Malaysia's northwestern coast, has powered back into view, fashioning itself as a subtropical Silicon Valley. Yet somehow few people have heard of this lovely flyspeck, and the omission seems more confounding the more time you spend here.

In the capital of Georgetown, a UNESCO World Heritage site, the streets are crammed with tile-roofed residences, centers of worship for nearly every religion, and opulent colonial mansions, linked by arcaded pedestrian passages; you can lose hours at a *kopi* (coffee) shop watching the street theater unfold. An increasing number of boutique hotels have opened in the midst of it all. Stay at the stylish Straits Collection, a four-suite compound carved from four restored 1920's shop-houses at the base of the heritage walk. It's just steps away from Jalan Masjid Kapitan Keling, also called Harmony Street, as well as three of Penang's most sacred temples: the Goddess of Mercy, Sri Maha Mariamman, and Khoo Kongsi. Also nearby is Clove Hall, six rooms in a 1920's Edwardian mansion on a former coconut plantation. For a more historic setting, opt for the Eastern & Oriental, built in 1885 on a promontory overlooking the Malaysian mainland and once frequented by the likes of Rudyard Kipling and Somerset Maugham.

You'll quickly adapt to the indolent pace of everyday life, which places a serious emphasis on food. Start your morning with a street breakfast of *putu mayam*—vermicelli noodles made from rice flour and coconut milk—then wind your way to the Chew Jetty, a 19th-century wooden dock flanked by tin-roofed fishermen's houses built on pilings over the water. The lunchtime scene is both pleasant and efficient at Pasar Air Itam, a market midway across the island that's a must for *assam laksa,* tamarind-flavored noodle soup. Head back to Georgetown and visit the Pinang Peranakan Mansion, an ornate house museum that counts Scottish ironwork and rare wooden opium beds as its treasures. Come evening, dine on traditional Chinese-Malay dishes—various pork stews; *inchee kabin* (fried chicken)—at Perut Rumah Nyonya Cuisine. When it comes time to leave Penang, you'll find yourself at one of the aforementioned temples, lighting joss sticks amid your fellow supplicants and invoking the travel gods for your speedy return to the island.

Inchee kabin (fried chicken) at Perut Rumah Nyonya Cuisine restaurant. Above: The Pinang Peranakan Mansion.

Staff members at
Six Senses Con Dao.

CON DAO

AWAY FROM IT ALL

INTREPID VISITORS IN SEARCH OF SOUTHEAST ASIA'S NEXT great destination are heading to Con Dao, an archipelago 60 miles off Vietnam's southeastern coast. An hour-long flight from Ho Chi Minh City brings you to Con Son, the largest (and only inhabited) member of the 16-island chain. Sheer granite cliffs border deserted beaches and crystal blue water—picture a tropical Amalfi Coast without the crowds. And with about 80 percent of the archipelago protected as part of a national park, the region will forever be an off-the-grid getaway.

Until recently, the island's accommodations have been charmingly basic, but Western-style luxury has arrived with the opening of the Six Senses Con Dao. Its 50 villas stretch along the sand facing the South China Sea; lounging on your patio, you can hear the call of macaques from the surrounding jungle. In classic Six Senses style, one of the hotel's Vietnamese restaurants is set up to resemble a market, with separate stalls "hawking" noodles and rolls and made-to-order dishes cooked outdoors in charcoal-fueled woks. For a glimpse of the real thing, visit the early morning Con Son Market, or Phuong Hanh, in the center of town.

The resort is as enticing as one might expect, but the rest of the eight-square-mile island is also worth exploring. Hire a private guide to bring you via motorbike to its most secluded spots, including a 19th-century hilltop lighthouse. Winding cliffside roads lead to the Dam Tre Bay lagoon and Bai Nhat beach, which only surfaces at low tide. Snorkel in the pristine waters to see wildlife such as the endangered dugong (a marine mammal similar to the manatee) and hawksbill turtles (which nest on neighboring Bay Canh Island from May through September). For now, Con Dao remains a relative secret—an escape all your own.

Fragrant frangipani at the Six Senses spa. Above: One of the hotel's private villas.

VIETNAM

A TASTE OF THE EXOTIC

Banh da ca (fish noodle soup) at the Quan An Ngon restaurant, in Hanoi. Opposite: The countryside outside the capital.

FOOD IS AT THE HEART OF VIETNAMESE CULTURE. Almost every aspect of social life revolves around the procurement, preparation, and shared pleasure of nourishment. It even has its place in commercial life: markets are on every corner, cooks on every curb. This is a cuisine rich with nuance.

The best way to tackle Hanoi, the country's capital, is to treat it as a progressive street buffet—you move from the spring-roll guy to the fermented-pork lady and onward into the night. Or you could make it easy and hit Quan An Ngon, where an all-star roster cooks signature dishes in the courtyard of an old villa. On the menu: *bun cha* (grilled pork marinated in sweetened fish sauce) and *banh da ca* (a tangy fish noodle soup laden with chunks of tilapia and *rau can*, a woody stalk with a cedary bite). Half of the city queues up for a seat at Pho Gia Truyen, in the Old Quarter, for the $2 helpings of *pho bo*, Vietnam's national dish, a beef soup topped with rice noodles, scallions, and sometimes bean sprouts.

A 90-minute flight south, Hue is the former imperial capital, renowned for its elaborate cuisine. In leafy Kim Long, the open-air canteen Huyen Anh offers only two dishes, but the *bun thit nuong* sums up everything that's delightful about Vietnamese cooking. Warm vermicelli noodles arrive drizzled in fish sauce and lime juice; tossed with banana blossoms, bean sprouts, and green papaya; and topped with glistening slices of pork.

Everything is sweeter in Saigon, another hour-and-a-half flight away. Its proximity to the Mekong Delta means it overflows with papaya, mango, coconut, soursop, and other exotic treats. They're blended into icy *sinh to* (smoothies) at Ben Thanh Market. Follow it up with a giant *banh xeo*—a rice-flour crêpe stuffed with pork, shrimp, bean sprouts, and mushrooms and wrapped in mustard leaves—at Banh Xeo An La Ghien. You won't find tastier *pho* than the varieties at Pho Hoa on Pasteur Street; for breakfast, order the *pho tai nam*, with rare beef and well-done flank. The atmosphere is decidedly more upscale at Cuc Gach Quan, a blend of historic details (antique armoires; a wall map of 1960's Saigon), contemporary touches (a floating staircase), and remarkable food. Clay-pot-stewed pork belly is flavorful but not heavy. Cloudlike house-made tofu comes lightly fried with lemongrass, shallots, and chiles. The sauce is so good, you'll want to bottle and smuggle it home with you.

Saigon's Pho Hoa
restaurant. From far left:
Selling produce by bicycle;
bun thit nuong (pork with
vermicelli noodles) at
Huyen Anh, in Hue.

Dining at Hanoi's Quan An
Ngon. Left: The makings of a
sinh to (smoothie) in Saigon's
Ben Thanh Market. Right: *Cuon
diep* (fresh shrimp rolls) at Cuc
Gach Quan, in Saigon.

Amandari's *nasi padang* (braised chicken, potato cakes, and egg-and-cassava-leaf curry). Below: Practicing a traditional Balinese dance at Hotel Tugu Bali.

BALI

TRANSCENDENT EXPERIENCES AT EVERY TURN

THE ALLURE OF BALI HAS ALWAYS BEEN ABOUT BOTH SPIRITUAL pursuits and sybaritic pleasures. Browse any hotel directory, and you find that lounging by the pool becomes "an opportunity to meditate"; a massage turns into a healing ritual; afternoon tea is recast as a ceremony; and a morning hike is nothing less than a pilgrimage. Now, more than ever, the island's resorts are making a priority of cultural relevance, promising unique entrée into Balinese art and architecture, music and dance, and cuisine and traditional medicine, as well as social and religious life. The best hotels actually come close to providing it, granting guests a compelling vantage on Bali itself.

At the Four Seasons Bali at Sayan, near the town of Ubud, you can spend the day planting rice with resident farmers and learning firsthand about the island's ingenious *subak* irrigation system. Not far away on the Ayung River Gorge, Amandari is literally on the path to a Balinese holy site and modeled on a historic village. One itinerary starts with an early trip to a food market, followed by a cooking class held in a nearby family's house; guests spend the day shopping for ingredients and stirring pots of green-papaya soup and duck curry before enjoying their multicourse feast on a breezy *bale* overlooking the river.

On the western coast, in Canggu, Hotel Tugu Bali offers much the same, including *pendet* (a traditional Balinese dance) lessons; the resort also sponsors a dance program for local children, who rehearse on the lawn. Farther south on the Bukit Peninsula, Alila Villas Uluwatu has a dense roster of immersive experiences. You can learn to play the gamelan, practice *djamoe* medicine, carve stone, or tour a hidden cave temple with a *mangku* (priest). It's all part of the sheer sensory overload that alternately enthralls and flummoxes foreign travelers; on this island, it's difficult to delineate art from artifice. At the end of the day, your eyes are exhausted. One's inner skeptic might ask, *"But what's real?"* In Bali, the answer is *everything*.

Warung restaurant at the
Alila Villas Uluwatu hotel, on
the Bukit Peninsula.

**Surfing off Nemberala
Beach, in Rote.**

ROTE

CATCH A WAVE

SURFERS HAVE A SOFT SPOT FOR ROTE, INDONESIA'S southernmost isle. Blessed with pink- and white-sand beaches, secluded coves, and 20-foot barrels of pure turquoise, the island was all but unknown until former world champion Felipe Pomar touched down on its shores 25 years ago. Fans of the sport followed suit, trailed in turn by a new breed of travelers—people plugged-in enough to have heard about this dot of land on the edge of global perception.

The two-hour ferry ride from Timor, Rote's neighbor to the east, leaves you in the main town of Ba'a, composed of little more than a few crumbling guesthouses. Do as the surfers do and head south to Nemberala. At the Nemberala Beach Resort, the four duplex bungalows feature locally quarried stone, regional hardwoods, and traditional *alang* roofs. A fleet of colorful dugouts arrive to take you to the center of the action—700 feet offshore—where you can try your luck on the legendary reef breaks.

Nonsurfers will also find much to enjoy. Join the kitchen staff for a trip to the weekly farmers' market, where resident artisans sell their wares. Rent a motorbike and drive south, past monkeys and mangroves, to a natural limestone arch near the town of Oeseli. Or charter a boat to the neighboring island of Pulau Ndao, which has powdery white beaches, a fishing village known for its rich ikat-weaving traditions, and residents who speak their own indigenous dialect. After dinner back at the resort's restaurant, walk along Nemberala beach and marvel at a sky brilliant with stars as waves crash in the distance and boats bob on inky midnight tides.

One of Banyan Tree Samui's
Gulf of Thailand views.
Above: A sampling of
tropical fruit at the resort.

KOH SAMUI

THIS SIDE OF PARADISE

IN THE 1960'S, VISITORS TO THE ISLAND OF KOH SAMUI WERE backpack-wielding vagabond-explorers who hopped a slow ferry from Bangkok and flopped down in no-frills hammocks on the beach. The roads were rough; there were no proper hotels. But even then, its evolution seemed preordained, its transformation inevitable: it would be plucked from obscurity like some future supermodel from a remote rural village.

These days, the average visitor stays only three nights on the island and spends most of that time on the grounds of a resort—lounging on the beach, indulging in the occasional massage. Koh Samui now has a number of outstanding places to do just that. The Banyan Tree Samui occupies a secluded peninsula on the southeastern coast; its 88 villas are scattered along steep, terraced hillsides and overlook the lush terrain and ocean. The W Retreat Koh Samui's setting is even more remarkable: an arrow-shaped headland with one beach facing sunrise and the other facing sunset. With their urbane-contemporary aesthetic, the Banyan Tree and the W represent a shift away from the indigenous architecture and design—pitched roofs, sala pavilions—that influenced slightly older resorts such as the Four Seasons, built only a few years before.

Secreted away in private jungles and coves, the resorts are increasingly removed from island life. The result is that there are two Koh Samuis: the private and the public, the luxe and the local. Venture beyond the hotel gates and you can take in a kickboxing match, browse the stalls at a night market, visit a 19th-century Buddhist temple, or wander among the Chinese shop-houses, where cobblers sell shoes made of lizard, stingray, and cobra skin. To the northeast, on Bang Po Beach, a family-run shack called Bang Po Seafood serves the best meals around—a spicy mango salad laced with sea urchin, or a turmeric-dusted red snapper, deep-fried to a golden crispy goodness. From your table you can see brightly colored longtail boats plying the water and fishermen walking along a dormant reef, waist-deep, as they hunt for squid. This at last is the Samui you've been dreaming of: a paradise found once more.

Sip Bar at the
W Retreat Koh Samui.

Eclectic finds at Gallery Sorrento, on Australia's Mornington Peninsula.

AUSTRALIA &
NEW ZEALAND

DNEY SURRY HILLS MORNINGTON PENINSULA MELBOURNE TA
AND GREAT BARRIER ISLAND SYDNEY SURRY HILLS MORNING
LBOURNE TASMANIA SOUTH ISLAND GREAT BARRIER ISLAND
ORNINGTON PENINSULA MELBOURNE TASMANIA SOUTH ISLAN
AND SYDNEY SURRY HILLS MORNINGTON PENINSULA MELBOU
UTH ISLAND GREAT BARRIER ISLAND SYDNEY SURRY HILLS MC
NINSULA MELBOURNE TASMANIA SOUTH ISLAND GREAT BARF
RRY HILLS MORNINGTON PENINSULA MELBOURNE TASMANIA
EAT BARRIER ISLAND SYDNEY SURRY HILLS MORNINGTON PEN

SYDNEY

STYLE AND SUSTENANCE

A view of Harbour Bridge and the Sydney skyline.

Butterfish *ankake* at Sake Restaurant & Bar. Clockwise from above: Willow boutique; fashion designer Josh Goot outside his store; riding the waves at Manly Beach.

Rolled quail breast at
Est, in the Establishment
Hotel. Below: Manly
Pavilion's dining room.

PART OUTSIZE BEACH RESORT, PART CULTURE CAPITAL,
Sydney exemplifies the art of relaxed urbanity. It's stylish but not
pretentious; cutting-edge but not aggressively hip. Beyond the
iconic opera house and picture-perfect harbor, there's a homegrown cosmopolitan scene that rivals some of the world's more
prominent metropolises.

Sydney's fashionable heart is the corner of Oxford Street and
Glenmore Road, in Paddington, where some of the most exciting
Australian designers are clustered. Kirrily Johnston represents the
easygoing down under aesthetic with her earthy, feminine clothes
(think billowy skirts with high cinched waists). At Kit Willow's bi-
level boutique, Willow, you'll find flirty draped frocks and cropped
jackets in organza and silk. The vibe is slightly more Op Art at Josh
Goot's light-filled showroom, where block-printed tunic dresses
come in colors as bright as the Sydney sun. The downtown men's
wear boutique BrentWilson sells updated classics such as tailored
suits and slim-fit pea coats.

Sydney's food and nightlife take advantage of the city's best
asset—its coast. In the harborside Rocks district, the well-heeled
flock to Sake Restaurant & Bar for superior sashimi and bite-size
shrimp tempura. Celebrity chef Neil Perry's Rockpool Bar & Grill
specializes in house-aged beef and wood-fired-grill poultry
(pheasant with smoked eggplant; partridge with roasted pear).
Downstairs, his sexy Spice Temple serves authentic Chinese dishes
in a sumptuous, red-tinged dining room. The Establishment
Hotel's Est attracts bright young things with a penchant for hyper-
local cuisine. A short ferry ride away is Manly Pavilion, lauded for
its fresh Italian fare. Pan-fried whiting comes wrapped in *lardo*,
and pappardelle arrives topped with a generous helping of wild-
boar *ragù*. Even more resplendent: the Pacific Ocean vistas
everywhere you look.

The entrance to the Belvoir Street Theatre. Right: Published Art bookshop.

SURRY HILLS

A NEW TAKE ON SUBURBIA

THINK OF SURRY HILLS AS A TINY VILLAGE JUST OUTSIDE Sydney's center—albeit one with the best shops, bars, and restaurants in town. The district started off as a manufacturing hub, lined with Victorian rowhouses that were near-slums for the immigrant workers who labored in its sweatshops. In the 1980's it became a grungy student hangout. But by the late 1990's fashion designers were swarming here for the cheap rents and charming architecture. This bohemian vibe and diversity lives on today.

Style is in Surry Hills' DNA. The best place to start exploring is Crown Street, a pleasant, walkable strip lined with plane trees. Breakfast at Bills is a must—order the moist and spongy ricotta hotcakes with banana slivers and sweet honeycomb butter.

Koskela's Aboriginal crafts. Left: Porcelain lampshades at Planet.

Another morning option: Fouratefive, a homey, hipsterish café with handmade wood tables, rattling vintage rock on the radio, and tattooed waitresses in floaty dresses. The Moroccan-style baked eggs with almonds and *labneh* (strained yogurt) arrive piping hot in a metal skillet with hunks of sourdough to scoop up the runny yolks. Afterward, visit the Published Art bookshop, on Mary Street, a neighborhood staple for more than a decade, to browse through the encyclopedic selection of obscure design tomes. Furniture store Planet carries Ross Longmuir's streamlined beds, tables, and sofas, all made from Australian hardwoods (don't worry, they ship). The lure at interiors haven Koskela is Aboriginal craftwork, such as the one-off lampshades traditionally woven with bush string. And Collect at Object Gallery is Surry

Hills' answer to New York City's MoMA store; look for high-gloss bowls made from macadamia-nut shells and Melinda Young's abstract plastic necklaces.

Many of Australia's top cultural commissars are making inroads here, too. The Belvoir Street Theatre, a nonprofit housed in an old tomato-sauce factory, counts Cate Blanchett and Geoffrey Rush among its alums. It still attracts A-list talent, including Academy Award–winning set designer (and wife of Aussie director Baz Luhrmann) Catherine Martin. Another set designer, Leon Krasenstein, runs the unconventional Friends of Leon Gallery, a showcase for female artists and fashion illustrators. The gallery is as much a labor of love as a moneymaking project. True to the neighborhood's tradition, the indie spirit lives on.

MORNINGTON PENINSULA

PLEASURES BY THE SEA

A brightly colored beach shack in Portsea. Opposite: The town's harbor, on Port Phillip Bay.

Point Nepean National Park.
Clockwise from above: Dining
at the Baths, in Sorrento;
diving into the water off Portsea;
a suite at the Hotel Sorrento.

Grilled calamari salad at the Baths. Below: Gallery Sorrento, on Ocean Beach Drive.

ON SUNNY FRIDAY AFTERNOONS FROM DECEMBER THROUGH February—the peak of Australian summer—you can trace the line of cars carrying weekenders out of Melbourne. Their destination: the Mornington Peninsula, 56 miles south, with its surf-worthy breaks, small-scale wineries, and twin beach towns of Portsea and Sorrento.

These are laid-back escapes, Aussie-style—surfing in the mornings, languid lunches, fish-and-chips on the beach at sunset. Sorrento is the area's shopping and dining hub, with top-notch restaurants and well-kept historic architecture. Base yourself in the Hotel Sorrento, an 1872 structure on a cliff above Port Phillip Bay, then hit the main drag on Ocean Beach Road. The eclectic Gallery Sorrento has rotating exhibitions by Australian artists such as Rick Matear, whose moody paintings often include vistas of the peninsula. Down the block, Seed sells playful children's clothing, including colorful bathing suits and snug knit cardigans. The restaurant Acquolina serves hearty northern Italian food—try the house-made spaghetti with fresh clams, mussels, and *bottarga* (tuna roe). Or order a calamari salad at the Baths, an informal waterfront staple with wooden tables and chairs. Five miles west of Sorrento lies the decidedly quieter Portsea, an enclave of exclusive villas. Watch the sun set over Front Beach from the Portsea Hotel's Beer Garden, where Aussie brews James Squire and Fat Yak are on tap.

The tip of the Mornington Peninsula is flanked by calm bay waters and ocean beaches known for their windswept beauty. At Shelley Beach, keep an eye out for pods of bottlenose dolphins offshore. Explore Point Nepean National Park, where you can see black wallabies, blue-winged parrots, and long-nosed bandicoots. Be sure to save time for wine tasting—another peninsula highlight, thanks to the 50-plus vineyards and cool maritime climate. Earthy Shiraz and pizzas from wood-fired ovens have given Moorooduc Estate a cult following, while Ten Minutes by Tractor Wine Co. has made a name for itself with its rich Chardonnays. The tasting room at Port Phillip Estate—a striking space with ribbed wood ceilings and views of the 60-acre property—is the most impressive around.

Atlantic chef
Donovan Cooke.
Left: Coffee at
the European.

MELBOURNE

A FOOD TOUR DOWN UNDER

AN EPICUREAN TOUR OF MELBOURNE? YES, INDEED: THE southern Australian city is rife with artisanal purveyors, sustainable local markets, and restaurants both classic and cutting-edge. Start your wanderings off right with perfect poached eggs and a side of strong espresso at the European, an old world–style café opposite Parliament House. Weekend mornings are the best time to visit the South Melbourne Market, which opened in 1867 but has a 21st-century outlook on global cuisine. Stop by for a range of specialty cheeses, helpings of "dim sim" (a cheeky play on the Chinese dumpling), and prime cuts of meat from an opera-singing butcher.

Private dining cabins at the Atlantic. Right: The Woolshed Pub's crisp kingfish with chickpea *skordalia* and vegetables.

On Acland Street, Clamms Fast Fish is owned by the company that provides Melbourne's best restaurants with seafood and serves up an excellent version of fish-and-chips. Get yours to go and venture to St. Kilda Beach to watch the waves roll onto the sand. After you've taken them in, make your way over to Bay Street, where Noîsette specializes in French-style cakes and baked goods (the dense walnut bread is irresistible).

The hot dinner ticket in town is the Atlantic, chef Donovan Cooke's seafood-centric restaurant at the Crown Entertainment Complex. Curtains resembling fishing nets line the dining room, spaces for private dining are referred to as "cabins," and appetizers (sliced abalone; kingfish *crudo*) are served in shells. For down-home dishes, follow Cooke himself and head straight to the Woolshed Pub, a converted cargo shed on the water that transcends its workaday roots with crisp-fried Berkshire pork belly in a coriander-and-red-chili sauce and a superb sticky date pudding. Cooke's pick for a nightcap: the Den, the retro-inspired bar downstairs from the Atlantic. Order the Cohiba No. 23—tobacco-infused *añejo* rum, pear eau-de-vie, fresh apple juice, and bitters, served in a balloon glass and delivered in (what else?) a humidor.

The two-bedroom Walter Pavilion at the Museum of Old & New Art.

On the grounds at MONA.
Below: Australian artist
Sidney Nolan's 1970's
mural *Snake*.

TASMANIA

ART'S UNLIKELY NEW PLAYGROUND

AN ICONOCLASTIC GALLERY IS THE LAST THING YOU'D EXPECT to find on far-flung Tasmania—known for its otherworldly landscapes, and not much else. The Museum of Old & New Art proves otherwise. With both ancient and contemporary works on view, the Southern Hemisphere's largest private museum has put this rugged, heart-shaped island on the cultural map.

This isn't your ordinary art outing. A 45-minute ferry ride up the Derwent River from Hobart's bustling harbor, the museum—the brainchild of gambler turned multimillionaire collector David Walsh—is a hulking mass of weathering steel and concrete carved into a waterfront clifftop. A spiral staircase leads to the structure's subterranean depths, where the nontraditional organizational scheme (Egyptian sarcophagi and Roman Empire mosaics next to 1990's work by the Young British Artists) encourages getting lost. Instead of curatorial notes stenciled on walls, you get an iPod loaded with information under a tab flagged ARTWANK. And most welcome of all: admission is free.

Once you've found your way back aboveground, tastings await at Moorilla, Walsh's on-site vineyard, which features boutique varietals by master winemaker Conor van der Reest. You can also sample the favorites at the Cellar Door lounge. More of a beer drinker? Tour the adjacent Moo Brew, which makes a classic Hefeweizen and a pleasantly hoppy Dark Ale. Come nightfall, the eight glass-and-steel Pavilion suites offer just as much visual stimulation as the museum itself, with pieces from Walsh's personal collection displayed on credenzas and on the walls.

Nugget Point, in the Catlins. Left: The lounge at Fiordland Lodge.

SOUTH ISLAND

A PRISTINE CROSS-COUNTRY DRIVE

NEW ZEALAND'S SOUTH ISLAND BEGS FOR HYPERBOLE. ITS geography is a location scout's dream, as anyone who's watched a *Lord of the Rings* film can attest. The people are as sunny and open as its skies. To spend a week driving through the landscape—in November, for perfect springtime weather—is to experience another, more ideal world.

From the airport in Queenstown, a kind of antipodean Aspen, follow the shore of Lake Wakatipu to Matakauri Lodge. The contemporary lakeside retreat has 11 simple, schist-and-wood guest rooms with views of the Remarkables Mountains. You'll need two days here to cruise on the century-old steamer *Earnslaw* and enjoy a white-water rafting trip on the Shotover River with adventure outfitter Real Journeys. Dinner at the lodge showcases the freshest

A church in the Catlins.
Left: The bar at Eichardt's
Private Hotel.

local produce—green-lipped mussels; Southland beef—courtesy of head chef Dale Gartland. Shop for cozy merino wool sweaters in Queenstown's lively center, 10 minutes away, and snag the window table at the restaurant in Eichardt's Private Hotel for shrimp and saffron *arancini* (rice balls), fried squid, and goat cheese with truffled honey and balsamic figs.

Drive two hours south to Te Anau and the start of the Southern Scenic route, traversing a sparsely populated wonderland of forests and wild coastlines. Check in to the rustic-modern Fiordland Lodge, owned by a veteran park ranger and a natural jumping-off point for Doubtful Sound. Larger and less touristy than Milford Sound (New Zealand's most famous fjord), it's best reached on a daylong excursion; look out for fur seals, bottlenose dolphins, and

penguins on your way. Evenings come to a close with an astronomy lesson back at the lodge.

Head toward the Catlins, a rugged region of waterfalls, blowholes, and petrified forests from the Jurassic era. (Beyond this remotest of Pacific shores, the next landfall is in Antarctica.) The Southern Scenic Route ends in Dunedin, a Scottish-influenced college town, but you'll want to travel 30 minutes more to the Otago Peninsula, where the timber-clad Kaimata Retreat is set amid untamed scenery. Decompress on the deck overlooking the inlet and a sheep ranch that clings to a precipitous, pea-green hillside. The next morning, follow Portobello Road back into Dunedin for lunch at the Mash Café before making your return to Queensland, a leisurely four hours away.

GREAT BARRIER ISLAND

LAST STOP AT THE END OF THE WORLD

An aerial view of the "Barrier" and its surrounding islands.

VISITING "THE BARRIER" IS LIKE TAKING A TRIP BACK IN TIME. There are no banks or malls, no supermarkets or traffic pileups. When you leave your hotel at night, you're advised to bring a flashlight along with you as there aren't streetlamps for miles. What the largest isle off New Zealand's North Island *does* have in spades is a nature enthusiast's dream: dense kauri forests, jagged coastal inlets, and some of the planet's most spectacular views.

After the 30-minute plane ride from Auckland, you'll find comforting traces of civilization in Puriri Bay. Seafood chowder and mussel fritters are on the menu at Tipi & Bobs Waterfront Lodge, a low-key hotel and restaurant on the harbor. For high design, venture across the island to the glass-walled Oruawharo Beach House, whose Modernist lines come courtesy of New Zealand architecture firm Fearon Hay.

From Port Fitzroy, on the western coast, you can cycle and tramp—that is, hike—through native flora, spotting threatened black petrels and New Zealand kaka birds on your way to Mount Hobson, the island's highest point. A guided tour of leafy Glenfern Sanctuary begins in a Unimog, a former army vehicle with a canvas-topped, open-air wagon, but the highlight occurs on your own two feet as you climb a wooden suspension bridge into the crown of a 600-year-old kauri tree. On the eastern side of the island, home to pristine beaches, aquatic pleasures reign: Kayak to secluded coves along the shore or simply sunbathe at the water's edge.

Pescheria La Lampara, a traditional fish market in Gallipoli, on Italy's Salentine Coast.

THE GUIDE

UITED STATES & CANADA CARIBBEAN MEXICO & CENTRAL & SOU
1ERICA EUROPE AFRICA & THE MIDDLE EAST ASIA AUSTRALIA &
ALAND UNITED STATES & CANADA CARIBBEAN MEXICO & CENT
UTH AMERICA EUROPE AFRICA & THE MIDDLE EAST ASIA AUSTR
W ZEALAND UNITED STATES & CANADA CARIBBEAN MEXICO &
NTRAL & SOUTH AMERICA EUROPE AFRICA & THE MIDDLE EAST
STRALIA & NEW ZEALAND UNITED STATES & CANADA CARIBBE
XICO & CENTRAL & SOUTH AMERICA EUROPE AFRICA & THE MID
ST ASIA AUSTRALIA & NEW ZEALAND UNITED STATES & CANAD

FOGO ISLAND

COWICHAN VALLEY

Portland

Montreal

Hudson

New York City

MONMOUTH COUNTY

CONTINENTAL DIVIDE

Park City

San Francisco

Chicago

Columbus

Las Vegas

Hollywood

Atlanta

Charleston

New Orleans

San Antonio

THE EVERGLADES

Miami

KAUAI

Honolulu

UNITED STATES & CANADA

WEST CHELSEA, NEW YORK CITY

STAY

Hôtel Americano Grupo Habita's sleek hotel with a rooftop pool and a subterranean bar. 518 W. 27th St.; 212/216-0000; hotel-americano.com; doubles from $$.

EAT

Bottino Salads and sandwiches in a whitewashed dining room. 246 10th Ave.; 212/206-6767; lunch for two ✗✗.

Ovest Pizzoteca Wood-fired Neapolitan pies and Italian wines by the glass. 513 W. 27th St.; 212/967-4392; dinner for two ✗✗.

Trestle on Tenth Swiss brasserie serving organic, locally sourced meals. 242 10th Ave.; 212/645-5659; dinner for two ✗✗✗.

Txikito Lively tapas bar that specializes in Basque cuisine. 240 Ninth Ave.; 212/242-4730; dinner for two ✗✗.

DO

Bryce Wolkowitz Gallery New-media installations by emerging artists. 505 W. 24th St.; 212/243-8830.

Gagosian Gallery Displays works by art-world icons such as Pablo Picasso and Roy Lichtenstein. 555 W. 24th St.; 212/741-1111.

Paul Kasmin Gallery Exhibits of contemporary pieces by the likes of David LaChapelle and Andy Warhol. 293 10th Ave.; 212/563-4474.

HARLEM, NEW YORK CITY

STAY

Aloft Harlem Tech-savvy hotel on one of Harlem's most historic thoroughfares. 2296 Frederick Douglass Blvd.; 877/462-5638; aloftharlem.com; doubles from $.

EAT

Amor Cubano Intimate, brick-walled restaurant with a focus on traditional Cuban cuisine. 2018 Third Ave.; 212/996-1220; dinner for two ✗✗.

Il Caffe Latte Low-key café with bracing coffee and flaky baked goods. 189 Malcolm X Blvd.; 212/222-2241; breakfast for two ✗.

Red Rooster Harlem Chef Marcus Samuelsson's mecca for Southern comfort food.

310 Lenox Ave.; 212/792-9001; dinner for two XX.

SHOP

Swing Internationally sourced housewares and apparel. 1960 Adam Clayton Powell Blvd.; 212/222-5802; swing-nyc.com.

DO

Apollo Theater Legendary performance space that stages musical productions and an infamous weekly amateur night. 253 W. 125th St.; 212/531-5300; apollotheater.org.

Conservatory Garden Six leafy acres of hedges, lawns, and fountains. E. 105th St., Central Park; centralparknyc.org.

Maysles Cinema Movies from compelling local filmmakers; don't miss the Harlem Homegrown series. 343 Lenox Ave.; 212/582-6050; mayslesinstitute.org.

Studio Museum in Harlem Of-the-moment works by artists of African descent, in a striking glass building. 144 W. 125th St.; 212/864-4500; studiomuseum.org.

HUDSON, NEW YORK

STAY

The Kaaterskill Unpretentious bed-and-breakfast and farm near the Catskill Mountains. 424 High Falls Rd. Ext., Catskill; 518/678-0026; thekaaterskill.com; doubles from $.

EAT

Café at Hudson Supermarket Mexican counter that serves creations like a complex roasted-poblano pork soup. 310 Warren St., Hudson; 518/822-0028; lunch for two XX.

DA|BA Upscale Swedish-inspired restaurant that also has standard pub fare. 225 Warren St., Hudson; 518/249-4631; dinner for two XXX.

Swoon Kitchenbar Neighborhood spot for crisp shoestring fries. 340 Warren St., Hudson; 518/822-8938; dinner for two XX.

SHOP

Carrie Haddad Gallery Hudson's first gallery displays up-to-the-minute photography and art. 622 Warren St., Hudson; 518/828-1915; carriehaddadgallery.com.

Historical Materialism Trove of old-world furniture and housewares. 601 Warren St., Hudson; 518/671-6151; historicalmaterialism.com.

Neven & Neven Moderne Vintage furnishings and decorative objects with a present-day focus. 618 Warren St., Hudson; 518/828-4214; nevenmoderne.com.

Rodgers Book Barn Filled with more than 50,000 items, including rare books and mint-condition records. 467 Rodman Rd., Hillsdale; 518/325-3610; rodgersbookbarn.com.

MONMOUTH COUNTY, NEW JERSEY

STAY

Bungalow Stylish 24-room hotel near the ocean in the Pier Village complex. 50 Laird St., Long Branch; 732/229-3700; bungalow hotel.net; doubles from $.

EAT

Avenue Oceanfront French restaurant known for its impressive seafood towers.

23 Ocean Ave., Long Branch; 732/759-2900; dinner for two XXX.

SHOP

Nirvana One-stop shop for designer jeans and T-shirts. 66 Centennial Dr., Long Branch; 732/222-7004.

DO

Count Basie Theater Named after the jazz great, a gilded 1926 auditorium turned concert venue. 99 Monmouth St., Red Bank; 732/842-9000; countbasietheater.org.

Monmouth Park Racetrack A 1946 track for competitive horse racing. Oceanport Ave., Oceanport; 732/222-5100; monmouthpark.com.

Stone Pony Live music venue; headliners have included Bruce Springsteen. 913 Ocean Ave., Asbury Park; 732/502-0600; drinks for two X.

CHARLESTON, SOUTH CAROLINA

STAY

Andrew Pinckney Inn Comfortable accommodations steps from King Street shops and restaurants. 40 Pinckney St.; 800/505-8983; andrewpinckneyinn. com; doubles from $.

Planters Inn Elegant rooms in the historic district. 112 N. Market St.; 800/845-7082; plantersinn.com; doubles from $$.

EAT

Bowens Island Local landmark where you can shuck your own oysters before they're roasted in an open-air kitchen. 1871 Bowens Island Rd.;

843/795-2757; dinner for two XX.

Charleston Pour House Cuban restaurant with two stages for live music. 1977 Maybank Hwy.; 843/571-4343; dinner for two XX.

Husk Upscale restaurant located in a 19th-century house on stately Queen Street. 76 Queen St.; 843/577-2500; dinner for two XXX.

DO

The Belmont Bourbon-centric bar with a civilized 46-person maximum. 511 King St.; no phone; drinks for two X.

ATLANTA

STAY

Loews Atlanta Hotel Elegant 414-room hotel with a spa and Turkish hammam. 1065 Peachtree St. N.E.; 800/235-6397 or 404/745-5000; loews hotels.com; doubles from $.

EAT

Abattoir Nose-to-tail cooking is the specialty. 1170 Howell Mill Rd.; 404/892-3335; dinner for two XXX.

JCT. Kitchen & Bar *The* place for fried chicken. 1198 Howell Mill Rd., suite 18; 404/355-2252; dinner for two XX.

KEY

LODGING
Under $250 = $
$250–$499 = $$
$500–$749 = $$$
$750–$999 = $$$$
$1,000 + up = $$$$$

DINING
Under $25 = X
$25–$74 = XX
$75–$149 = XXX
$150–$299 = XXXX
$300 + up = XXXXX

Miller Union New Southern dishes such as farm eggs baked in celery purée. 999 Brady Ave. N.W.; 678/733-8550; dinner for two ✗✗✗.

Yeah Burger The focus of the mix-and-match menu is on local and sustainable meats and produce. 1168 Howell Mill Rd., suite E; 404/496-4393; dinner for two ✗✗.

SHOP

Ann Mashburn Shop stocked with stylishly preppy staples like ballerina flats and poplin shirtdresses. 1198 Howell Mill Rd.; annmashburn.com.

Sid Mashburn Gentlemanly suits and accoutrements such as silk tartan ties. 1198 Howell Mill Rd.; sidmashburn.com.

DO

Saltworks Cutting-edge video and sculptural installations by emerging talents. 664 11th St. N.W.; 404/881-0411; saltworks gallery.com.

THE EVERGLADES, FLORIDA
STAY

Ivey House Eco-lodge with guided kayaking tours through neighboring cypress swamps. 107 Camellia St., Everglades City; 877/567-0679; iveyhouse.com; doubles from $.

EAT

Camellia Street Grill The day's catch is prepared with house-grown herbs. 202 Camellia St., Everglades City; 239/695-2003; dinner for two ✗✗.

City Seafood Café & Market Funky restaurant along the water. 702 Begonia St., Everglades City; 239/695-4007; lunch for two ✗.

DO

Everglades National Park Vast protected wetlands in southern Florida. 305/242-7700; nps.gov/ever.

Fakahatchee Strand Preserve State Park A 20-mile-long slough filled with ghost orchids, otters, mink, and roseate spoonbills. 137 Coastline Dr., Copeland; 239/695-4593; floridastate parks.org/fakahatcheestrand.

Swamp Buggy Races A ritual of mud and supercharged engines held three times a year. Collier Blvd. and Rattlesnake Hammock Rd., Naples; 800/897-2701; swampbuggy.com.

MIAMI
STAY

Hotel Beaux Arts Miami Ultramodern boutique hotel with an NBA-approved basketball court. 255 Biscayne Blvd. Way, Miami; 888/717-8850; marriott.com; doubles from $$.

JW Marriott Marquis Miami Downtown's most recent addition, inside a sleek, 41-story tower. 255 Biscayne Blvd. Way, Miami; 888/717-8850; marriott.com; doubles from $$.

One Bal Harbour Resort & Spa Luxury accommodations located near the tony Bal Harbour shopping center. 10295 Collins Ave., Bal Harbour; 877/455-5410; oneluxuryhotels.com; doubles from $$.

Soho Beach House Public spaces feature heavy ye-olde-English-club leather chairs and a 150-plus-piece contemporary art collection. 4385 Collins Ave., Miami Beach; 786/507-7900; sohobeach house.com; doubles from $$.

EAT

Wynwood Kitchen & Bar Farm-to-table dishes with international flair, served in an urban art space. 2550 N.W. Second Ave., Miami; 305/722-8959; dinner for two ✗✗✗.

DO

Bal Harbour Shops Upscale boutiques, plus art nights and free concerts, near Miami Beach. 9700 Collins Ave., Bal Harbour; 305/866-0311; balharbourshops.com.

De la Cruz Collection Contemporary Art Space A 30,000-square-foot museum with high-end boutiques and showrooms. 23 N.E. 41st St., Miami; 305/576-6112; delacruz collection.org.

New World Center Frank Gehry's sleek performing-arts venue that helped spur the downtown revival. 500 17th St., Miami Beach; 305/428-6748; newworld center.com.

Wynwood Walls Graffiti garden with a restaurant and bar. N.W. Second Ave. at 25th St., Miami; 305/531-4411; thewynwoodwalls.com.

CHICAGO
STAY

Peninsula Chicago Sleek tower on the Magnificent Mile, with two first-rate restaurants: the Lobby and Shanghai Terrace. 108 E. Superior St.; 866/382-8388 or 312/337-2888; peninsula.com; doubles from $$$.

EAT

The Bristol Chris Pandel's unpredictable daily menu lures off-duty chefs and locavores. 2152 N. Damen Ave.; 773/862-5555; dinner for two ✗✗.

Jam Sunday brunch takes a turn toward the savory, thanks to items such as buckwheat crêpes with braised lamb neck and Asian pears. 937 N. Damen Ave.; 773/489-0302; brunch for two ✗✗.

The Southern Bar-centric restaurant where you'll find "the dirtiest fried chicken north of the Mason-Dixon." 1840 W. North Ave.; 773/342-1840; dinner for two ✗✗.

COLUMBUS, INDIANA
STAY

Conrad Indianapolis A 23-story hotel in the heart of downtown. 50 W. Washington St., Indianapolis; 800/266-7237 or 317/713-5000; conradhotels.com; doubles from $.

DO

Architectural Tour Guided bus tour of 70 renowned buildings and public art installations. Columbus Area Visitors Center, Columbus; 800/468-6564; columbus.in.us.

Indianapolis Museum of Art Over 50,000 works of art; also runs the Miller House, an iconic minimalist glass structure and Modernist gardens. 4000 N. Michigan Rd., Indianapolis; 317/923-1331; imamuseum.org.

KEY

LODGING
Under $250 = $
$250–$499 = $$
$500–$749 = $$$
$750–$999 = $$$$
$1,000 + up = $$$$$

DINING
Under $25 = ✗
$25–$74 = ✗✗
$75–$149 = ✗✗✗
$150–$299 = ✗✗✗✗
$300 + up = ✗✗✗✗✗

NEW ORLEANS

STAY

International House Hotel Boho-chic boutique property on the edge of the French Quarter. 221 Camp St.; 504/553-9550; ihhotel.com; doubles from $.

EAT

Antoine's Restaurant French-Creole favorite since 1840. 713 Rue St.Louis; 504/581-4422; dinner for two ✗✗✗.

Mondo Eclectic small plates (ceviche and guacamole; Thai shrimp-and-pork meatballs) in Lakeview. 900 Harrison Ave.; 504/224-2633; dinner for two ✗✗.

Satsuma Café Cozy lunch spot in Bywater that serves innovative sandwiches and salads. 3218 Dauphine St.; 504/304-5962; lunch for two ✗.

DO

Preservation Hall French Quarter locale dedicated to traditional New Orleans jazz. 726 St. Peter St.; 504/522-2841; preservationhall.com.

Prospect.2 Exhibition that focuses on local artists. Oct. 22–Jan. 29, 2012; citywide; prospectneworleans.org.

St. Claude Avenue and Julia Street Galleries Don't miss Arthur Roger Gallery (432 and 434 Julia St.; 504/522-1999) and Good Children Gallery (4037 St. Claude Ave.; 504/975-1557).

SAN ANTONIO, TEXAS

STAY

Hotel Havana Restored 1914 hacienda with 27 rooms. 1015 Navarro St.; 210/222-2008; havanasanantonio.com; doubles from $.

JW Marriott San Antonio Hill Country Resort & Spa Huge compound with 1,002 rooms, a water park, spa, and two golf courses. 23808 Resort Pkwy.; 866/882-4420; jwmarriott.com; doubles from $$.

EAT

Il Sogno Upscale Italian specialties in an industrial setting. 200 E. Grayson St.; 210/223-3900; dinner for two ✗✗✗.

La Gloria Mexican street-food café. 100 E. Grayson St.; 210/267-9040; dinner for two ✗✗.

SHOP

Tienda de Cocina Hard-to-find housewares from Central and South America. 200 E. Grayson St.; 877/875-2665; melissaguerra.com.

THE CONTINENTAL DIVIDE

STAY

Casitas de Gila Guesthouses Five southwestern-style cottages surrounded by juniper and piñon trees. 50 Casita Flats Rd., Gila, N. Mex.; 877/923-4827; casitasdegila.com; doubles from $.

Old Faithful Inn Rustic lodge that has a stone fireplace. Yellowstone National Park, Wyo.; 866/439-7375; yellowstonenationalparklodges.com; doubles from $.

Rising Sun Motor Inn Simple yet comfortable rooms next to St. Mary Lake. Glacier National Park, Mont.; 866/875-8456; nationalparkreservations.com; doubles from $.

Sky Hotel Stylish Kimpton hotel with ski-in access at the base of Aspen Mountain. 709 E. Durant Ave., Aspen, Colo.; 800/882-2582; theskyhotel.com; doubles from $$.

EAT

Largo Café Hole-in-the-wall burger joint. 3896 Hwy. 60, Quemado, N. Mex.; 575/773-4686; lunch for two ✗.

Two-Bit Cowboy Saloon One of Wyoming's best selections of single-malt whiskeys in a cozy, living-room-style setting. 290 Atlantic City Rd., Atlantic City, Wyo.; 307/332-0248; drinks for two ✗.

DO

El Malpais National Monument Landscape filled with craters, caves, and other eerie formations caused by one million years of volcanic activity. 123 E. Roosevelt Ave., Grants, N. Mex.; 505/783-4774; nps.gov/elma.

Glacier National Park More than 700 miles of trails through wilderness, lakes, and mountains. 406/888-7800; nps.gov/glac.

Little Nell Aspen's most glamorous address and the go-to destination for après-ski cocktails. 675 E. Durant Ave., Aspen, Colo.; 970/420-9700; drinks for two ✗✗.

Mad Dog & the Pilgrim Booksellers A selection of 60,000 antiquarian books. 4176 Hwy. 789, Sweetwater Station, Wyo.; 307/544-2203.

LAS VEGAS

STAY

Mandarin Oriental, Las Vegas Modernist hotel in the slick CityCenter complex. 3752 Las Vegas Blvd. S.; 888/881-9578; mandarinoriental.com; doubles from $.

EAT

Archi Thai Kitchen Stucco hut where you'll find the ultimate chicken *satay*. 6360 W. Flamingo Rd.; 702/880-5550; lunch for two ✗.

Bachi Burger Pork buns and Asian-inflected burgers in a fuss-free setting. 470 E. Windmill Lane; 702/242-2244; lunch for two ✗.

Bartolotta Ristorante di Mare Coastal Italian restaurant known for expensive fresh fish. Wynn Las Vegas, 3131 Las Vegas Blvd. S.; 702/770-9966; dinner for two ✗✗✗✗.

Joël Robuchon Grand dining room featuring a 16-course tasting menu. MGM Grand Hotel & Casino, 3799 Las Vegas Blvd. S.; 702/891-7925; dinner for two ✗✗✗✗✗.

Lotus of Siam Considered the country's best Thai restaurant. 953 E. Sahara Ave.; 702/735-3033; dinner for two ✗✗.

PARK CITY, UTAH

STAY

Montage Deer Valley Resort with 220 rooms and suites,

an Alpine-inspired spa, and three restaurants. 9100 Marsac Ave.; 888/604-1301; montagedeervalley.com; doubles from $$$$.

Sky Lodge Cool boutique hotel in Old Town. 201 Heber Ave.; 888/876-2525; theskylodge.com; doubles from $$$.

St. Regis Deer Valley Slope-facing resort with a sprawling spa and butler service. 2300 Deer Valley Dr. E.; 877/787-3447; stregis.com; doubles from $$$$.

Waldorf Astoria Park City Ski-in resort at the Canyons with one of only six Golden Door spas in the country. 2100 W. Frostwood Dr.; 866/279-0843; waldorfastoria.com; doubles from $$$.

EAT

Bar Bohème The Sky Lodge's cozy fireside bar. 201 Heber Ave.; 435/658-9425; dinner for two ✗✗✗.

No Name Saloon The locals' watering hole of choice. 447 Main St.; 435/649-6667; dinner for two ✗.

Talisker on Main Intimate restaurant with an extensive wine list. 515 Main St.; 435/658-5479; dinner for two ✗✗✗.

PORTLAND, OREGON
STAY

Ace Hotel A 78-room retreat with eco-friendly elements and vintage furniture. 1022 S.W. Stark St.; 503/228-2277; acehotel.com; doubles from $.

EAT

Beast Vegetables and salads get as much careful attention as the meaty entrées. 5425

N.E. 30th Ave.; 503/841-6968; dinner for two ✗✗✗✗.

Bunk Sandwiches Inventive subs such as the pork-belly *cubano*. 621 S.E. Morrison St.; 503/477-9515; lunch for two ✗.

Clyde Common Cozy hipster restaurant in the Ace Hotel. 1014 S.W. Stark St.; 503/228-3333; dinner for two ✗✗.

Le Pigeon Celebrated Lower Burnside bistro with a hyper-local ethos. 738 E. Burnside St.; 503/546-8796; dinner for two ✗✗✗.

Meat Cheese Bread Stop in for a BLB sandwich (bacon, lettuce, and golden beets). 1406 S.E. Stark St.; 503/234-1700; lunch for two ✗.

Ned Ludd The wood-burning oven turns out everything from slow-roasted chops to flatbreads. 3925 N.E. Martin Luther King Jr. Blvd.; 503/288-6900; dinner for two ✗✗.

Sugar Cube Whipping up the city's best confections. 4262 SE Belmont St.; 503/890-2825; dessert for two ✗.

Voodoo Doughnut Quirky late-night snack stop (get the bacon-maple-glazed). 22 S.W. Third Ave.; 503/241-4704; doughnuts for two ✗.

SAN FRANCISCO
STAY

Inn San Francisco A 21-room hotel with Victorian details and a rooftop deck. 943 S. Van Ness Ave.; 415/641-0188; innsf.com; doubles from $.

SHOP

Afterlife Boutique Well-edited shop that carries reconstructed antique jewelry and collectible

concert tees. 988 Valencia St.; 415/796-2398; afterlifeboutique.com.

Gravel & Gold Sells treasures like Japanese paper goods and Canadian wool blankets. 3266 21st St.; 415/552-0112; gravelandgold.com.

Libros Latinos Imported books from the Caribbean and Latin America. 2141 Mission St.; 415/503-1800; libroslatinos.com.

Paxton Gate One-of-a-kind jewelry, taxidermy, and gardening accessories. 824 Valencia St.; 415/824-1872; paxtongate.com.

HOLLYWOOD, CALIFORNIA
STAY

The Redbury Designed by photographer Matthew Rolston, with 57 apartment-style suites. 1717 Vine St.; 877/962-1717; theredbury.com; doubles from $$.

SHOP

Bettie Page Offering styles made famous by the cheerfully sexy dominatrix. 6650 Hollywood Blvd.; 323/461-4014; bettiepageclothing.com.

Decades Celebrities flock to this light-filled boutique for high-end vintage gowns. 8214½ Melrose Ave.; 323/655-0223; decadesinc.com.

Hollywood Movie Posters Antique movie posters and ephemera from recent blockbusters. 6727⅝ Hollywood Blvd.; 323/463-1792.

It's a Wrap Consignment store that specializes in pieces that have been worn on or purchased for a film set. 1164 S. Robertson Blvd.;

310/246-1183; itsawraphollywood.com.

Larry Edmunds Bookshop Emporium of entertainment-related books and photos. 6644 Hollywood Blvd.; 323/463-3273; larryedmunds.com.

Prop Store Filled floor-to-ceiling with movie-set pieces and costumes. 9000 Fullbright Ave., Chatsworth; 818/727-7829; propstore.com.

DO

Hollywood Museum Memorabilia from cinema's golden age. 1660 N. Highland Ave.; 323/464-7776; thehollywoodmuseum.com.

HONOLULU
STAY

Modern Honolulu A 353-room hotel designed by Yabu Pushelberg. 1775 Ala Moana Boulevard; 866/971-2782; themodernhonolulu.com; doubles from $$$.

EAT

Jimbo Bustling eatery known for its house-made noodles. 1936 S. King St.; 808/947-2211; lunch for two ✗✗.

Shimazu Store New and unexpected flavors of shave ice. 330 N. School St.; 808/371-8899; dessert for two ✗.

Town Seasonal ingredients are front and center on the restaurant's ever-changing menu. 3435 Waialae Ave.; 808/735-5900; dinner for two ✗✗✗.

Yama's Fish Market Concrete-floor takeout joint specializing in Hawaiian plate lunches. 2332 Young St.; 808/941-9994; lunch for two ✗.

SHOP

Anne Namba The designer's latest creations, using vintage Japanese kimono and obi fabrics. 324 Kamani St.; 808/589-1135; annenamba.com.

Cindy's Family-owned lei-making shop in Chinatown. 1034 Maunakea St.; 808/536-6538; cindysleishoppe.com.

Kawamoto Orchids Three-acre nursery selling hardy buds. 2630 Waiomao Rd.; 808/732-5808; kawamoto orchids.com.

Lin's Known for leis made with fragrant pikake and plumeria. 1017 Maunakea St.; 808/537-4112; linsleishop.com.

Tincan Mailman 1950's-era kitsch, including silk Aloha shirts, hand-tinted postcards, and mahogany ukuleles. 1026 Nuuanu Ave.; 808/524-3009; tincanmailman.net.

KAUAI, HAWAII

STAY

St. Regis Princeville Resort On Hanalei Bay, 251 cheery rooms and the friendliest staff around. 5520 Ka Haku Rd., Princeville; 877/787-3447; stregisprinceville.com; doubles from $$$$.

Waimea Plantation Cottages Former sugar-field bungalows on 27 acres of coconut palms and banyan trees. 9400 Kaumualii Hwy., Waimea; 808/338-1625; waimeaplantation. com; doubles from $$.

EAT

Kauai Grill Jean-Georges Vongerichten's French-Asian-influenced bayside restaurant in the St. Regis Princeville.

5520 Ka Haku Rd.; 808/826-9644; dinner for two ✗✗.

Wrangler's Steakhouse Hawaiian cowboy-themed dining with fresh fish and great steaks. 9852 Kaumualii Hwy., Waimea; 808/338-1218; dinner for two ✗✗.

DO

Beach at Polihale State Park At the end of a dirt road north from Mana village. Off Kaumualii Hwy. (Rte. 50); 808/274-3444; hawaii stateparks.org.

Pali Ke Kua Beach (Hideaways) Near the community path in Princeville, a perfect stretch of sand shaded by a canopy of false kamani trees and hidden from view by massive black lava-rock.

FOGO ISLAND, NEWFOUNDLAND

STAY

Foley's Place Historic B&B that dates back a century. 709/658-7244; foleysplace.ca; doubles from $.

EAT

Nicole's Café Known for its house-made seafood chowder. 159 Main Rd., Joe Batt's Arm; 709/658-3663; lunch for two ✗✗.

DO

Fogo Island Arts Corporation Venue that hosts an artist-in-residency program. 709/270-1981; artscorpfogoisland.ca.

Outings with Roy Dwyer The nature writer leads day trips while discussing Fogo's colonial past. 709/658-3538; roydwyer@ eastlink.ca.

MONTREAL

STAY

Casa Bianca Inside a century-old château with claw-foot tubs and views of Mount Royal. 4351 Ave. de l'Esplanade; 866/775-4431; casabianca.ca; doubles from $.

Le Petit Hôtel Boutique hideaway with 24 contemporary rooms. 168 Rue St.-Paul Ouest; 877/530-0360; petithotel montreal.com; doubles from $.

EAT

Boucherie Abu Elias Lebanese grill joint that serves dishes such as *kafta* and *shish taouk*. 733 Blvd. de la Côte-Vertu; 514/747-7754; dinner for two ✗.

La Salle à Manger French bistro highlighting house-cured charcuterie. 1302 Ave. du Mont-Royal; 514/522-0777; dinner for two ✗✗✗.

DO

Bixi Bikes Public bike system that offers 24-hour service at 400 docks around the city. 514/789-2494; bixi.com.

Marché Jean-Talon North America's largest outdoor food market. 7070 Ave. Henri-Julien.

COWICHAN VALLEY, BRITISH COLUMBIA

STAY

Fairburn Farmstay & Guesthouse An 1896 farmhouse on 130 acres. 3310 Jackson Rd., Duncan; 250/746-4637; fairburnfarm. bc.ca; doubles from $.

Sooke Harbour House The 28-room inn and fine-dining restaurant serves Dungeness crabs and sweet Weathervane scallops. 1528 Whiffen Spit

KEY

LODGING
Under $250 = **$**
$250–$499 = **$$**
$500–$749 = **$$$**
$750–$999 = **$$$$**
$1,000 + up = **$$$$$**

DINING
Under $25 = ✗
$25–$74 = ✗✗
$75–$149 = ✗✗✗
$150–$299 = ✗✗✗✗
$300 + up = ✗✗✗✗✗

Rd., Sooke; 250/642-3421; sookeharbourhouse.com; doubles from $$; dinner for two ✗✗.

EAT

Craig Street Brew Pub Its Shawnigan Irish Ale is the best of several house-made beers. 25 Craig St., Duncan; 250/737-2337; dinner for two ✗✗.

Spinnakers Gastro Brewpub The pub's own ESB cask ale is served on a deck overlooking the harbor. 308 Catherine St., Victoria; 250/386-2739; lunch for two ✗✗.

SHOP

True Grain Bread & Mill Crusty organic loaves and German pretzels get equal billing. 1725 Cowichan Bay Rd., Cowichan Bay; 250/746-7664.

DO

Duncan Farmers' Market Sample local products in the valley's workaday hub. City Square, Duncan; 250/732-1723.

Merridale Ciderworks Tops for heirloom apple cider. 1230 Merridale Rd., Cobble Hill; 250/743-4293.

Tugwell Creek Honey Farm & Meadery House-harvested honey and mead. 8750 West Coast Rd., Sooke; 250/642-1956.

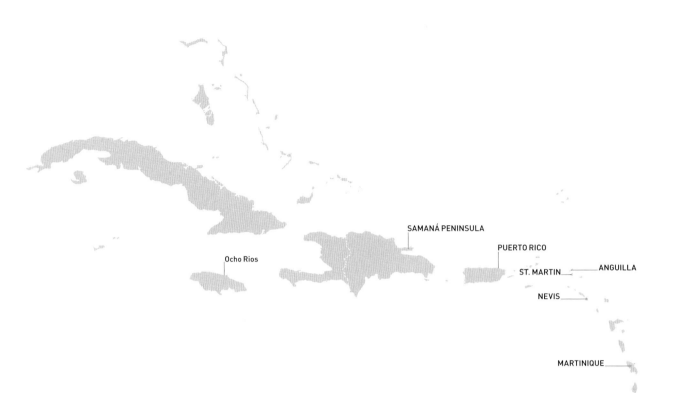

SAMANÁ PENINSULA

Ocho Rios

PUERTO RICO

ST. MARTIN — ANGUILLA

NEVIS →

MARTINIQUE →

BARBADOS →

CARIBBEAN

STAY

**Conrad Condado Plaza &
Casino** Atlantic-facing
high-rise with a casino that
stays open 24 hours. 999 Avda.
Ashford, Condado, San Juan;
888/722-1274; condadoplaza.
com; doubles from $$.

EAT

Budatai Iron Chef Roberto
Treviño's fun, Latin-Asian
fusion cuisine. 1056 Avda.
Ashford, Condado, San Juan;
787/725-6919; dinner for
two ✗✗✗.

José Enrique Local hangout
near La Placita square. 176
Calle Duffaut, Santurce, San
Juan; 787/725-3518; dinner for
two ✗✗✗.

L'Auxerre Urbane continental
fare in a charming 1871 house.
16 Calle Estrella, San Germán;
787/892-8844; dinner for
two ✗✗.

Pikayo Celebrated chef Wilo
Benet's formal flagship in the
Conrad Condado Plaza. 999
Avda. Ashford, Condado, San
Juan; 787/721-6194; dinner for
two ✗✗✗.

Piñones kiosks Look for deep-
fried *alcapurrias* made fresh.
Rte. 187, east of Isla Verde,
San Juan; snacks for two ✗.

OCHO RIOS, JAMAICA
STAY

Couples Tower Isle
Beachside all-inclusive,
with an impressive roster of
activities. 800/268-7537;
couples.com; doubles from
$$$ per person.

Sandals Royal Plantation
Luxe all-inclusive with
designated butlers for each

room. 800/726-3257; sandals.
com; doubles from $$ per
person, three-night minimum.

SAMANÁ PENINSULA,
DOMINICAN REPUBLIC
STAY

Balcones del Atlántico A
RockResort property with 86
villas on a protected crescent.
Las Terrenas; 866/513-7625;
rockresorts.com; doubles
from $$.

**Bannister Luxury
Condominium Hotel**
Marina-side hotel with access

to an equestrian center. Km 5, Crta. Sánchez-Samaná, Samaná Bay; 809/503-6363; thebannisterhotel.com; doubles from $.

Peninsula House Intimate gingerbread-trimmed Victorian that tops out at 12 guests. Calle Coson, Las Terrenas; 809/962-7447; thepeninsulahouse.com; doubles from $$$, including breakfast.

BARBADOS
STAY

Atlantis Hotel Ten 500-square-foot suites on the water. Tent Bay, Bathsheba, St. Joseph; 246/433-9445; atlantishotelbarbados.com; doubles from $$.

Lush Life Nature Resort On a hilltop fringed by rain forest, 10 spacious cottages made from indigenous wood. Suriname, St. Joseph; 246/433-1300; lushlife.bb; cottages from $.

Sandy Lane Grande dame with 112 marble-floor rooms and a Rolls-Royce Phantom to shuttle guests to and from the airport. St. James; 866/444-4080; sandylane. com; doubles from $$$$$.

EAT

Bajan Blue In the Sandy Lane resort, a modern spin on West Indian, Polynesian, and Asian cuisine. St. James; 246/444-2000; dinner for two XXXX.

Nishi Briton Paul Edwards's upscale Japanese restaurant. Second St., Holetown, St. James; 246/432-8287; dinner for two XXX.

DO

Old Pharmacy Gallery & Star Bar Former apothecary turned art gallery that hosts outdoor movie screenings. Queen St., Speightstown; 246/234-2494.

NEVIS
STAY

Four Seasons Resort Nevis Ten tennis courts, a spa, a golf course, and a pristine beach. Pinney's Beach, Charlestown; 800/332-3442; fourseasons. com; doubles from $$$.

Golden Rock Inn Six pastel cottages on the side of a green hill. Gingerland; 869/469-3346; golden-rock.com; doubles from $$.

Nisbet Plantation Beach Club Bright, tidy bungalows on a 30-acre former sugar plantation. St. James Parish; 800/742-6008; nisbetplantation. com; doubles from $$$, including breakfast and dinner.

EAT

Sunshine's Beach Bar & Grill Open-air restaurant on Pinney's Beach that serves addictive rum drinks known as Killer Bees. Charlestown; 869/469-5817; dinner for two XX.

DO

Alexander Hamilton Museum Set in the house where he was born, the museum chronicles the history of the island. Charlestown; 869/469-5786.

ST. MARTIN
STAY

Love Hotel Seven colonial-style rooms on the French side. Grand Case; 590-590/298-714; love-sxm.com; doubles from $.

EAT

L'Escapade Upscale French restaurant with a carefully curated wine cellar. 94 Blvd. de Grand Case; 590-590/877-504; dinner for two XXX.

Rainbow Café Casual beachfront bistro. 176 Blvd. de Grand Case; 590-590/875-580; dinner for two XXX.

DO

Princess Casino at Port de Plaisance One of the island's best casinos. Cole Bay; 599/544-4311.

ANGUILLA
STAY

Cap Juluca Lining a calm bay, 98 rooms with Frette linens and Moroccan-style rugs. Maundays Bay; 888/858-5822; capjuluca.com; doubles from $$, including breakfast.

EAT

B&D's Barbecue Standout roadside grill with smoky pork ribs to go. Long Bay; 264/497-6670; dinner for two XX.

E's Oven West Indian specialties (goat curry; conch stew) in a no-frills setting. South Hill Village; 264/498-8258; dinner for two XXX.

KoalKeel In a 200-year-old limestone cottage serving refined French-Anguillan fare and a lavish rum-truffle tower. The Valley; 264/497-2930; dinner for two XXX.

Straw Hat Restaurant Famous for its grilled Anguillan crayfish. Meads Bay; 264/497-8300; lunch for two XX.

DO

Dune Preserve Driftwood bar

owned by Anguilla-born reggae artist and raconteur Bankie Banx. Rendezvous Bay; 264/772-9259; drinks for two X.

Pumphouse Rum punches, reggae bands, and weekly calypso nights are the draw. Sandy Ground, Road Bay; 264/497-5154; drinks for two X.

MARTINIQUE
STAY

Maison d'Hôte de L'Ilet Oscar Antiques-filled plantation house on a private island. Le François; 596-696/453-330; ilet-oscar.com; doubles from $.

EAT

Chez Tante Arlette Informal restaurant where locals gather on Sundays. Grand-Rivière; 596-596/557-575; lunch for two XXX.

Le Brédas The chef's signature dish: a mille-feuille of foie gras and plantains. St. Joseph; 596-596/576-552; dinner for two XXX.

Le Petibonum Beachside shack featuring freshly caught fish (try the marlin ceviche). Le Carbet; 596-596/780-434; lunch for two XXX.

KEY

LODGING
Under $250 = $
$250–$499 = $$
$500–$749 = $$$
$750–$999 = $$$$
$1,000 + up = $$$$$

DINING
Under $25 = X
$25–$74 = XX
$75–$149 = XXX
$150–$299 = XXXX
$300 + up = XXXXX

San Miguel de Allende

VERACRUZ

Mexico City

CAYE CAULKER

Acapulco

JICARO ISLAND

Lima

SACRED VALLEY

EASTER
ISLAND

São Paulo

IGUAZÚ FALLS

COLONIA
Buenos Aires

PATAGONIAN
LAKES REGION

MEXICO &
CENTRAL &
SOUTH
AMERICA

MEXICO CITY
STAY

Condesa DF One of the city's most fashionable addresses, thanks to its vintage-inspired design. 102 Avda. Veracruz; 52-55/5241-2600; condesadf. com; doubles from $.

Las Alcobas Intimate escape (embroidered linens; whirlpool tubs) in buzzy Polanco. 390 Avda. Presidente Masaryk; 52-55/3300-3900; lasalcobas. com; doubles from $$.

St. Regis Mexico City Yabu Pushelberg–designed rooms with panoramic city views. 438 Paseo de la Reforma; 877/787-3447 or 52-55/5228-1818; stregis.com; doubles from $$.

EAT

El Patio Japanese-Mexican fusion fare on the rooftop of the Condesa DF hotel.

102 Avda. Veracruz; 52-55/5241-2600; dinner for two ✗✗.

DO

Kurimanzutto Former timber yard turned exhibition space for emerging art. 94 Calle Gob. Rafael Rebollar; 52-55/5256-2408; kurimanzutto.com.

Museo Universitario Arte Contemporáneo Showcases modern international and Mexican artists in a soaring, light-filled building. 3000 Avda. Insurgentes Sur; 52-55/5622-6972; muac.unam.mx.

Museo Universitario del Chopo Enrique Norten–designed experimental art and performance hall. 10 Calle Enrique González Martínez; 52-55/5546-5484; chopo.unam.mx.

OMR Contemporary gallery in the Roma district, home of the city's leading art scene. 54 Plaza Río de Janeiro; 52-55/5525-4368; galeriaomr.com.

Proyectos Monclova Showroom known for its cutting-edge exhibitions. 31 Calle Gral. Antonio León; 52-55/4754-3546; proyectos monclova.com.

ACAPULCO, MEXICO
STAY

Banyan Tree Cabo Marqués Asian-style resort off Puerto Marqués Bay with a spa, three restaurants, and infinity pools in each villa. Blvd. Cabo Marqués, Lote 1; 800/591-0439 or 52-744/434-0100; banyan tree.com; doubles from $$$.

Hotel Boca Chica Grupo Habita's updated 1950's beach club. Playa Caletilla, Fracc. Las Playas; 800/337-4685 or 52-744/482-7879; hotel-boca chica.com; doubles from $.

Hotel Encanto Rooms in this all-white, geometric building feature Mexican pillow covers and marble floors. 51 Jacques Cousteau, Fracc. Brisas del Marqués;

877/337-1260 or 52-744/446-7101; hotelencanto.com.mx; doubles from $$.

EAT

Becco al Mare Italian food and fine wines in a minimalist white dining room with superb views of Acapulco Bay. 14 Crta. Escénica; 52-744/446-7402; dinner for two ✗✗✗.

Zibu Mex-Thai fusion under a *palapa* with three mosaic-floor rooms overlooking Puerto Marqués Bay. Avda. Escénica, Fracc. Glomar; 52-744/433-3058; dinner for two ✗✗.

SAN MIGUEL DE ALLENDE, MEXICO
STAY

Rosewood San Miguel de Allende Luxury resort tucked away on four palm-studded acres near the historic center. 11 Nemesio Diez; 888/767-3966; rosewoodhotels.com; doubles from $$.

EAT

Café Rama Downtown lunch spot where international dishes are made with indigenous ingredients. 7 Calle Nueva; 52-415/154-9655; lunch for two ✗.

SHOP

Fábrica La Aurora A 1902 factory that's home to more than three dozen galleries and boutiques. Stock up on ceramic tiles at Superficies. Colonia Aurora; no phone; fabricalaaurora.com.

DO

La Azotea Laid-back terrace bar frequented by well-heeled locals. 6 Umarán; 52-415/152-8265; drinks for two ✗.

VERACRUZ, MEXICO
STAY

Emporio Modern hotel with three restaurants, three pools, and a spa along the port. 244 Paseo del Malecón; 866/280-6073 or 52-55/5062-6161; hotelesemporio.com; doubles from $.

EAT

El Acamalín Go to this friendly restaurant for the house-made tamales. 40 Calle Venustiano Carranza, Xico; no phone; dinner for two ✗✗.

Tomy Orange-and-blue-walled local hangout that dishes up flavorful seafood on the outskirts of town. Calle Roque Espinoso Domínguez, Zempoala; 52-296/971-4796; lunch for two ✗✗.

DO

Parque Juárez Terraced green space that looks out on the Sierra Madre Oriental mountains. Calle J. J. Herrera, Xalapa Enríquez.

Parque Los Berros Expansive parkland that is a favored spot for residents' morning runs. Avda. Miguel Hidalgo, Xalapa Enríquez.

Parque Los Tecajetes Ecological conservation area filled with protected plants native to Mexico's cloud forests. Calle Guadalupe Victoria, Xalapa Enríquez.

JICARO ISLAND, NICARAGUA
STAY

Jicaro Island Ecolodge Environmentally minded resort comprising nine wooden casitas with slatted walls and mosquito-netted

beds. 505/8403-1236; jicarolodge.com; doubles from $$, including meals.

CAYE CAULKER, BELIZE
STAY

Seaside Cabanas Ten rooms and six colorful cabins, each with its own roof terrace facing the Caribbean Sea. 011-501/226-0498; seasidecabanas.com; doubles from $.

EAT

Jolly Roger's Grill & Restaurant Casual roadside eatery that's a must for fresh-caught fish. Ave. Hicaro; 011-501/664-3382; dinner for two ✗✗.

DO

Ambergris Cay A neighboring isle (30 minutes away by boat) with scores of upscale shops and dining spots. ambergris caye.com.

Underwater Adventures The world's second-largest reef is the ideal site for snorkeling and diving. Don't miss Hol Chan Marine Reserve and the Blue Hole. gocayecaulker.com.

LIMA, PERU
STAY

Hotel Paracas Whitewashed rooms and adobe-colored

KEY

LODGING
Under $250 = **$**
$250–$499 = **$$**
$500–$749 = **$$$**
$750–$999 = **$$$$**
$1,000 + up = **$$$$$**

DINING
Under $25 = ✗
$25–$74 = ✗✗
$75–$149 = ✗✗✗
$150–$299 = ✗✗✗✗
$300 + up = ✗✗✗✗✗

façades in Lima's version of the Hamptons. 173 Avda. Paracas; 51-56/581-333; luxurycollection.com; doubles from $$.

Westin Lima Hotel & Convention Center Modernist retreat in the city center, with an undulating glass exterior. 450 Calle Las Begonias; 51-1/201-5000; starwood hotels.com; doubles from $$.

EAT

Central Tasting menus include updated Peruvian classics such as braised baby-goat leg with herbs from the chef's rooftop garden. 376 Calle Santa Isabel; 51-1/242-8575; dinner for two ✕✕✕.

Pescados Capitales *Limeños* flock to this congenial dining room for inventive ceviches and an easygoing atmosphere. 1337 Avda. La Mar; 51-1/421-8808; lunch for two ✕✕.

SHOP

Dédalo Arte y Artesanía The place to buy flatware and jewelry made by Peruvian artisans. 295 Paseo Sáenz Peña; 51-1/652-5400.

Indigo Arte y Artesanía Craft shop that sells locally made alpaca-wool clothing. 260 Avda. El Bosque; 51-1/441-2232.

DO

Fundación Museo Amano Collection of woven textiles from the country's central coast. 160 Calle Retiro; 51-1/441-2909.

Islas Ballestas and San Gallán Untouched islands teeming with pelicans, penguins, and sea lions. Day

trips can be arranged through the concierge at Hotel Paracas. 51-56/581-333; aluque@tikariy.com.pe.

Museo Enrico Poli Museum spotlighting ancient Peruvian gold and silver. 466 Calle Lord Cochrane; 51-1/422-2437; by appointment.

Museo Larco Pre-Columbian artifacts in a renovated 18th-century mansion built atop the remains of a seventh-century pyramid. 1515 Avda. Bolívar; 51-1/461-1312; museolarco.org.

SACRED VALLEY, PERU

STAY

Hotel Monasterio In a 16th-century former monastery. Oxygen is pumped into the rooms to ward off altitude sickness. 136 Calle Palacio, Plazoleta Nazarenas; 51-1/610-8300; monasterio hotel.com; doubles from $$$, including breakfast.

EAT

Map Café Glass-walled gem serving upscale Nouveau Andean dishes such as guinea pig confit. 231 Plaza de las Nazarenas; 51-8/424-2476; dinner for two ✕✕.

SHOP

Kuna Opulent wool hats, shawls, and ponchos made by Peruvian artisans. 127 Portal de Panes, Plaza de Armas; 51-8/424-3191; kuna.com.pe.

PATAGONIAN LAKES REGION, CHILE

STAY

Espejo de Luna Quirky eight-room hotel and restaurant

with a main lodge built in the shape of a shipwreck. Km 35, Camino Queilen; 56-91/458-933; espejodeluna.cl; doubles from $$.

Palafito 1326 Hotel Boutique Twelve muted rooms with blond-wood furnishings, on Castro Bay. 1326 Calle Ernesto Riquelme; 56-65/530-053; palafito1326.cl; doubles from $.

Quincho Country Home Rustic lodge overlooking Lake Llanquihue and surrounded by boxwood and wildflowers. Km 7.5, Ruta 225; 56-65/330-737; quinchocountryhome.cl; doubles from $$$.

EAT

Mercado Angelmó Open-air market where vendors hawk local goods and musicians play in the dining area above. Palafitos de Angelmó; no phone; lunch for two ✕.

Restaurant Quetelmahue Residents come here for the region's *curanto al hoyo* (chicken, shellfish, sausage, and potatoes, cooked beneath *nalca* leaves). Quetelmahue; 56-9/8791-9410; lunch for two ✕✕.

DO

MAM-Museo de Arte Moderno Chiloé Modern Chilote art housed in a spartan gallery inside a restored shingled farmhouse. Parque Municipal de Castro; 56-65/635-454; mamchiloe.cl.

Vicente Pérez Rosales National Park More than 600,000 acres of forested landscape; you can see

surging waterfalls at Saltos del Petrohué.

EASTER ISLAND, CHILE

STAY

Posada de Mike Rapu Eco-chic rooms with modern amenities. Guests choose their activities (hiking *moai* paths; biking; fishing) with the help of an on-site guide. 866/750-6699 or 56-2/395-2800; explora.com; $$$$$ per person, including meals, drinks, and expeditions, minimum three nights.

BUENOS AIRES

STAY

Algodon Mansion French Classical hotel with 10 ebony wood-floored suites and round-the-clock butler service. 1647 Montevideo; 54-11/3530-7777; algodon mansion.com; suites from $$.

Palacio Duhau-Park Hyatt Buenos Aires Centennial magnolia trees shade a 1932 palace with crystal chandeliers and contemporary furniture. 1661 Avda. Alvear; 800/233-1234 or 54-11/5171-1234; park. hyatt.com; doubles from $$.

EAT

Almacén Secreto In-the-know diners seek out the intimate Villa Crespo restaurant, behind an unmarked doorway, for the venison *raviolones* and oven-baked Paraná fish. 1242 Aguirre; 54-11/4854-9131; dinner for two ✕✕.

Casa Coupage *Puerta cerrada* where the sommelier-owners serve dense Argentinean specialties such as skirt steak with quinoa. 5518 Soler;

54-11/4777-9295; dinner for two ✖✖✖✖.

SHOP

Arte Étnico Argentino Rustic hand-finished furniture sourced from villages in Santiago del Estero. 4656 El Salvador; 54-11/4832-0516; arteetnicoargentino.com.

ArtePampa Tribal-style dolls, llama-motif mirrors, and textured-paper lampshades—all handcrafted in the La Pampa district. 917 Defensa; 54-11/4362-6406; artepampa.com.

Marcelo Toledo Shop where the master silversmith of the same name creates ornate silver-lined gourds for sipping maté. 462 Humberto Primo; 54-11/4362-0841; marcelo toledo.net.

Pick Market Airy food hall in the Recoleta neighborhood that carries imported spices, locally sourced preserves, fresh produce, and gourmet foods. 1212 Libertad; 54-11/ 4519-8046; thepickmarket. com.ar.

DO

El Zanjón Below San Telmo, a labyrinth of worn dwellings and courtyards that reveal centuries of urban living. 755 Defensa; 54-11/4361-3002; elzanjon.com.ar.

La Peña del Colorado Leading Argentinean folk musicians stamp out complex rhythms at this popular music venue in Palermo. 3657 Güemes; 54-11/4822-1038; lapeniadel colorado.com.

Palacio Barolo The city's first skyscraper still offers some of the best views of the skyline. 1370 Avda. de Mayo; 54-11/4381-1885; palacio barolotours.com.ar.

IGUAZÚ FALLS, ARGENTINA

STAY

Sheraton Iguazú Resort & Spa On the Argentine side, the only place to stay in Iguazú National Park. Balconies in 91 of the hotel's spacious rooms provide stunning views of the waterfalls. Iguazú National Park; 800/325-3535 or 54-3757/491-800; sheraton. com; doubles from $$$.

COLONIA, URUGUAY

STAY

Casa los Jazmines Rustic guesthouse with 400-thread-count Egyptian cotton sheets, iPod docking stations, and a selection of Uruguayan and Argentine wines. Camino del Caño; 598/4520-2799; casalos jazmineshotel.com; doubles from $.

Four Seasons Resort Carmelo Twenty private bungalows with views of the eucalyptus-lined Río de la Plata. Km 262, Ruta 21; 800/332-3442 or 598/4542-9000; fourseasons.com; doubles from $$.

EAT

Bodega y Granja Narbona Sprawling complex that includes a rural restaurant, a restored 1909 wine cellar stocked with local Tannat wines, and a dairy farm. Km 268, Ruta 21; 598/540-4778; puertocarmelo.com; doubles from $; lunch for two ✖✖✖.

El Drugstore Funky restaurant filled with brightly colored chairs and bold paintings, with two vintage cars for alfresco dining parked out front. 174 Portugal; 598/522-5241; lunch for two ✖✖.

SHOP

Almacén la Carlota Stylish general store stocked with papier-mâché toys, zinc bowls, and works by local painters. 150 Calle Real; 598/522-6717.

Oveja Negra Designer Silvia Sarti uses traditional looming techniques to make soft merino- wool clothing. 114 De la Playa; 598/522-1323; ovejanegraweb.com.

SÃO PAULO, BRAZIL

STAY

Hotel Fasano Über-cool red-brick hotel in São Paulo's stylish Jardins district, with 60 rooms, two restaurants, a spa, and a ground-level bar that draws the city's fashionable set. 88 Rua Vittorio Fasano; 55-11/ 3896-4000; fasano. com.br; doubles from $$$.

EAT

A Figueira Rubaiyat Steak house known for its legendary Saturday *feijoada* buffet, eaten in the shade of a hundred-year-old fig tree on the patio. 1738 Rua Haddock Lobo; 55-11/3087-1399; dinner for two ✖✖✖.

Bar Original Located in the bar-rich southern Moema district and pouring diminutive pulls of draft beer known as *chopp.* 137 Rua Graúna; 55-11/ 5093-9486; drinks for two ✖.

Bráz On Sundays, the city's *futebol* fans head to this upscale pizzeria for perfectly charred pies and Calabrian sausage bread. 125 Rua Graúna; 55-11/5561-1736; dinner for two ✖✖.

Dalva e Dito Casual, adobe-hued space that serves updated regional dishes such as *moqueca,* a seafood stew from the Afro-Brazilian Bahia region. 115 Rua Padre João Manuel; 55-11/3068-4444; lunch for two ✖✖✖.

Kinoshita White-hot restaurant that presents beguiling Japanese-Mediterranean cuisine with a tropical flourish. 405 Rua Jacques Félix; 55-11/3849-6940; dinner for two ✖✖✖✖.

Maní Husband-and-wife chefs Helena Rizzo and Daniel Redondo give Brazilian favorites the post-molecular-gastronomy treatment. 24 Rua dos Estudantes; 55-11/3277-4939; dinner for two ✖✖✖✖.

Mocotó Cult favorite for artisanal cachaça and home-style specialties. 100 Avda. Nossa Senhora do Loreto; 55-11/2951-3056; lunch for two ✖✖.

KEY

LODGING
Under $250 = $
$250–$499 = $$
$500–$749 = $$$
$750–$999 = $$$$
$1,000 + up = $$$$$

DINING
Under $25 = ✖
$25–$74 = ✖✖
$75–$149 = ✖✖✖
$150–$299 = ✖✖✖✖
$300 + up = ✖✖✖✖✖

ICELAND · St. Petersburg · COLONSAY · Copenhagen · Dublin · EAST SUSSEX · London · Ghent · Paris · Vienna · THE ALPS · Beaune · CAP FERRET · ITALIAN LAKES · ASTURIAS · Florence · Istanbul · SKOPELOS · SALENTO · Sintra · GOZO

EUROPE

ICELAND
STAY

Hótel Buðir Iceland's finest country-house hotel; many rooms overlook a glacier. Buðir Snæfellsnes; 011-354/ 435-6700; budir.is; doubles from $; dinner for two ✗✗✗.

101 Hotel Modern, art-focused property with 38 rooms. Reykjavík; 011-354/580-0101; 101hotel.is; doubles from $$.

EAT

Dill Museum cafeteria of the Alvar Aalto–designed Nordic House by day and cutting-edge dining destination at night.

5 Sturlugötu, Reykjavík; 011-354/552-1522; dinner for two ✗✗✗.

COLONSAY, SCOTLAND
STAY

Colonsay Hotel Nine-room Georgian inn built in 1750, with sloping slate roofs and spare furnishings. Colonsay Estate; Argyll; 44-1951/200-316; colonsayestate.co.uk; doubles from $.

SHOP

General Store Country market that specializes in regional delicacies such as

Laphroaig single-malt scotch. 44-1951/ 200-265; colonsay shop.net.

DO

Colonsay Guide Service Budding naturalist Kevin Byrne and others offer private guided walks across the island. 44-1951/200-320; colonsayguide.co.uk.

Colonsay House & Garden Stately 1772 residence nestled within 20 woodland acres, including Scotland's best rhododendron gardens. Colonsay Estate, Argyll; 44-1951/200-316.

DUBLIN
STAY

Merrion Hotel Four Georgian town houses with luxurious furnishings in the heart of the city center. 21 Upper Merrion St.; 353-1/603-0600; merrion hotel.com; doubles from $$.

EAT

Cake Café Cheerful bakery and café that serves up seasonal comfort food. 62 Pleasants Place; 353-1/478-9394; lunch for two ✗✗.

Winding Stair Restaurant and bookstore overlooking the river Liffey and Ha'Penny

Bridge. 40 Lower Ormond Quay; 353-1/872-7320; dinner for two ✗✗✗.

SHOP

Sheridan's Cheesemongers Irish farmhouse selections in a light-filled shop; try the St. Tola, an organic, raw, goat variety, and the washed-rind Gubbeen. 11 S. Anne St.; 353-1/679-3143.

DO

Archbishop Marsh's Library Opened in 1701, Ireland's first public library, located behind St. Patrick's Cathedral. St. Patrick's Close; 353-1/454-3511; marshlibrary.ie.

Buswell's Bar Local gathering spot with brocade wallpaper and a vast mahogany bar. Molesworth St.; 353-1/614-6500; drinks for two ✗.

Cobblestone Long and narrow, the rustic taproom doubles as a music venue. Smithfield Square; 353-1/872-1799; drinks for two ✗.

Dublin Writers Museum Displaying manuscripts and memorabilia from Samuel Beckett, James Joyce, and more. 18 Parnell Square; 353-1/872-2077; writersmuseum.com.

Long Room Library at Trinity College Collection of 200,000 rare books on an expanse of shelves that reaches from floor to ceiling. College Green; 353-1/896-1000; tcd.ie/library.

Stag's Head One of the oldest pubs in town, situated just outside the din of the Temple Bar neighborhood. 1 Dame Court; 353-1/679-3687; drinks for two ✗.

EAST SUSSEX, ENGLAND

DO

Dixter House & Gardens One of England's most beloved green spaces. The caretaker hosts a yearly series of intensive gardening courses. Northiam, East Sussex; 44-1797/252-878; greatdixter.co.uk; weeklong classes $$$$$ per person, including meals and lodging.

EAST END, LONDON

STAY

Boundary A 17-room boutique hotel, plus a French restaurant, brasserie, and rooftop bar for the stylish set. 2-4 Boundary St.; 44-20/7729-1051; theboundary.co.uk; doubles from $$.

Shoreditch House The Soho House group's eastern outpost, with a strictly enforced no-suits-or-ties dress code. Ebor St.; 44-20/7739-5040; shoreditchrooms.com; doubles from $.

SHOP

Aesop Fashionable apothecary that sells luxe plant-based products in a slick storefront. 5A Redchurch St.; 44-20/7613-3793.

Broadway Market Equal parts farmers' market and urban style show. From London Fields to Regent's Canal; broadwaymarket.co.uk.

Columbia Road Shops & Flower Market London's favorite Sunday-morning destination, where you can bargain for Dutch tulips, Kenyan lisianthus, and English roses. columbiaroad.info.

Hostem Men's wear store that appeals to both hedge fund managers and East London hipsters. 41-43 Redchurch St.; 44-20/7739-9733.

Old Truman Brewery Weekend market featuring almost 200 independent creative companies with a fiercely loyal local following. 91 Brick Lane; trumanbrewery.com.

Spitalfields Market Various food stalls and stores are open throughout the week. 16 Horner Square; visitspitalfields.com.

DO

Gallery in Redchurch Street Former hat factory turned contemporary exhibition space. 50 Redchurch St.; 44-20/7287-8408; galleryinredchurchstreet.com.

SINTRA, PORTUGAL

STAY

Hotel Tivoli Palácio de Setais Neoclassical property that has frescoed rooms, gilded antiques, and a roster of famous guests. 10 Avda. Barbosa do Bocage; 351/219-233-200; tivolihotels.com; doubles from $$, including breakfast.

DO

Parques de Sintra Tour landmarks and over-the-top estates built by royalty in the 18th and 19th centuries. 351/219-237-300; parquesdesintra.pt.

ASTURIAS, SPAIN

STAY

La Cepada Outfitted like a hotel three times the price, with quirky design, an innovative restaurant, and a panoramic view of the mountains. Avda. Contranquil, Canegas de Onís; 34/98-584-9445; hotellacepada.com; doubles from $.

EAT

Bar Rompeolas Ramshackle fish house that produces fried calamari, egg-battered monkfish, and basketball-size crabs cooked to perfection. San Roque, Tazones; 34/98-589-7013; dinner for two ✗✗.

Casa Gerardo Michelin-starred restaurant that serves *vanguardista* specialties such as razor clams in almond butter and an updated *fabada*. Km 8, Crta. AS-19, Prendes; 34/98-588-7797; dinner for two ✗✗✗.

Restaurante La Huertona Traditional Asturian dishes presented in a wood-paneled dining room overlooking the Picos de Europa national park. Crta. AS-19, Ribadesella; 34/98-588-7797; dinner for two ✗✗✗.

PARIS

STAY

Hôtel Amour Boldface-name patrons, cheeky décor, and

KEY

LODGING
Under $250 = **$**
$250–$499 = **$$**
$500–$749 = **$$$**
$750–$999 = **$$$$**
$1,000 + up = **$$$$$**

DINING
Under $25 = ✗
$25–$74 = ✗✗
$75–$149 = ✗✗✗
$150–$299 = ✗✗✗✗
$300 + up = ✗✗✗✗✗

a youthful vibe. 8 Rue Navarin, Ninth Arr.; 33-1/48-78-31-80; hotelamourparis.fr; doubles from $.

Hôtel Joyce Immaculate, affordable rooms with great beds and lots of light. 29 Rue la Bruyère, Ninth Arr.; 33-1/ 55-07-00-01; astotel.com; doubles from $$.

Hôtel Jules Boutique property whose lobby resembles a space-age library. 49-51 Rue La Fayette, Ninth Arr.; 33-1/42-85-05-44; hoteljules. com; doubles from $$.

EAT

À la Mère de Famille
Traditional *confiserie* full of froufrou offerings. 33-35 Rue du Faubourg Montmartre, Ninth Arr.; 33-1/47-70-83-69; pastries for two ✗.

Astier The down-at-the-heels interiors belie the fine French cooking; there are also more than 350 wine choices. 44 Rue Jean-Pierre Timbaud, 11th Arr.; 33-1/43-57-16-35; lunch for two ✗✗✗.

Le Bouchon et L'Assiette
Well-priced restaurant where food is painstakingly sourced and globally minded (scallops in ginger bouillon; velouté of garbanzo beans with *sobrasada* sausage). 127 Rue Cardinet, 17th Arr.; 33-1/42-27-83-93; dinner for two ✗✗✗.

Pain de Sucre *Boulangerie* equally renowned for its delicious breads and flaky pastries. 14 Rue Rambuteau, Third Arr.; 33-1/45-74-68-92; pastries for two ✗.

SHOP

Papiers Peints Art and

furniture gallery set in a former wallpaper store designed by Le Corbusier. 11 Rue de la Vieuville, 18th Arr.; 33-1/42-59-99-90.

Spree Store featuring a mix of European and Asian fashion labels casually strewn over Midcentury furniture. 16 Rue de la Vieuville, 18th Arr.; 33-1/42-23-41-40.

BEAUNE, FRANCE
EAT

Charcuterie Raillard
Unexpected delights such as *jambon persillé* more than make up for the unremarkable storefront. 4 Rue Monge; 33-3/80-22-23-04.

Fromagerie Hess The well-curated selection of artisanal cheeses and a knowledgeable staff mark this shop as Beaune's best. 7 Place Carnot; 33-3/80-24-73-51.

Le Jardin des Ramparts
The city's most ambitious restaurant, set in an old house with walls the color of olive oil. 10 Rue de l'Hôtel Dieu; 33-3/80-24-79-41; dinner for two ✗✗✗✗.

DO

Maison Joseph Drouhin
Tranquil cellar and tasting room that houses a sampling of the winery's latest bottlings, built above tunnels that extend below the city. 7 Rue d'Enfer; 33-3/80-24-68-88; drouhin.com.

CAP FERRET, FRANCE
STAY

Côté Sable On the bay side of the peninsula, the hotel

has soothing neutral-toned rooms and a Clarins spa. 37 Blvd. de la Plage; 33-5/57-17-07-27; cotesable.fr; doubles from $$.

Hôtel des Pins White, country-chic rooms with raw-wood accents. 23 Rue des Fauvettes; 33-5/56-60-60-11; hotel despins.eu; doubles from $.

La Co(o)rniche Philippe Starck's buzzy hotel, set in a split-timber former hunting lodge. 46 Ave. Louis Gaume, Pyla-sur-Mer; 33-5/56-22-72-11; lacoorniche-pyla.com; doubles from $$.

La Maison du Bassin Crisp interiors, nautical antiques, and sisal rugs scented with orange-flower water remain true to the area's shabby-chic spirit. 5 Rue des Pionniers; 33-5/56-60-60-63; lamaison dubassin.com; doubles from $.

EAT

Chez Boulan Laid-back spot where platters of oysters are served with lemon wedges and ice-cold white wine. 2 Rue des Palmiers; 33-5/56-60-77-32; lunch for two ✗✗.

Chez Hortense Known for its down-home charm and garlicky mussels; it's also the toughest reservation in town. Ave. Sémaphore; 33-5/56-60-62-56; dinner for two ✗✗✗.

Le Père Ouvrard Popular for its fish-based tapas during cocktail hour on high-season weekends. 4 Rue des Pionniers; no phone; snacks for two ✗✗.

Sail Fish The bottle-service set's go-to bistro, sushi bar, and occasional dance party venue. 38 Rue Bernaches;

33-5/56-60-44-84; dinner for two ✗✗✗.

THE ALPS
STAY

Hotel Alpenrose Centrally located, family-friendly accommodations a short walk from medieval Schattenburg Castle. 4-6 Rosengasse, Feldkirch, Austria; 43-5522/ 72175; hotel-alpenrose.net; doubles from $.

Hotel Post Classic country inn with modern flair, designed by architect Oskar Leo Kaufmann. 35 Brugg, Bezau, Austria; 43-5514/2207; hotelpostbezau. com; doubles from $$, including breakfast and dinner.

Hotel Therme Vals Modernist spa hotel built on the site of stunning natural thermal pools. Vals, Switzerland; 41-81/926-8080; therme-vals. ch; doubles from $$.

EAT

Confiserie Roggwiller
A 50-year-old shop known for its *Galler Biber* (a traditional gingerbread-style confection filled with almond paste). 17 Multergasse, St. Gallen, Switzerland; 41-71/222-5092; pastries for two ✗.

Engel Local favorite that specializes in hearty Austrian classics such as cured pork belly. 29 Platz, Bezau, Austria; 43-5514/2203; dinner for two ✗✗✗.

Schattenburg Castle Taste Austria's largest schnitzels in the 13th-century fortress's grand hall. 1 Burggasse, Feldkirch, Austria; 43-5522/ 71982; dinner for two ✗✗.

Ustria Casa da Luzi Swiss chef Reto Derung's focus at this tavern is on ultra-fresh ingredients. 7115 Surcasti, Uors, Switzerland; 41-81/931-1010; dinner for two ✗✗✗.

SHOP

Devich Shoe store that sells handmade, surprisingly chic wooden clogs. 186 Ellenbogen, Bezau, Austria; 43-5514/2236.

Käsekeller Minimalist cheese co-op in a building designed by Oskar Leo Kaufman. 423 Zeihenbühl, Lingenau, Austria; 43-5513/42870.

Textil Hirschbül Here, you'll find one-of-a-kind gifts, from unique schnapps glasses to knitted children's clothing. 2 Hof, Schwarzenberg, Austria; 43-5512/2994.

DO

Abbey of St. Gall Home to more than 2,100 medieval and Renaissance manuscripts. 6A Klosterhof, St. Gallen, Switzerland; 41-71/227-3416.

Kunsthaus Bregenz Contemporary art museum set in a glass-and-steel building. Karl-Tizian-Platz, Bregenz, Austria; 43-574/485-940.

GHENT, BELGIUM
STAY

Chambreplus Three spacious bedrooms in the heart of the city. The husband-and-wife owners run a cooking school in the cellar. 31 Hoogpoort; 32-9/225-3775; chambreplus.be; doubles from $.

SHOP

Eva Bos Custom vintage-style jackets and dresses and tailored Audrey Hepburn-inspired evening gowns. 66 Vlaanderenstraat; 32/495-496-164.

Het Oorcussen Edgy boutique showcasing pieces by Belgian designers, including Ann Demeulemeester and Dries Van Noten. 7 Vrijdagmarkt; 32-9/233-0765.

Obius Clothing store that offers Martin Margiela sweaters and Veronique Branquinho heels. 4 Meerseniersstraat; 32-9/233-8269.

DO

Design Museum Gent Re-creations of 18th-century domestic life housed in a mansion from the same era. 5 Jan Breydelstraat; 32-9/267-9999; design.museum.gent.be.

St. Bavo Cathedral Gothic landmark that holds Jan van Eyck's 15th-century altarpiece *Adoration of the Mystic Lamb.* St. Bavo Square; 32-9/269-2045; sintbaafskathedraal-gent.be.

Stedelijk Museum voor Actuele Kunst (S.M.A.K.) Museum featuring late-20th-century works. Citadelpark; 32-9/240-7601; smak.be.

ITALIAN LAKES
STAY

Grand Hotel a Villa Feltrinelli World War II residence of Benito Mussolini, with more than 1,000 19th-century paintings and antiques. 38-40 Via Rimembranza, Gargnano; 39-0365/798-000; villafeltrinelli.com; doubles from $$$$$.

Relais Regina Teodolinda Six simple but stylish suites in an 1800's villa with a 200-year-old garden. 58 Via Vecchia Regina, Laglio; 39-031/400-031; relaisreginateodolina.it; doubles from $$.

Villa Arcadio Hotel & Resort White wooden rafters, stone walls, and present-day art in a 13th-century former convent. 2 Via Palazzina, Salò; 39-0365/42281; hotelvillaarcadio.it; doubles from $$.

Villa Crespi Moorish-style estate with four-poster beds, damask draperies, and a Michelin-starred restaurant. 18 Via G. Fava, Orta San Giulio; 39-0322/911-902; villacrespi.it; doubles from $$$; dinner for two ✗✗✗✗.

Villa d'Este Along with 152 opulent rooms, the property has 25 acres of parkland, three restaurants, tennis courts, and a newly renovated spa. 40 Via Regina, Cernobbio; 39-031/3481; villadeste.it; doubles from $$$.

EAT

Navedano Seafood is served on a flower-fringed veranda at this 19th-century windmill. Via Giuseppe Velzi, Como; 39-031/308-080; dinner for two ✗✗✗✗.

Vassalli Pasticcerie Salò's foremost confectioner. 84/86 Via S. Carlo, Salò; 39-0365/20752; pastries for two ✗.

SHOP

Guerrieri Rizzardi Azienda Agricola A 550-year-old estate whose wine production is personally overseen by Countess Maria Cristina Rizzardi. 4 Via Verdi, Bardolino; 39-045/721-0028; tours by appointment.

SALENTO, ITALY
STAY

Masseria Bernardini Seven suites with streamlined kitchens and artwork and fragrant rosemary and lavender gardens. Contrada Agnano, Nardò; 39-02/5843-1058; masseriabernardini.com; suites from $$.

Suite 68 Hip B&B in a private palazzo, located around the corner from the Awaiting Table Cookery School. 7 Via Leonardo Prato, Lecce; 39-0832/303-506; kalekora.it; doubles from $.

EAT

Alle due Corti Family-run place where the menu is written in dialect (and English). 1 Corte dei Guigni, Lecce; 39-0832/242-223; dinner for two ✗✗.

Antica Pasticceria G. Portaluri Old-timey bakery and pastry shop near the town square. 18 Via Alcide de Gasperi, Maglie; 39-0380/356-5236; pastries for two ✗.

SHOP

La Cartapesta di Claudio Riso Showroom specializing in detailed papier-mâché figurines that depict rural life.

KEY

LODGING
Under $250 = **$**
$250–$499 = **$$**
$500–$749 = **$$$**
$750–$999 = **$$$$**
$1,000 + up = **$$$$$**

DINING
Under $25 = ✗
$25–$74 = ✗✗
$75–$149 = ✗✗✗
$150–$299 = ✗✗✗✗
$300 + up = ✗✗✗✗✗

27 Via Vittorio Emanuele, Lecce; 39-0832/243-410; cartapestariso.it.

Terrarossa Arte Salentina Quirky crafts made by native Salentine artisans. 28 Piazza Salandra, Nardò; 39-0833/572-685; terrarossasalento.it.

DO

Awaiting Table Cookery School You can learn to make fresh *burrata* on the patio of an 18th-century castle at this well-run culinary school. Lecce; awaitingtablecookery school.com; February– December; classes from $$.

FLORENCE

STAY

Gallery Hotel Art Design hotel with photography and art at every turn as well as rooms outfitted with Asian woods and Tuscan stones. 5 Vicolo dell'Oro; 39-055/2726-4000; gallery hotelart.com; doubles from $$.

J.K. Place Firenze Twenty rooms with thoughtful residential touches. 7 Piazza Santa Maria Novella; 39-055/ 264-5181; jkplace.com; doubles from $$.

DO

Art Bar Creative types flock to this pocket-size bar for its fresh cocktails. 4R Via del Moro; 39-055/287-661; drinks for two ✗.

Brancolini Grimaldi Bookstore and gallery that shows edgy international photography. 12R Vicolo dell'Oro; 39-055/239-6263; brancolinigrimaldi.com.

FOR Gallery Photography and video showroom dedicated to cutting-edge talent. 45R Via dei Fossi; 39-055/ 215-457; forgallery.it.

Galleria Biagiotti American Carole Biagiotti represents the likes of Italian street painter Ericailcane, known for his whimsical fauna drawings. 39R Via delle Belle Donne; 39-055/214-757; biagiotti.com.

La Strozzina Themed exhibitions by young area talents. Piazza Strozzi; 39-055/ 277-6461; strozzina.org.

Museo Marino Marini Various sculptures by mid-20th-century Tuscan artist Marino Marini, famous for his stylized equestrian works. Piazza San Pancrazio; 39-055/219-432; museomarinomarini.it.

Poggiali e Forconi Hosts impressive rotating shows that have included Patti Smith and David LaChapelle. 35A Via della Scala; 39-055/287-748; poggialieforconi.it.

Sangallo Art Station Gallery and café displaying pieces by rising and established names. 5R Via Fra Giovanni Angelico; 39-055/051-7157; sangallo artstation.it.

COPENHAGEN

STAY

Nimb Hotel Thirteen rooms with oiled-oak floors, silver wallpaper, and Philippe Starck bathtubs. 5 Bernstorffsgade; 45/8870-0000; tivoli.dk; doubles from $$, including breakfast.

Tivoli Hotel Accommodations inspired by the amusement park, with circus-striped

headboards and staffers in harlequin attire. 2 Arni Magnussons Gade; 45/8870-0000; tivolihotel.com; doubles from $.

EAT

Nimb Brasserie Seasonal, locally sourced Scandinavian restaurant has three open kitchens and offers views of Tivoli Gardens. Nimb Hotel, 5 Bernstorffsgade; 45/8870-0000; dinner for two ✗✗.

Nimb Herman Michelin-starred restaurant serving international cuisine within the Nimb complex. 5 Bernstorffsgade; 45/8870-0000; dinner for two ✗✗✗✗.

DO

Tivoli Gardens A charmingly compact amusement park that dates to 1843 and is a birthplace of Danish Modern design. 3 Vesterbrogade; 45/3315-1001; tivoli.dk.

VIENNA

STAY

Hotel Hollmann Beletage Near St. Stephen's Cathedral, 25 contemporary rooms (orange accents; espresso-hued furniture; steel-wire chairs). 6 Köllnerhofgasse; 43-1/961-1960; hollmann-beletage.at; doubles from $.

EAT

Café Central An 1876 tradition-minded coffeehouse located in the shop-filled Palais Ferstel complex. 17 Herrengasse; 43-1/533-3764; coffee for two ✗.

Café Korb Old Town coffeehouse with marble-topped tables, bentwood chairs,

and formally clad waiters. 9 Brandstätte; 43-1/533-7215; coffee for two ✗.

Café Landtmann Glass-enclosed winter garden and wood-paneled interior lit by ornate brass chandeliers. 4 Dr.-Karl-Lueger-Ring; 43-1/ 2410-0100; coffee for two ✗.

Café Museum Onetime haunt of Egon Schiele, originally designed by architect Adolf Loos. 7 Operngasse; 43-1/ 2410-0620; coffee for two ✗.

Café Ritter Opened in 1867 in a former aristocratic palace. 73 Mariahilferstrasse; 43-1/ 587-8238; coffee for two ✗.

Café Weimar Classic meeting spot in Vienna's Ninth district. 68 Währingerstrasse; 43-1/ 317-1206; coffee for two ✗.

SKOPELOS, GREECE

STAY

Adrina Beach Hotel Serene pastel-colored rooms facing the pine-studded coastline. Panormos; 34-24240/23371; adrina.gr; doubles from $.

Adrina Resort & Spa New sister resort to Adrina Beach Hotel; 16 terraced rooms and 22 villas overlook the azure Aegean. Panormos; 30-24240/ 23371; theresort.gr; doubles from $.

EAT

Perivoli Garden-side restaurant serving Greek specialties (grilled lamb; pork with prunes). Skopelos Town; 30-24240/23758; dinner for two ✗✗.

DO

Mercurius Bar & Café Open-air watering hole

where you can listen to live *rebetika* music. Skopelos Town; 30-24240/24593; drinks for two ✗.

Ouzeri Anatoli Revelers drink ouzo while the owner and his sons treat the audience to an impromptu performance. Skopelos Town; 30-24240/22851; drinks for two ✗✗.

National Marine Park On the neighboring island of Alonnisos, protected turquoise waters provide shelter for the Mediterranean monk seal. Alonnisos; 30-24240/66378; alonissos-park.gr.

GOZO, MALTA
STAY

Hotel Ta' Cenc & Spa Nestled in a 370-acre nature preserve, 85 stone bungalows that look out on the sea. Cenc St., Sannat; 356-22/191-000; tacenchotel.com; doubles from $$.

St. Augustine Convent Atmospheric 15th-century building perched on a hill above Victoria's mazelike streets and Baroque town houses. St. Augustine Square, Victoria; 356/2155-6060; doubles from $.

EAT

Ta' Frenc Restaurant Restored farmhouse with tables set in a fragrant organic herb garden. Ghajn Damma St., Xaghra; 356-21/553-888; dinner for two ✗✗✗.

Tapie's Bar Hole-in-the-wall local hangout known for its people-watching and excellent *pastizzi* (ricotta-filled pastries). St. Francis Square, Victoria; lunch for two ✗.

SHOP

Gozo Glass Handblown objets d'art made from patterned glass. Ta Dbiegi Crafts Village, Gharb; 356-21/561-974.

ISTANBUL
STAY

Çirağan Palace Kempinski Imperial Ottoman Palace with 22 suites decked out in silk fabrics, rich wood paneling, and private terraces. 32 Çirağan Cad., Beşiktaş; 90-212/326-4646; kempinski.com; doubles from $$.

EAT

Asitane Restaurant that features an extensive menu of painstakingly researched former sultans' fare. 6 Kariye Camii Sk., Edirnekapi; 90-212/635-7997; dinner for two ✗✗✗.

Cercis Murat Konaği Where well-heeled Turks feast on a fusion of Turco-Arabic dishes from the southeastern city of Mardin. 22 Yazmaci Tahir Sk., Suadiye; 90-216/410-9222; dinner for two ✗✗.

Çiya Sofrasi Pilgrimage site for global foodies, thanks to Musa Dagdeviren's acclaimed folk-inspired creations. 43 Güneşlibahçe Sk., Kadiköy; 90-216/330-3190; dinner for two ✗✗.

Kiva Han Ethnic Anatolian food (Japanese plums stuffed with ground meat; bulgur dumplings), plus a picturesque view. 4 Galata Tower Square, Beyoğlu; 90-212/292-9898; dinner for two ✗✗.

Zarifi Pays tribute to the cuisines of the city's old minorities, including Greeks, Armenians, and Sephardic Jews. 13 Çukurluçeşme Sk., Beyoğlu; 90-212/293-5480; dinner for two ✗✗.

ST. PETERSBURG
STAY

Antique Hotel Rachmaninov Hub for creative types that occupies two sprawling floors of a Soviet-era apartment building. 5 Kazanskaya Ul.; 7-812/571-7618; hotel rachmaninov.com; doubles from $.

Grand Hotel Europe Gilded 1875 landmark overlooking Mikhailovsky Palace, once frequented by Dostoyevsky. 1/7 Mikhailovskaya Ul.; 7-812/329-6888; grandhotel europe.com; doubles from $$.

EAT

Probka Groundbreaking modern Italian cuisine in a wine-bar setting. 5 Ul. Belinskogo; 7-812/273-4904; dinner for two ✗✗✗.

SHOP

Generator Nastroenia Store specializing in tongue-in-cheek gifts, including journals that reinterpret Soviet-era symbols. 7 Karavannaya Ul.; 7-812/314-5351; generator-nastroenia.ru.

LowFat Studio Open-door workshop and showroom for the eco-friendly fashion line of the same name. 17 Vilensky Per.; 7-812/579-2639; lowfatwear.com.

Lyyk Design Market Showroom for Russian fashion designers' avant-garde looks. 74 Nab. Kanala Griboyedova; 7-812/939-6051; lyyk.ru.

DO

Concert Hall at the Mariinsky Theatre The historic venue's newer performance space for opera, theatrical productions, and more. 37 Ul. Dekabristov; 7-812/326-4141; mariinsky.ru.

Erarta Museum set in a 20th-century columned building that showcases up-and-coming Russian talent. 2, 29-ya Liniya; 7-812/324-0809; erarta.com.

Loft Project Etagi Industrial-chic exhibition space housed in a former bread factory. 74 Ligovsky Prospekt; 7-812/458-5005; loftprojetetagi.ru.

Novy Museum Specializes in paintings and sculptures from genre-defining artists. 29, 6-ya Liniya; 7-812/323-5090; novymuseum.ru.

Rosphoto Eclectic photography gallery that displays international and local works. 35 Bolshaya Morskaya Ul.; 7-812/314-1214; rosphoto.org.

KEY

LODGING
Under $250 = $
$250–$499 = $$
$500–$749 = $$$
$750–$999 = $$$$
$1,000 + up = $$$$$

DINING
Under $25 = ✗
$25–$74 = ✗✗
$75–$149 = ✗✗✗
$150–$299 = ✗✗✗✗
$300 + up = ✗✗✗✗✗

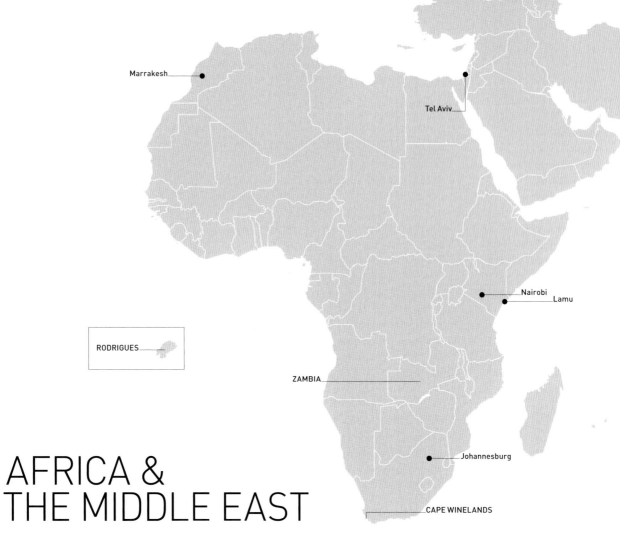

Marrakesh

Tel Aviv

Nairobi
Lamu

RODRIGUES

ZAMBIA

Johannesburg

CAPE WINELANDS

AFRICA &
THE MIDDLE EAST

STAY

Royal Mansour Marrakech
Extravagant resort owned by
the king of Morocco. Rue Abou
Abbas El Sebti; 212-5/2980-
8080; royalmansour.com;
*riad*s from $$$$$.

EAT

Al Baraka Informal counters
for house-made *tagines*
and wood-fired flatbreads.
Rte. 24 Commune Annakhil,
Sidi Youseff Ben Ali; lunch
for two ✗✗.

Chez Lamine Haj Mostapha
N'Guyer's no-frills lamb joint
in the Guéliz neighborhood.
19 Ibn Aicha St.; 212-524/
431-164; lunch for two ✗.

Dar Moha *Nouvelle marocaine*
fare served in Pierre Balmain's
former *riad*. 81 Rue Dar el Bacha;
212-524/386-264; dinner for
two ✗✗✗.

Haj Mostapha A street stall
known for its *mechoui* (roasted
lamb); sister to Chez Lamine.
Souk Quessabine, off Jamaâ El
Fna square; lunch for two ✗.

Hassan *Merguez* sausages are
devoured at a tin counter
thronged by big families. Stall
no. 32, Jamaâ El Fna square;
snacks for two ✗.

Le Grande Table Ornate jewel
box of a restaurant, overseen
by Yannick Alléno. Rue Abou
Abbas El Sebti; 212-529/808-
080; dinner for two ✗✗✗✗✗.

DO

Café de France Roof-terrace
tables offer the best vantage
of the city. Jamaâ El Fna
square; 212-524/442-319; tea
for two ✗.

STAY

Lamu House Two Swahili
houses with 10 traditional
guest rooms. Lamu Old Town;
254/735-874-428; lamuhouse.
com; doubles from $$.

Peponi Hotel Whitewashed
rooms with ocean views. The
veranda is a popular jet-set
watering hole. Shela Village;
254/208-023-655; peponi-
lamu.com; doubles from $$.

EAT

Olympic Unpretentious café
offering Old Town specialties
(tandoori snapper, lime pickle;
biryani). Lamu Town; 254/728-
667-692; dinner for two ✗.

DO

Petley's Inn Convivial rooftop
bar. Lamu Town; 254/724-251-
955; drinks for two ✗.

STAY

Hogmead The patrician
country-house hotel has
wood-paneled soaking tubs
and leather club chairs.
Kikenni Rd., Langata;
254/712-579-999; doubles
from $$$.

Nairobi Tented Camp
An eco-chic safari camp.
Nairobi National Park; 254/
771-977-404; nairobitented
camp.com; doubles from
$$$$, including meals.
Tribe Hotel Urbane building
where hipsters and dignitaries
mingle. Limuru Rd., Gigiri;
254/207-200-000; tribe-hotel.
com; doubles from $$$.
EAT
Seven Seafood & Grill
White-on-white space that
dishes up fresh fish flown
in from the coast. ABC Place,
Waiyaki Way; 254/737-776-
677; dinner for two XX.
Talisman Chef Marcus
Mitchell's eclectic gastropub,
set in a 1920's bungalow. 320
Ngong Rd., Karen; 254/203-
883-213; dinner for two XX.

ZAMBIA
STAY
**Bushcamp Company
Zungulila** Four thatched-roof
dwellings with canopy beds
and plunge pools. 260-216/
246-041; bushcampcompany.
com; from $$ per person,
all-inclusive.
Remote Africa Safaris
Authentic bush experience
reminiscent of a private
homestay. 260-216/246-185;
remoteafrica.com; from $$$
per person, all-inclusive.
**Sanctuary Retreats Zebra
Plains** Four luxe tents in the
wildlife-rich South Luangwa
National Park. 44-20/7190-7728;
sanctuaryretreats.com; from
$$$ per person, all-inclusive.
Sanctuary Sussi & Chuma
Elegant adventure camp near

Victoria Falls. 44-20/7190-7728;
sanctuaryretreats.com; from
$$$ per person, all-inclusive.
Wilderness Safaris Toka Leya
Pine walkways link 12 canvas
tents overlooking the Zambezi
River. wilderness-safaris.com;
from $$$ per person,
all-inclusive.

JOHANNESBURG,
SOUTH AFRICA
STAY
**Saxon Boutique Hotel, Villas
& Spa** Set on six acres of
landscaped gardens, where
Nelson Mandela completed
Long Walk to Freedom. 36 Saxon
Rd.; 27-11/292-6000; thesaxon.
com; doubles from $$$$$.
EAT
Attic Antiques-filled spot
serving a varied menu
inspired by the travels of its
globe-trotting owners. Fourth
Ave. and 10th St.; 27-11/880-
6102; dinner for two XX.
Moemas Pocket-size café and
bakery with inventive salads
and photo-ready sweets. Third
Ave. at Seventh Ave.; 27-11/788-
7725; lunch for two X.
SHOP
Arts on Main Shopping and
gallery complex that lures
top local artists. 264 Fox St.;
artsonmain.co.za.
44 Stanley Boutique shops
showcasing creative young
talent. 44 Stanley Ave.; 27-11/
482-4444; 44stanley.co.za.
DO
Apartheid Museum
Exhibitions offer an invaluable
primer on South Africa's
historic race divisions.
Northern Pkwy. at Gold Reef

Rd.; 27-11/309-4700;
apartheidmuseum.org.
Circa on Jellicoe
Contemporary South African
art in a striking space.
2 Jellicoe Ave.; 27-11/788-
4805; circaonjellicoe.co.za.

CAPE WINELANDS,
SOUTH AFRICA
STAY
Babylonstoren Working guest
farm with 14 minimalist
cottages modeled on Boer
residences. Klapmuts/
Simondium Rd., Franschhoek
Valley; 27-21/863-3852;
babylonstoren.com; doubles
from $$$.
Delaire Graff Lodges & Spa
A 55-acre property with
interiors conceived by London
designer David Collins.
Helshoogte Pass, Stellenbosch;
27-21/885-8160; delaire.co.za;
doubles from $$$$$.
EAT
La Motte A 420-acre estate
with a world-class restaurant.
R45, Main Rd., Franschhoek
Valley; 27-21/876-8800; lunch
for two XX.

TEL AVIV
STAY
Gordon Hotel Streamlined
waterfront boutique hotel
with an on-site Mediterranean
bistro. 2 Gordon St.; 972-3/
520-6100; gordontlv.com;
doubles from $$.
SHOP
Aqua Creations Showroom
Israeli artist Ayala Serfaty's
unique furniture shop.
319 Hayarkon St.; 972-3/515-
1222; aquagallery.com.

Made in TLV In a former train
station, design books, tabletop
items, and photographs.
Old Station; 972-3/510-4333;
madeintlv.com.
Retro TLV A spacious boutique
filled with restored furniture
by Midcentury masters.
123 Yehuda HaLevy; 972-3/
685-0663; retro-tlv.com.
Talents Design Works by
up-and-coming Israeli artists.
34 Nachmani St.; 972-3/685-
0666; talentsdesign.com.

RODRIGUES, MAURITIUS
STAY
Mourouk Ebony Hotel
Waterfront Creole-style
retreat; don't miss the
twice-weekly *sega tambour*
performance. 011-230/832-
3351; mouroukebonyhotel.
com; doubles from $.
EAT
Coralie la Diffe'rence A must
for freshly caught seafood.
Countour Oblasse; 011-230/
832-1071; dinner for two XX.
DO
**François Leguat Tortoise
& Cave Reserve**
Protected park for resident
Aldabra species. tortoises
cavereserve-rodrigues.com.

KEY

LODGING
Under $250 = $
$250–$499 = $$
$500–$749 = $$$
$750–$999 = $$$$
$1,000 + up = $$$$$

DINING
Under $25 = X
$25–$74 = XX
$75–$149 = XXX
$150–$299 = XXXX
$300 + up = XXXXX

GOBI DESERT

Tokyo

Beijing

Shanghai
Hangzhou

Lhasa

Hong Kong

Mumbai

Hyderabad

Bangkok

VIETNAM

KOH KONG

Puducherry

CON DAO

KO SAMUI

PENANG

SINGAPORE

BALI

ROTE

ASIA

TOKYO

STAY

Peninsula Tokyo 314 rooms with warm wood touches and Imperial Palace views. 1-8-1 Yurakucho, Chiyoda-ku; 866/382-8388; peninsula.com; doubles from $$$.

EAT

Kondo Tempura restaurant in the Ginza district. Sakaguchi Bldg., ninth floor, 5-5-13 Ginza, Chuo-ku; 81-3/5568-0923; dinner for two ✖✖✖✖.

Owan Intimate counter serving an affordable *omakase*. Okada

Bldg., 2-26-7 Ikejiri, Setagaya-ku; 81-3/5486-3844; dinner for two ✖✖✖✖.

Restaurant Kinoshita Upscale Francophile cooking. Estate Bldg., 3-37-1 Yoyogi, Shibuya-ku; 81-3/3376-5336; dinner for two ✖✖✖.

Rokukakutei Go here for *kushiage* (fried, skewered morsels). Kojun Bldg., fourth floor, 6-8-7 Ginza, Chuo-ku; 81-3/5537-6008; dinner for two ✖✖✖✖✖.

Sushi Takumi Okabe Superior sushi in an unprepossessing

space. 5-13-14 Shirokanedai, Minato-ku; 81-3/5420-0141; dinner for two ✖✖✖✖✖.

SHOP

Takashimaya Department store with a food hall of global gourmet edibles. 2-4-1 Nihonbashi, Chuo-ku; 81-3/3211-4111.

HONG KONG

STAY

Hullett House Hotel Ten suites in the 1881 former maritime police headquarters. 2A Canton Rd., Tsim Sha Tsui;

852/3988-0000; hulletthouse. com; doubles from $$$.

Ritz-Carlton Luxe comforts at the world's tallest hotel. 1 Austin Rd. W., West Kowloon; 800/241-3333; ritzcarlton. com; doubles from $$$.

EAT

Nanhai No. 1 Cantonese food in a harbor-facing dining room. iSquare, 30th floor, 63 Nathan Rd., Tsim Sha Tsui; 852/2487-3688; dinner for two ✖✖✖.

SHOP

Ecols Green-minded space that carries items made from

reused materials. The One, Level 6, 100 Nathan Rd., Tsim Sha Tsui; 852/3106-4918.

Forest Bird Modern clothing and jewelry by European and Japanese labels. 39 Staunton St., Central; 852/2810-1166.

Homeless Whimsical home-goods store. 28 Gough St., Central; 852/2851-1160.

Kotur Intricate clutches in silk brocade, snakeskin, and shell are the draw. Ground floor, 60 Po Hing Fong, Sheung Wan; 852/2815-8708.

Moustache Pick up 1960's-inspired knit sweaters and pajamas at this men's wear emporium. 31 Aberdeen St., Sheung Wan; 852/2541-1955.

DO

Sugar Alfresco bar on the East Hotel's 32nd floor. 29 Taikoo Shing Rd., Island East; 852/3968-3738; drinks for two ✘.

SHANGHAI
STAY

Park Hyatt Minimalist rooms on the upper floors of a tower overlooking the city and the Huangpu River. 100 Century Ave., Pudong; 877/875-4658; park.hyatt.com; doubles from $$.

Ritz-Carlton Shanghai Pudong The standard in modern swank, with copper-clad bathtubs and a sky-high bar. 8 Century Ave., Pudong; 800/241-3333; ritzcarlton.com; doubles from $$$.

Waterhouse at South Bund Quirky hotel inside a concrete and steel-beamed 1930's warehouse. 1-3 Maojiayuan Rd., Shiliupu; 800/337-4685; waterhouseshanghai.com; doubles from $.

EAT

Jia Jia Tang Bao Cafeteria-style hangout known for *xiao long bao* (soup dumplings). 90 Huanghe Rd., Huangpu; 86-21/6327-6878; lunch for two ✘.

Shouning Road Night Food Market Alley lined with street grills and late-night snackers. Luwan; dinner for two ✘.

DO

El Cóctel Trendy bar in the French Concession. 47 Yongfu Rd., Xuhui; 86-21/6433-6511; drinks for two ✘.

HANGZHOU, CHINA
STAY

Amanfayun Surrounded by bamboo groves, 42 suites housed in brick-and-timber dwellings. 22 Fayun Nong; 800/477-9180; amanresorts.com; doubles from $$$.

Banyan Tree Villas styled with Chinese antiques; abuts the Xixi National Wetland Park. 21 Zijingang Rd.; 800/591-0439; banyantree.com; doubles from $$$.

Four Seasons Hotel Hangzhou at West Lake Graceful green spaces give way to 78 guest rooms and three villas. 5 Lingyin Rd.; 800/819-5053; fourseasons.com; doubles from $$.

SHOP

Qi Family Hospitable tea stall that lets you sample before you buy. No. 19, Longjing Village; 86-571/8799-9413.

DO

Guo's Villa Courtyard where locals gather for tea.

28 Yanggong Causeway; 86-571/8798-6026; tea for two ✘.

Huqingyu Tang A 140-year-old medicine shop that specializes in ancient remedies. 95 Dajing Lane; 86-571/8781-5209.

Lingyin Temple Striking Buddhist prayer grounds. 1 Fayun Rd.; 86-571/8796-8665; lingyinsi.org.

Old Dragon Well Imperial Tea Garden Historic plantation favored by emperors. 148 Lion's Hill; 86-571/8799-7711.

BEIJING
STAY

China World Summit Wing Taking up the top 18 floors of Beijing's tallest building, 278 serene rooms with vistas. 1 Jianguomenwai Ave., China World Trade Center; 866/565-5050; shangri-la.com; doubles from $$.

Opposite House Slick, light-filled boutique hotel near Sanlitun nightlife. 11 Sanlitun Rd., Bldg. 1; 86-10/6417-6688; theoppositehouse.com; doubles from $$.

DO

Apothecary Creative cocktails and house-made mixers. Nali Patio, third floor, D302, 81 Sanlitun Bei Rd.; 86-10/5208-6040; drinks for two ✘.

D.Lounge Brick-walled gallery that morphs into a nighttime hot spot. Courtyard 4, Gongti Bei Lu; 86-10/6593-7710; drinks for two ✘✘.

Ichikura Japanese whiskey den stocked with rare varieties. 36 Dongsanhuan Bei Lu; 86-10/6507-1107; drinks for two ✘.

KEY

LODGING
Under $250 = $
$250–$499 = $$
$500–$749 = $$$
$750–$999 = $$$$
$1,000 + up = $$$$$

DINING
Under $25 = ✘
$25–$74 = ✘✘
$75–$149 = ✘✘✘
$150–$299 = ✘✘✘✘
$300 + up = ✘✘✘✘✘

Xiu Fashionistas flock to this rooftop bar for live music and Asian tapas. Beijing Yintai Centre, Bldg. 8, sixth floor, 2 Jianguomenwai Ave.; 86-10/8567-1108; drinks for two ✘.

SINGAPORE
STAY

Marina Bay Sands Supersized resort with 2,561 rooms, seven restaurants, and a 500-foot-long infinity pool. 10 Bayfront Ave.; 65/6688-8868; marinabaysands.com; doubles from $$.

EAT

Lavender Street Hawker Centre Famous for *assam laksa* (noodle soup). 195 Lavender St; lunch for two ✘.

DO

Asian Civilisations Museum Heritage displays set in a riverside colonial-era structure. 1 Empress Place; 65/6332-7798; acm.org.sg.

Peranakan Museum Highlights the mix of immigrant cultures. 39 Armenian St.; 65/6332-7591; peranakanmuseum.sg.

BANGKOK
STAY

Asadang Channels Old Bangkok in a 19th-century

mansion furnished with antiques. 94 Asadang Rd.; 66-2/622-2239; theasadang.com; doubles from $.

EAT

Gaggan A disciple of Ferran Adrià presents updated Indian classics in a white dining room. 68/1 Soi Langsuan; 66-2/652-1700; dinner for two ✗✗✗.

Gedhawa Specializing in northern Thailand's subtle, herb-scented cuisine. 24 Soi 35, Sukhumvit Rd.; 66-2/662-0501; dinner for two ✗.

Or Tor Kor Market Stalls filled with exotic produce and street-food staples (curries; fish dumplings). Thanon Kamphaengphet; snacks for two ✗.

Phuket Town Shop-house restaurant with a focus on southern Thai standouts. 160/8 Soi 55, Sukhumvit Rd.; 66-2/714-9402; dinner for two ✗✗.

Soul Food Mahanakorn Thai comfort dishes made with organic ingredients. 56/10 Soi 55, Sukhumvit Rd.; 66-2/714-7708; dinner for two ✗✗.

Sra Bua by Kiin Kiin Inventive local cuisine with a Danish molecular twist. Siam Kempinski Hotel, 991/9 Rama I Rd.; 66-2/162-9000; dinner for two ✗✗✗✗.

KOH KONG, CAMBODIA
STAY

Chi Phat Community-based tourism site: eight homestays and 11 guesthouses. 855-92/720-925; wildlifealliance.org; $ per person.

4 Rivers Floating Lodge Along the Tatai River, plush tents on recycled-wood decks. Koh Andet Island, Tatai Village; eco lodges.asia; doubles from $.

Rainbow Lodge Family-friendly eco-retreat with seven solar-powered, thatched-roof bungalows. Tatai; 855-99/744321; rainbowlodgecambodia.com; doubles from $, including meals.

HYDERABAD, INDIA
STAY

The Park Sleek hotel overlooking the lake in the city center. 22 Raj Bhawan Rd.; 91-40/2345-6789; thepark hotels.com; doubles from $$.

Taj Banjara A 122-room retreat near Hyderabad's shopping and business districts. Rd. No. 1, Banjara Hills; 866/969-1825; tajhotels.com; doubles from $.

Taj Falaknuma Palace Opulent onetime residence of the nizam. Engine Bowli, Falaknuma; 866/969-1825; tajhotels.com; doubles from $$$.

DO

Ramoji Film City Watch movies being made at the world's largest facility. 91-84/1524-6555; ramojifilmcity.com.

MUMBAI
STAY

Taj Mahal Palace Book one of the 285 rooms in the Palace Wing, which have glass-walled bathrooms. Apollo Bunder; 866/969-1825; tajhotels.com; doubles from $$$.

EAT

Koh by Ian Kittichai Haute contemporary Thai restaurant in the InterContinental Marine Drive hotel. 135 Marine Dr.; 91-22/3987-9999; dinner for two ✗✗✗.

SHOP

Bandit Queen Home-goods emporium selling handmade linens. 130 Dinshaw Petit Lane; 91-22/2294-8752.

Bungalow 8 Cutting-edge clothing by an Yves Saint Laurent vet. Grants Bldg., 17 Arthur Bunder Rd.; 91-22/2281-9880.

Neemrana Boutique that stocks cotton saris, blouses, and robes. 6 Purshotam Bldg., New Queen's Rd.; 91-22/2361-4436.

DO

Gallery BMB The focus here is on burgeoning Indian sculptors and painters. Queens Mansion, G. T. Marg; 91-22/6171-5757; gallerybmb.com.

Gallery Maskara Cavernous former warehouse showing groundbreaking installations. 6/7 Third Pasta Lane; 91-22/2202-3056; gallerymaskara.com.

Volte New-media video and art installations in a seafront space. 2/19 Kamal Mansion, Arthur Bunder Rd.; 91-22/2204-1220; volte.in.

PUDUCHERRY, INDIA
STAY

Hôtel De l'Orient Airy rooms in a charming 18th-century mansion. 17 Rue Romain Rolland; 91-413/234-3067; neemranahotels.com; doubles from $.

Le Dupleix Heritage hotel housed in a former mayor's villa. 5 Rue De La Caserne; 91-413/222-6999; sarovar hotels.com; doubles from $.

EAT

Le Café Seafront spot for fresh lime sodas, salads, and sandwiches. Goubert Ave.; no phone; lunch for two ✗.

GOBI DESERT, MONGOLIA
STAY

Three Camel Lodge Twenty luxury *gers* with wood-burning stoves and private bathrooms. 800/998-6634; threecamel lodge.com; doubles from $$.

DO

Flaming Cliffs One of the world's richest deposits of dinosaur fossils. mongolia tourism.gov.mn.

Gurvan Saikhan National Park The main attractions are Yolyn Am, a gorge layered in ice and snow, and Hongoryn Els, or the Singing Dunes. mongoliatourism.gov.mn.

LHASA, TIBET
STAY

St. Regis Lhasa Resort Striking hotel with a spa and locally minded restaurant. 22 Jiangsu Rd.; 877/787-3447; stregis.com; doubles from $$; dinner for two ✗✗.

SHOP

Lhasa Village Handicraft Center Nonprofit market for artisanal wares. 11 Chak Tsal Gang Rd.; tibetcraft.com.

DO

Jokhang Temple One of Tibet's holiest sites. Barkhor Square; 86-891/632-3129.

Norbulingka The traditional summer palace of the Dalai Lama. norbulingka.org.

PENANG, MALAYSIA

STAY

Clove Hall Edwardian bungalow of six suites, some with vaulted ceilings and colonial antiques. 11 Jalan Clove Hall; 60-4/229-0818; clovehall.com; doubles from $.

Eastern & Oriental An 1885 hotel that has hosted the likes of Rudyard Kipling. 10 Lebuh Farquhar; 60-4/222-2000; e-o-hotel.com; doubles from $$.

Straits Collection Four suites built inside five 1920's shop-houses. 89-95 Lebuh Armenian; 60-4/263-7299; straitscollection.com.my; suites from $.

EAT

Pasar Air Itam Open-air storefront known for *assam laksa* (noodle soup). Jalan Pasar Hawker Center, Air Itam; no phone; lunch for two ✗.

Perut Rumah Nyonya Cuisine Elegant restaurant serving traditional Peranakan dishes. 17 Jalan Kelawei; 60-4/227-9917; dinner for two ✗✗.

DO

Goddess of Mercy Temple (Kuan Yin Teng) Bustling, smoke-wreathed devotional site. Lorong Stewart.

Khoo Kongsi Wealthy clan's outrageously opulent temple. 18 Medan Cannon; 60-4/261-4609; khookongsi.com.my.

Pinang Peranakan Mansion House museum on Chinese-Malay culture. 29 Lebuh Gereja; 60-4/261-2929; pinang peranakanmansion.com.my.

Sri Maha Mariamman Hindu temple to the fertility goddess. Lebuh Queen.

CON DAO, VIETNAM

STAY

Six Senses Ultra-luxe resort with 50 spacious villas, each with its own private plunge pool. Dat Doc Beach; 800/591-7480; sixsenses.com; villas from $$$$.

DO

Con Dao National Park Lush natural landscape made up of mangrove forests and pristine lagoons for snorkeling. condao park.com.

VIETNAM

STAY

La Résidence Hotel & Spa The top choice in Hue, for its Art Deco details and riverside location. 5 Le Loi St., Hue; 84-54/383-7475; la-residence-hue.com; doubles from $.

Park Hyatt Centrally located, with great service and the best buffet breakfast in town. 2 Lam Son Square, District 1, Ho Chi Minh City; 877/875-4658; park.hyatt.com; doubles from $$.

Sofitel Legend Metropole A 1901 colonial landmark with a spa and three restaurants. 15 Ngo Quyen St., Hoan Kiem District, Hanoi; 800/763-4835; sofitel.com; doubles from $$.

EAT

Banh Xeo An La Ghien A must for stuffed rice-flour crêpes. 74 Suong Nguyet Anh St., District 1, Ho Chi Minh City; 84-8/3833-0534; lunch for two ✗.

Ben Thanh Market Exotic fruits and vegetables for sale; try them in an icy smoothie. Intersection of Le Loi and Tran Hung Dao Sts., District 1, Ho Chi Minh City; snacks for two ✗.

Cuc Gach Quan Upscale Vietnamese classics. 10 Dang Tat, Tan Dinh Ward, District 1, Ho Chi Minh City; 84-8/3848-0144; dinner for two ✗.

Huyen Anh No-fuss canteen with pared-down menu. 52/1 Kim Long St., Hue; 84-54/352-5655; lunch for two ✗.

Pho Gia Truyen Serving bargain-priced helpings of Vietnam's national dish, *pho bo*. 49 Bat Dan St., Hoan Kiem District, Hanoi; no phone; *pho* for two ✗.

Pho Hoa Another popular *pho* spot. 260C Pasteur St., District 3, Ho Chi Minh City; 84-8/829-7943; lunch for two ✗.

Quan An Ngon Vendors cook specialties in a villa courtyard. 18 Phan Boi Chau, Hoan Kiem District, Hanoi; 84-4/3942-8162; dinner for two ✗.

BALI, INDONESIA

STAY

Alila Villas Uluwatu Refined, eco-consious resort with a stellar Indonesian restaurant. Jalan Belimbing Sari, Banjar Tambiyak, Desa Pecatu; 62-361/848-2166; alilahotels.com; doubles from $$$$$.

Amandari Thatched-roof villas laid out like Balinese houses. Kedewatan, Ubud; 800/477-9180; amanresorts.com; doubles from $$$.

Four Seasons Bali at Sayan Sprawling resort with a roster of immersive experiences. 800/332-3442; fourseasons.com; doubles from $$.

KEY

LODGING
Under $250 = $
$250-$499 = $$
$500-$749 = $$$
$750-$999 = $$$$
$1,000 + up = $$$$$

DINING
Under $25 = ✗
$25-$74 = ✗✗
$75-$149 = ✗✗✗
$150-$299 = ✗✗✗✗
$300 + up = ✗✗✗✗✗

Hotel Tugu A 22-suite space filled with Indonesian objets. Jalan Pantai Batu Bolong, Canggu Beach; 62-361/731-701; tuguhotels.com; doubles from $$.

ROTE, INDONESIA

STAY

Nemberala Beach Resort Four duplex bungalows made with locally quarried stone and regional hardwoods. 888/669-7873; nemberalabeachresort.com; $ per person.

KOH SAMUI, THAILAND

STAY

Banyan Tree Samui On a white-sand crescent, 88 villas with private plunge pools. 99/9 Moo 4, Maret; 800/591-0439; banyantree.com; doubles from $$$$$.

W Retreat The resort features mod design and exudes a youthful vibe. 4/1 Moo 1, Tambol, Maenam; 877/946-8357; whotels.com; doubles from $$$$.

EAT

Bang Po Seafood Family-run shack for fresh fish. 92/3 Moo 6, Tambon, Maenam; 66-77/420-010; dinner for two ✗✗.

Sydney •

Melbourne •

GREAT BARRIER ISLAND

MORNINGTON PENINSULA

NEW ZEALAND

TASMANIA

SOUTH ISLAND

AUSTRALIA & NEW ZEALAND

SYDNEY

STAY

Establishment Hotel
The 31 Modernist rooms have granite tubs and Japanese-wood floors. 5 Bridge St.; 61-2/9240-3000; merivale. com; doubles from $$.

EAT

Est Mediterranean restaurant in the Establishment Hotel. 252 George St.; 61-2/9240-3000; dinner for two **XX**.

Manly Pavilion Italian dishes that compete with the Pacific vistas. W. Esplanade; 61-2/9949-9011; dinner for two **XXX**.

Rockpool Bar & Grill
Wood-fired poultry and house-aged beef in an Art Deco space. 66 Hunter St.; 61-2/8078-1900; dinner for two **XXXX**.

Sake Restaurant & Bar
Sushi and bite-size shrimp

tempura lure the well-heeled. 12 Argyle St.; 61-2/9259-5656; dinner for two **XXX**.

Spice Temple Upscale Chinese food in a red-tinged setting. 10 Bligh St.; 61-2/8078-1888; dinner for two **XXXX**.

SHOP

BrentWilson Men's wear store selling updated classics such as slim-fit peacoats. Galeries Victoria, 500 George St.; 61-2/9283-2339.

Josh Goot Airy showroom for the designer's bright block-printed tunic dresses. 104 Glenmore Rd.; 61-2/8399-0533.

Kirrily Johnston Feminine pieces (billowy skirts with high, cinched waists) in a light-filled space. 6 Glenmore Rd.; 61-2/9380-7775.

Willow Bi-level boutique that stocks flirty draped frocks

and luxe cropped jackets. 3A Glenmore Rd.; 61-2/9358-4477.

SURRY HILLS, SYDNEY

STAY

Diamant Hotel Simple, design-driven rooms and courtyard suites with views of Sydney's skyline. 14 Kings Cross Rd.; 61-2/9295-8888; diamant. com.au; doubles from $.

EAT

Bills Sleek breakfast joint that attracts residents with its spongy ricotta hotcakes. 359 Crown St.; 61-2/9360-4762; breakfast for two **X**.

Fouratefive Laid-back neighborhood café. 485 Crown St.; 61-2/9698-6485; breakfast for two **XX**.

SHOP

Collect Eclectic housewares in a slick store inside Object

Gallery. 417 Bourke St.; 61-2/9361-4511; object.com.au.

Koskela Striking Aboriginal craftwork is the draw. 91 Campbell St., Level 1; 61-2/9280-0999; koskela.com.au.

Planet Handmade Australian furniture. 114 Commonwealth St.; 61-2/9211-5959; planet furniture.com.au.

Published Art An encyclopedic selection of visual-arts tomes abound at this bookshop. 2/23-33 Mary St.; 61-2/9280-2839; publishedart.com.au.

DO

Belvoir Street Theatre
Prestigious nonprofit that brings in A-list talent. 25 Belvoir St.; 61-2/9699-3444; belvoir.com.au.

Friends of Leon Gallery
Pop art illustrations by local female artists. 82 Marlborough

St.; 61-4/0324-8978; friendsof
leon.com.

MORNINGTON PENINSULA, AUSTRALIA

STAY

Hotel Sorrento Set above the bay, 41 rooms with exposed stone walls. 5-15 Hotham Rd., Sorrento; 61-3/5984-8000; hotelsorrento.com.au; doubles from $$, including breakfast.

EAT

Acquolina Come for hearty house-made pasta with local shellfish. 26 Ocean Beach Rd., Sorrento; 61-3/ 5984-0811; dinner for two XXX.

The Baths Waterfront staple serving fresh fish and salads. 3278 Point Nepean Rd., Sorrento; 61-3/5984-1500; lunch for two XXX.

Beer Garden Aussie brews are on tap at this oasis in the Portsea Hotel. 3746 Point Nepean Rd., Portsea; 61-3/ 5984-2213; drinks for two XX.

SHOP

Seed Women and children's clothing in a tailored store. 108 Ocean Beach Rd., Sorrento; 61-3/5984-1617.

DO

Gallery Sorrento Rotating exhibitions feature Australian artists. 141 and 152 Ocean Beach Rd., Sorrento; 61-3/5984-4933.

Point Nepean National Park Natural landscape that is home to blue-winged parrots, black wallabies, and long-nosed bandicoots. Point Nepean Rd., Portsea; parkweb.vic.gov.au.

Port Phillip Estate A 60-acre wine-producing property. 263 Red Hill Rd., Red Hill

South; 61-3/5989-4444; portphillipestate.com.au.

MELBOURNE

STAY

Park Hyatt Art Deco–style interiors and a top-notch spa. 1 Parliament Square; 877/875-4658 or 61-3/9224-1234; hyatt. com; doubles from $$.

EAT

Atlantic Donovan Cooke's seafood-inspired restaurant in the Crown complex. 8 Whiteman St.; 61-3/9698-8888; dinner for two XXXX.

Clamms Fast Fish No-fuss counter selling crisp fish-and-chips. 141 Acland St.; 61-3/ 9534-1917; lunch for two X.

The European Old-world-style café opposite Parliament House. 161 Spring St.; 61-3/9654-0811; breakfast for two XX.

Noîsette The place for just-baked French cakes and pastries. 84 Bay St.; 61-3/ 9646-9555; pastries for two X.

Woolshed Pub English comfort food in a converted cargo shed. Shed 9, Central Pier, 161 Harbour Esplanade; 61-3/ 8623-9640; dinner for two XX.

DO

The Den Retro lounge beneath the Atlantic. 8 Whiteman St.; 61-3/ 9698-8888; drinks for two XX.

South Melbourne Market Collection of food stalls that dates to 1867. 322 Coventry St., Fitzroy; 61-3/9209-6295.

TASMANIA, AUSTRALIA

STAY

Pavilions Glass-and-steel apartments look out on the Derwent River. 655 Main Rd.,

Berriedale; 61-3/6277-9900; mona.net.au; doubles from $$$.

DO

Moorilla & Moo Brew Vineyard and adjacent brewery. 655 Main Rd., Berriedale; 61-3/6277-9900; mona.net.au.

Museum of Old & New Art Collector David Walsh's acquisitions are on view in a subterranean space. 655 Main Rd., Berriedale; 61-3/6277-9900; mona.net.au.

SOUTH ISLAND, NEW ZEALAND

STAY

Fiordland Lodge Rustic-modern escape near Fiordland National Park. 472 Te Anau-Milford Hwy., Te Anau; 64-3/249-7832; fiordlandlodge. co.nz; doubles from $$$$.

Kaimata Retreat Remote eco-lodge in a pristine setting. 297 Cape Saunders Rd., Dunedin; 64-3/456-3443; kaimatanz.com; doubles from $$.

Matakauri Lodge Lakeside hotel with views of the Remarkables Mountains. 569 Glenorchy Rd., Queenstown; 64-3/441-1008; matakauri.co. nz; doubles from $$$$$, including dinner.

EAT

Eichardt's Private Hotel Bar The city's best tapas. Marine Parade, Queenstown; 64-3/441-0450; lunch for two XX.

Mash Café Panini served beneath the Regent Theatre. 16 The Octagon, Dunedin; 64-3/471-7372; lunch for two X.

KEY		
LODGING		
Under $250	=	**$**
$250–$499	=	**$$**
$500–$749	=	**$$$**
$750–$999	=	**$$$$**
$1,000 + up	=	**$$$$$**
DINING		
Under $25	=	**X**
$25–$74	=	**XX**
$75–$149	=	**XXX**
$150–$299	=	**XXXX**
$300 + up	=	**XXXXX**

DO

Real Journeys This travel outfitter arranges rafting trips along the Shotover River. 64-3/ 249-7416; realjourneys.co.nz.

Royal Albatross Centre The Southern Hemisphere's sole mainland breeding colony for the rare birds. Taiaroa Head, Otago Peninsula; 64-3 /478-0499; albatross.org.nz.

GREAT BARRIER ISLAND, NEW ZEALAND

STAY

Oruawharo Beach House Glass-walled hotel with four modern rooms and views of Oruawharo Bay. 5 Ringwood St., Torbay; 64-9/473-6031; ihu.co.nz; doubles from $$.

EAT

Tipi & Bob's Waterfront Lodge Low-key hotel and restaurant on a tranquil harbor; don't miss the mussel fritters. 38 Puriri Bay Rd., Puriri Bay; 64-9/429-0550; dinner for two XX.

DO

Glenfern Sanctuary Protected parkland for native species of flora and fauna. Glenfern Rd., Port FitzRoy; 64-9/429-0091; glenfern.org.nz.

trips directory

ADVENTURE

Alps, 146
Caye Caulker, Belize, 106
Continental Divide, 46-47
Easter Island, Chile, 112-113
Everglades, Florida, 32-33
Gobi Desert, Mongolia, 214
Great Barrier Island,
  New Zealand, 250-251
Iguazú Falls, Argentina, 116-117
Jicaro Island, Nicaragua, 104-105
Koh Kong, Cambodia, 207
Park City, Utah, 50-51
Patagonian Lakes Region, Chile,
  110-111
Rote, Indonesia, 228-229
Sacred Valley, Peru, 108-109
Veracruz, Mexico, 102-103
Zambia, 178-179

AFFORDABLE

Acapulco, Mexico, 96-99
Alps, 146
Asturias, Spain, 136-137
Atlanta, 30-31
Bangkok, 206
Barbados, 74-77
Buenos Aires, 114-115
Cap Ferret, France, 142-145
Caye Caulker, Belize, 106
Charleston, South Carolina, 28-29
Colonsay, Scotland, 130-131
Columbus, Indiana, 39
Continental Divide, 46-47
Cowichan Valley, British Columbia,
  66-67
Everglades, Florida, 32-33
Fogo Island, Newfoundland, 62-63
Ghent, Belgium, 147
Gozo, Malta, 159
Harlem, New York City, 18-19
Hudson, New York, 20-23
Iceland, 124-127

Iguazú Falls, Argentina, 116-117
Kauai, Hawaii, 58-59
Las Vegas, 48-49
London, 132-133
Martinique, 86-89
Melbourne, 244-245
Mexico City, 92-95
Monmouth County, New Jersey,
  24-27
Montreal, 64-65
Mornington Peninsula, Australia,
  240-243
New Orleans, 40-43
Paris, 138-139
Patagonian Lakes Region, Chile,
  110-111
Penang, Malaysia, 216-219
Portland, Oregon, 52-53
Salento, Italy, 150-153
San Antonio, Texas, 44-45
San Francisco, 54-55
Shanghai, 198-201
Skopelos, Greece, 158
St. Martin, 82-83
St. Petersburg, Russia, 162-165
Veracruz, Mexico, 102-103
Vienna, 156-157
Vietnam, 222-225

ARTS + CULTURE

Alps, 146
Atlanta, 30-31
Bali, Indonesia, 226-227
Cape Winelands, South Africa,
  184-185
Columbus, Indiana, 39
Copenhagen, 155
Dublin, 128-129
Easter Island, Chile, 112-113
Florence, 154
Fogo Island, Newfoundland, 62-63
Ghent, Belgium, 147
Harlem, New York City, 18-19

Hollywood, California, 56-57
Johannesburg, South Africa,
  180-183
Lhasa, Tibet, 215
Lima, Peru, 107
Mexico City, 92-95
Miami, 34-37
Mumbai, 212
Nairobi, Kenya, 176-177
New Orleans, 40-43
Puducherry, India, 213
San Antonio, Texas, 44-45
San Miguel de Allende, Mexico,
  100-101
Singapore, 205
St. Petersburg, Russia, 162-165
Surry Hills, Sydney, 238-239
Tasmania, Australia, 246-247
West Chelsea, New York City,
  14-17

BEACHES

Acapulco, Mexico, 96-99
Anguilla, 84-85
Barbados, 74-77
Cap Ferret, France, 142-145
Caye Caulker, Belize, 106
Colonsay, Scotland, 130-131
Con Dao, Vietnam, 220-221
Gozo, Malta, 159
Great Barrier Island,
  New Zealand, 250-251
Honolulu, 60-61
Jicaro Island, Nicaragua,
  104-105
Kauai, Hawaii, 58-59
Koh Samui, Thailand, 230-231
Lamu, Kenya, 172-175
Lima, Peru, 107
Martinique, 86-89
Miami, 34-37
Monmouth County, New Jersey,
  24-27

Mornington Peninsula, Australia,
  240-243
Nevis, 78-81
Ocho Rios, Jamaica, 72
Puerto Rico, 70-71
Rodrigues, Mauritius, 188-189
Rote, Indonesia, 228-229
Salento, Italy, 150-153
Samaná Peninsula, Dominican
  Republic, 73
Skopelos, Greece, 158
St. Martin, 82-83
Sydney, 234-237
Veracruz, Mexico, 102-103

CITIES

Atlanta, 30-31
Bangkok, 206
Beijing, 204
Buenos Aires, 114-115
Charleston, South Carolina, 28-29
Chicago, 38
Copenhagen, 155
Dublin, 128-129
Florence, 154
Ghent, Belgium, 147
Hangzhou, China, 202-203
Hollywood, California, 56-57
Hong Kong, 196-197
Honolulu, 60-61
Hyderabad, India, 208-211
Istanbul, 160-161
Johannesburg, South Africa, 180-183
Las Vegas, 48-49
Lima, Peru, 107
London, 132-133
Marrakesh, Morocco, 168-171
Melbourne, 244-245
Mexico City, 92-95
Miami, 34-37
Montreal, 64-65
Mumbai, 212
Nairobi, Kenya, 176-177

New Orleans, 40-43
New York City, 14-19
Paris, 138-139
Portland, Oregon, 52-53
San Antonio, Texas, 44-45
San Francisco, 54-55
São Paulo, Brazil, 120-121
Shanghai, 198-201
Singapore, 205
St. Petersburg, Russia, 162-165
Sydney, 234-239
Tel Aviv, 186-187
Tokyo, 192-195
Vienna, 156-157
Vietnam, 222-225

COUNTRYSIDE

Alps, 146
Asturias, Spain, 136-137
Bali, Indonesia, 226-227
Beaune, France, 140-141
Cape Winelands, South Africa,
    184-185
Colonia, Uruguay, 118-119
Colonsay, Scotland, 130-131
Continental Divide, 46-47
Cowichan Valley, British Columbia,
    66-67
East Sussex, England, 134
Fogo Island, Newfoundland, 62-63
Gobi Desert, Mongolia, 214
Hudson, New York, 20-23
Italian Lakes, 148-149
Kauai, Hawaii, 58-59
Koh Kong, Cambodia, 207
Patagonian Lakes Region, Chile,
    110-111
Sacred Valley, Peru, 108-109
Salento, Italy, 150-153
Sintra, Portugal, 135
South Island, New Zealand,
    248-249
Veracruz, Mexico, 102-103

DRIVES

Alps, 146
Asturias, Spain, 136-137
Barbados, 74-77
Cape Winelands, South Africa,
    184-185
Continental Divide, 46-47
Cowichan Valley, British Columbia,
    66-67
Everglades, Florida, 32-33
Gobi Desert, Mongolia, 214
Hudson, New York, 20-23
Iceland, 124-127
Italian Lakes, 148-149
Mornington Peninsula, Australia,
    240-243
Patagonian Lakes Region, Chile,
    110-111
Salento, Italy, 150-153
South Island, New Zealand,
    248-249
Veracruz, Mexico, 102-103

FAMILY

Acapulco, Mexico, 96-99
Alps, 146
Atlanta, 30-31
Barbados, 74-77
Caye Caulker, Belize, 106
Chicago, 38
Colonia, Uruguay, 118-119
Continental Divide, 46-47
Copenhagen, 155
Everglades, Florida, 32-33
Honolulu, 60-61
Hudson, New York, 20-23
Iguazú Falls, Argentina, 116-117
Jicaro Island, Nicaragua,
    104-105
Kauai, Hawaii, 58-59
Lima, Peru, 107
Monmouth County, New Jersey,
    24-27

Mornington Peninsula, Australia,
    240-243
Park City, Utah, 50-51
Patagonian Lakes Region, Chile,
    110-111
Portland, Oregon, 52-53
Puerto Rico, 70-71
Salento, Italy, 150-153
San Antonio, Texas, 44-45
San Francisco, 54-55
St. Martin, 82-83
Surry Hills, Sydney, 238-239
Zambia, 178-179

FOOD + WINE

Alps, 146
Asturias, Spain, 136-137
Atlanta, 30-31
Bangkok, 206
Barbados, 74-77
Beaune, France, 140-141
Buenos Aires, 114-115
Cape Winelands, South Africa,
    184-185
Cap Ferret, France, 142-145
Charleston, South Carolina, 28-29
Chicago, 38
Cowichan Valley, British Columbia,
    66-67
Dublin, 128-129
Harlem, New York City, 18-19
Honolulu, 60-61
Hudson, New York, 20-23
Iceland, 124-127
Istanbul, 160-161
Italian Lakes, 148-149
Las Vegas, 48-49
Marrakesh, Morocco, 168-171
Martinique, 86-89
Melbourne, 244-245
Montreal, 64-65
New Orleans, 40-43
Paris, 138-139

Portland, Oregon, 52-53
Puerto Rico, 70-71
Salento, Italy, 150-153
San Antonio, Texas, 44-45
São Paulo, Brazil, 120-121
Sydney, 234-237
Tokyo, 192-195
Vietnam, 222-225

NIGHTLIFE

Beijing, 204
Charleston, South Carolina, 28-29
Dublin, 128-129
Hong Kong, 196-197
Las Vegas, 48-49
Melbourne, 244-245
Miami, 34-37
New Orleans, 40-43
São Paulo, Brazil, 120-121
Shanghai, 198-201

SHOPPING

Atlanta, 30-31
Buenos Aires, 114-115
Colonia, Uruguay, 118-119
Ghent, Belgium, 147
Hollywood, California, 56-57
Hong Kong, 196-197
Honolulu, 60-61
Hudson, New York, 20-23
Johannesburg, South Africa,
    180-183
Lima, Peru, 107
London, 132-133
Mornington Peninsula, Australia,
    240-243
Mumbai, 212
Nairobi, Kenya, 176-177
Paris, 138-139
San Francisco, 54-55
St. Petersburg, Russia, 162-165
Sydney, 234-239
Tel Aviv, 186-187

INDEX

A

Acapulco, Mexico, 96-99
The Alps, 146
Anguilla, 84-85
Arenas de Cabrales, Spain, 136
Argentina, 114-117
Asbury Park, New Jersey, 27
Aspen, Colorado, 47
Asturias, Spain, 136-137
Atlanta, 30-31
Atlantic City, Wyoming, 47
Australia, 234-247
Austria, 146, 156-157

B

Bali, Indonesia, 226-227
Bangkok, 206
Barbados, 74-77
Beaune, France, 140-141
Beijing, 204
Belgium, 147
Belize, 106
Bezau, Austria, 146
Brazil, 120-121
Bregenz, Austria, 146
British Columbia, 66-67
Buenos Aires, 114-115

C

California, 54-57
Cambodia, 207
Canada, 62-67
Cangas de Onís, Spain, 136-137
Cape Winelands, South Africa,
   184-185
Cap Ferret, France, 142-145
Cardel, Mexico, 102
Carmelo, Uruguay, 118-119
Castro, Chile, 110-111

Catskill, New York, 20-23
Caye Caulker, Belize, 106
Chachalacas, Mexico, 102
Charleston, South Carolina,
   28-29
Chicago, 38
Chile, 110-113
Chiloé, Chile, 110-111
China, 196-204
Chinchero, Peru, 108
Chi Phat, Cambodia, 207
Colonia, Uruguay, 118-119
Colonsay, Scotland, 130-131
Colorado, 47
Columbus, Indiana, 39
Con Dao, Vietnam, 220-221
Continental Divide, 46-47
Copenhagen, 155
Cowichan Valley, British Columbia,
   66-67
Cuzco, Peru, 108-109

D

Denmark, 155
Dominican Republic, 73
Dublin, 128-129
Dunedin, New Zealand, 249

E

Easter Island, Chile 112-113
East Sussex, England, 134
England, 132-134
The Everglades, Florida, 32-33
Everglades City, Florida, 33

F

Feldkirch, Austria, 146
Florence, 154
Florida, 32-37

Fogo Island, Newfoundland, 62-63
France, 138-145

G

Gallipoli, Italy, 150-153
Georgetown, Malaysia, 216-219
Georgia, 30-31
Ghent, Belgium, 147
Gobi Desert, Mongolia, 214
Gozo, Malta, 159
Grand Case, St. Martin, 82-83
Great Barrier Island, New
   Zealand, 250-251
Greece, 158
Green Valley, Nevada, 49

H

Hangzhou, China, 202-203
Hanoi, Vietnam, 222-225
Harlem, New York City, 18-19
Hawaii, 58-61
Ho Chi Minh City, Vietnam,
   224-225
Hollywood, California, 56-57
Hong Kong, 196-197
Honolulu, Hawaii 60-61
Hudson, New York, 20-23
Hue, Vietnam, 224-225
Hyderabad, India, 208-211

I

Iceland, 124-127
Iguazú Falls, Argentina, 116-117
Illinois, 38
India, 208-213
Indiana, 39
Indonesia, 226-229
Ireland, 128-129
Israel, 186-187

Istanbul, 160-161
Italian Lakes, 148-149
Italy, 148-154

J

Jamaica, 72
Japan, 192-195
Jicaro Island, Nicaragua, 104-105
Johannesburg, South Africa
   180-183

K

Kalispell, Montana, 47
Kauai, Hawaii, 58-59
Kenya, 172-177
Koh Kong, Cambodia, 207
Koh Samui, Thailand, 230-231

L

Lamu, Kenya, 172-175
Las Vegas, 48-49
Lecce, Italy, 150-153
Lhasa, Tibet, 215
Lima, Peru, 107
Lingenau, Austria, 146
Llanes, Spain, 136-137
London, 132-133
Long Branch, New Jersey, 24-27
Louisiana, 40-43

M

Maglie, Italy, 150-153
Maienfeld, Switzerland, 146
Malaysia, 216-219
Malta, 159
Marigot, St. Martin, 82-83
Marrakesh, Morocco, 168-171
Martinique, 86-89
Mauritius, 188-189

Melbourne, 244-245
Mexico, 92-103
Mexico City, 92-95
Miami, 34-37
Mongolia, 214
Monmouth County, New Jersey, 24-27
Montana, 46-47
Montreal, 64-65
Mornington Peninsula, Australia, 240-243
Morocco, 168-171
Mumbai, 212

N
Nairobi, Kenya, 176-177
Naples, Florida, 32-33
Nardò, Italy, 150-153
Nemberala, Indonesia
Nevada, 48-49
Nevis, 78-81
Newfoundland, 62-63
New Jersey, 24-27
New Mexico, 47
New Orleans, 40-43
New York City, 14-19
New York State, 20-23
New Zealand, 248-251
Nicaragua, 104-105

O
Oceanport, New Jersey, 24-27
Ocho Rios, Jamaica, 72
Oregon, 52-53
Oviedo, Spain, 136-137

P
Paracas, Peru, 107
Paris, 138-139

Park City, Utah, 50-51
Patagonian Lakes Region, Chile, 110-111
Penang, Malaysia, 216-219
Peru, 107-109
Port Fitzroy, New Zealand, 250-251
Portland, Oregon, 52-53
Portsea, Australia, 240-243
Portugal, 135
Puducherry, India, 213
Puerto Rico, 70-71
Puerto Varas, Chile, 110-111

Q
Quebec, 64-65
Queenstown, New Zealand, 248-249
Quemado, New Mexico, 47

R
Red Bank, New Jersey, 27
Reykjavík, Iceland, 124-127
Ribadesella, Spain, 136-137
Rodrigues, Mauritius, 188-189
Rote, Indonesia, 228-229
Russia, 162-165

S
Sacred Valley, Peru, 108-109
Salento, Italy, 150-153
Samaná Peninsula, Dominican Republic, 73
San Antonio, Texas, 44-45
San Francisco, 54-55
San Germán, Puerto Rico, 71
San Juan, Puerto Rico, 70-71
San Miguel De Allende, Mexico, 100-101

Santa Maria di Leuca, Italy, 152
São Paulo, Brazil, 120-121
Schwartzenberg, Austria, 146
Scotland, 130-131
Shanghai, 198-201
Silver City, New Mexico, 47
Singapore, 205
Sintra, Portugal, 135
Skopelos, Greece, 158
Sorrento, Australia, 240-243
South Africa, 180-185
South Carolina, 28-29
South Island, New Zealand, 248-249
Spain, 136-137
St. Gallen, Switzerland, 146
St. Martin, 82-83
St. Petersburg, Russia, 162-165
Surcasti, Switzerland, 146
Surry Hills, Sydney, 238-239
Switzerland, 146
Sydney, 234-239

T
Tasmania, Australia, 246-247
Tazones, Spain, 136-137
Te Anau, New Zealand, 248-249
Tel Aviv, 186-187
Texas, 44-45
Thailand, 206, 230-231
Tibet, 215
Tokyo, 192-195
Turkey, 160-161

U
Uruguay, 118-119
Utah, 50-51

V
Veracruz, Mexico, 102-103
Victoria, British Columbia, 66-67
Victoria, Malta, 159
Vienna, 156-157
Vietnam, 220-225

W
West Chelsea, New York City, 14-17
Wyoming, 47

X
Xalapa, Mexico, 102-103
Xico, Mexico, 102-103

Z
Zambia, 178-179

Hanging out at the pier off Les Anses d'Arlet, in Martinique.

contributors

Christine Ajudua
Gini Alhadeff
Tom Austin
Colin Barraclough
Raul Barreneche
Thomas Beller
Laura Begley Bloom
Danny Bonvissuto
Anya von Bremzen
Marie Brenner
Dominique Browning
Karen Burshtein
Claudia Caruana
Aric Chen
Jennifer Chen
Tanvi Chheda
Christine Ciarmello
María José Cortés

Anthony Dennis
Yolanda Edwards
Mark Ellwood
Erin Florio
Jennifer Flowers
Meghann Foye
Michael Frank
Peter Frank
Gael Greene
Jaime Gross
Michael Gross
Margot Guralnick
Catesby Holmes
Karrie Jacobs
Howie Kahn
David Kaufman
Melik Kaylan
Stirling Kelso
Josh Krist

Christopher Kucway
Sandy Lang
Matt Lee
Ted Lee
Peter Jon Lindberg
Naomi Lindt
Heather Smith MacIsaac
Francine Maroukian
Alexandra Marshall
Andrew McCarthy
Clark Mitchell
Heidi Mitchell
Shane Mitchell
Saúl Peña
Katerina Roberts
Sean Rocha
Douglas Rogers

Julian Rubenstein
Adam Sachs
Bruce Schoenfeld
Kate Sekules
Maria Shollenbarger
Gary Shteyngart
Paola Singer
Adam Skolnick
Sarah Spagnolo
Valerie Stivers-Isakova
Guy Trebay
Jeremy Tredinnick
Daniela Vaca
Diane Vadino
José Luis Aguilera Velasco
Valerie Waterhouse
Sally Webb
Michael Z. Wise
Lynn Yaeger

Examining a vintage camera outside the Old Truman Brewery, in London's East End.

photographers

Gregory Allen, 92, 93, 94, 95

Malù Alvarez, 44, 45

Cedric Angeles, 38, 40, 41, 42, 43, 112, 113, 128, 129, 214

Jessica Antola, 64, 65, 86, 87, 88, 89, 284

Ball & Albanese, 12, 50, 51

Jose Bernad, 142, 143, 144, 145

Walter Bibikow, 188-189

Jonathan Bloom, 176, 177

Laura Begley Bloom, 120

Massimo Borchi, 159

Aya Brackett, 192-193, 194, 195

Simon Brown, 134

Jan Butchofsky/Corbis, 110 (left)

James Camp Photography, 30 (left)

Brown W. Cannon III, 8, 190, 222, 223, 224, 225

João Canziani, 84, 85

Fred Castleberry, 30 (right)

David Cicconi, 10, 150, 151, 152, 153, 180, 181, 182, 183, 252

Noe DeWitt, 34, 35, 36, 37

Tara Donne, 66, 67, 70, 71

DOOK, 185

Peter Frank Edwards, 28, 29, 58, 59, 74, 75, 76, 77

Philipp Engelhorn, 196, 197

Blasius Erlinger, 32, 33

Andrea Fazzari, 140, 141, 208, 209, 210, 211, 220, 221, 230, 231

Juan Jose Gabaldon/LatinStock, 111 (right)

Beth Garrabrant, 2, 3, 17 (top), 18, 19, 20, 24, 25, 26, 27

Oberto Gili, 148, 149

Nicholas Gill/Alamy, 111 (left)

Andres Gonzalez, 160, 161 (bottom)

Emiliano Granado, 14, 15, 16, 17 (bottom)

Eugenio Gravino, 228-229

Frank Herfort, 162, 163, 164, 165

Monika Hoefler & Jens Schwarz, 172-173, 174, 175

Matthew Hranek, 146

John Huba, 236 (bottom right)

Jasper James, 204

Mans Jensen, 155

Hamish Johnson, 250-251

Steve Kepple, 52, 53, 54 (bottom left, right), 55 (top)

Christian Kerber, 124, 125, 126, 127, 132, 133, 286

Frederic Labaune, 46-47

Dave Lauridsen, 100, 101

Whitney Lawson, 55 (bottom), 82-83

Amanda Marsalis, 54 (top left)

Anne Menke, 68, 78, 79, 80, 81

Morgan & Owens, 198-199, 200, 201, 206

David Naugle, 31 (left)

David Nicolas, 104, 105, 114, 115

Marcus Nilsson, 5, 166, 168, 169, 170, 171

Anders Overgaard, 121

David Pearson/Alamy, 213

Javier Pierini, 116, 117

Sean Rocha, 147

Mark Roper, 232, 240, 241, 242, 243

Jessica Sample, 6, 21, 56 (left), 57 (right), 122, 156, 157

Kieran Scott, 246, 247

Susan Seuberg, 60-61

Katie Shapiro, 56 (right), 57 (left)

John Short/Corbis, 130-131

Darren Soh, 202, 203

Hugh Stewart, 226, 227

Buff Strickland, 106, 107

John Sylvester/Alamy, 62-63

Petrina Tinslay, 234-235, 236 (top, bottom left), 237 (bottom), 238, 239

TrujilloPaumier, 90, 96, 97, 98, 99

Richard Truscott, 138, 139

Mikkel Vang, 190, 216, 217, 218, 219

Daryl Visscher/Redux, 212

Coral von Zumwalt, 48, 49

Anna Wolf, 22, 23

Jarrett Wrisley, 206 (right)

A magazine of modern global culture, *Travel + Leisure* examines the places, ideas, and trends that define the way we travel now. T+L inspires readers to explore the world, equipping them with expert advice and a better understanding of the endless possibilities of travel. Delivering clear, comprehensive service journalism, intelligent writing, and evocative photography, T+L is the authority for today's traveler. Visit us at TravelandLeisure.com.